IMAGES
of America

FORT STOCKTON

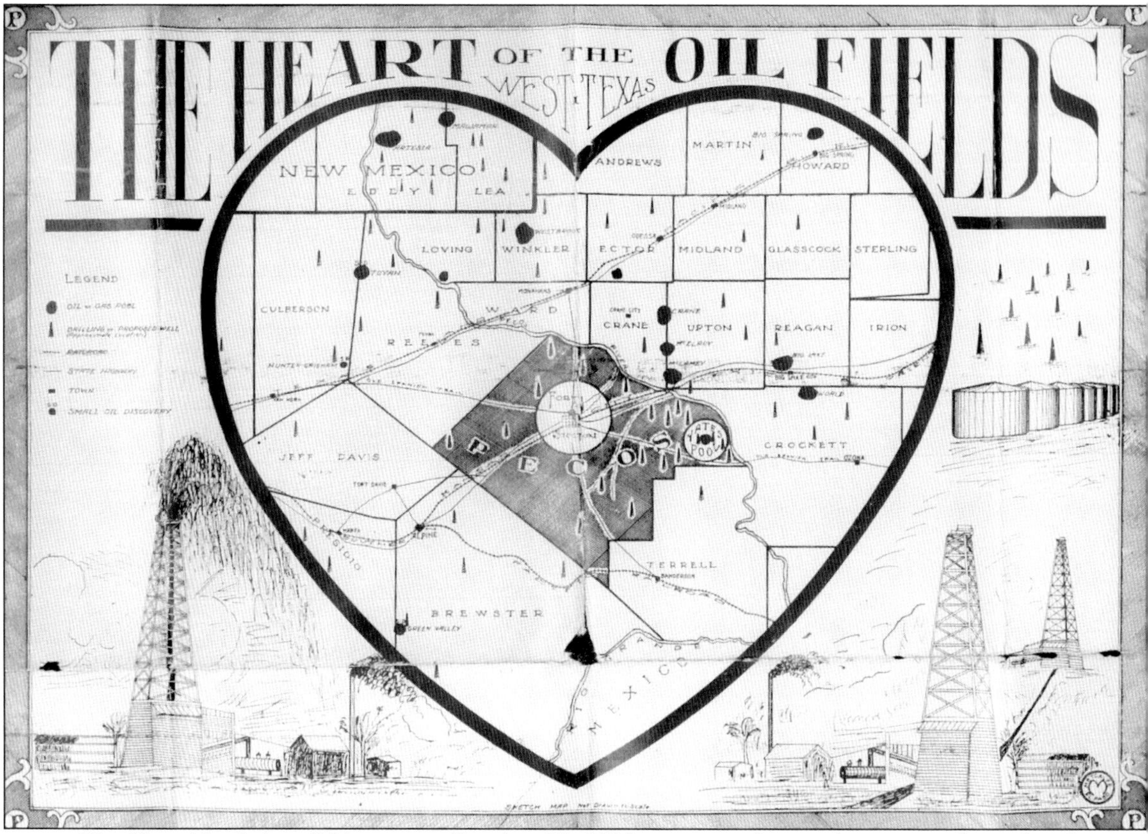

The Yates No. 1-A well blew in on October 28, 1926, covering the nearby mesa with crude oil, forever changing West Texas history. The Yates Oil Field in eastern Pecos County launched a new era of oil exploration and fueled the growth of towns across the region. Fort Stockton community leaders quickly developed an advertising campaign. This map from an undated special edition of the *Fort Stockton Pioneer* touted the city as "the Heart of the Oil Fields." The map detailed a shaded Pecos County dotted with drilling rigs, but the paper focused on "other resources that are just as great as our oil." The vision of a diverse economy combining multiple enterprises has been a regular theme in the city's history. (Courtesy of Fort Stockton Historical Society.)

ON THE COVER: Comanche Springs and the network of irrigation canals constructed along Comanche Creek gave rise to large groves of trees lining their banks. These spots provided shady sites for social events, especially picnics on the Fourth of July. In 1902, Lon Sanders and May Rooney (center) dance to the violin and harp music of the Gomez brothers, Chico and Edubijan, while other picnic events unfold in the background. Fort Stockton's water and trees provided a welcome oasis in arid West Texas. A 1922 calendar of old photographs printed by the Rooney Mercantile Company included this picnic shot. (Courtesy of Fort Stockton Historical Society.)

IMAGES
of America

FORT STOCKTON

James Collett and the
Fort Stockton Historical Society

ARCADIA
PUBLISHING

ISBN 978-0-7385-8494-2

Published by Arcadia Publishing
Charleston, South Carolina

Printed in the United States of America

Library of Congress Control Number: 2011926344

For all general information, please contact Arcadia Publishing:
Telephone 843-853-2070
Fax 843-853-0044
E-mail sales@arcadiapublishing.com
For customer service and orders:
Toll-Free 1-888-313-2665

Visit us on the Internet at www.arcadiapublishing.com

To all the Pecos County pioneers—gracias.

Contents

ACKNOWLEDGMENTS

The Fort Stockton Historical Society has a long history of preserving the story and the sites of Fort Stockton. Every day, local citizens and travelers touch the past in a very literal way as they stroll across the parade ground of historic Fort Stockton or walk through the rooms of the Annie Riggs Memorial Museum. The archives of the historical society were an invaluable visual and written record and served as the foundation for this book. Unless otherwise noted, photographs are from the Fort Stockton Historical Society collection. The Fort Stockton Historical Society board provided superb assistance in the creation of this book. The 2011 board includes Terry Whigham, president Diane Indorf, Sal Salazar Jr., vice-president Debbie Teich, Nancy Hammond, treasurer Robert Card, Frank Carpenter, Sheridan Porter Purvis, Sam Calderon III, Jean Lockhart, secretary George Riggs, and M.R. Gonzalez. Special thanks also to Jennifer Justison, director of the Annie Riggs Memorial Museum, for her help, to Charlie and Sixie Davis for their assistance with the Hovey School records, and to Mary Ibarra for assistance with local family interviews. Thanks also to all those individuals who shared photographs from family collections.

INTRODUCTION

For centuries, nomadic Native Americans crossing the arid Stockton Plateau in West Texas sought out the oasis formed by the springs at the head of Comanche Creek. At one time the third largest in Texas, they poured out over 60 cubic feet of fresh water per second. The Jumano Indians developed simple irrigation projects along the Creek to grow corn, beans, and pumpkins. Whatever names they gave to the springs are forever lost.

In 1684, Spanish explorer Juan de Mendoza, on an expedition eastward from El Paso, named the springs San Juan del Rio. The Spaniards never established a foothold in West Texas, and this name also faded into obscurity.

With the acquisition of horses, Apache and Comanche Indians pushed into Texas, disrupting tribes there and clashing with the Spanish and, later, the Anglos moving into western Texas. The West Texas springs became part of the route by which the Comanche swept down from Oklahoma and the Texas Panhandle to raid into Mexico.

By 1849, routes were developing through the area to the California gold fields for traders and travelers. The Chihuahua Trail provided a lengthy, dangerous path from Presidio to San Antonio. In the spring of 1849, the expedition of Capt. William Whiting, who was mapping what developed into the San Antonio to El Paso Road, became the first to record the site as Comanche Springs. Over the next decade, stage companies established routes through the area, and thousands of travelers took this southern road west. In 1851, Henry Skillman began the first mail service from San Antonio to El Paso. The Butterfield Overland Mail line shifted its route south in 1859 to include Comanche Springs, which became a regular relay station.

The United States military established Camp Stockton in 1859 to provide greater protection for travelers and to disrupt use of the Comanche War Trail. Company H of the First US Infantry, under the command of Capt. Stephen Carpenter, constructed several adobe buildings in April of that year. By the end of 1860, what was now designated Fort Stockton was one of the best built and arranged posts in the region.

With the outbreak of the Civil War, all federal troops left the state. The Texas Mounted Rifles occupied Fort Stockton briefly, abandoning it in August 1862. This first Fort Stockton quickly fell into disrepair. The only pre–Civil War structure remaining is the ruin of J.D. Holliday's sutler store, now known as Fort Stockton's Oldest House.

After the war, federal troops reoccupied the springs as part of the campaign to regain control of West Texas from the Indians. In July 1867, Col. Edward Hatch made it the headquarters of the 9th Cavalry, a newly established regiment of black troops that became known as the Buffalo Soldiers. The new post was on the bank of Comanche Creek, a half-mile north of the old fort. Hatch employed Mexican workers for the fort's construction. Stone was quarried from nearby mesas for the guardhouse and for the foundations of other post buildings, the walls of which were adobe. The post served as a staging point for patrols and scouts monitoring Apache activity in the area. As the Indian threat diminished, troops were withdrawn. The last troops left in June 1886, and Fort Stockton was closed.

In 1862, Peter Gallagher, an Irishman from San Antonio, was among those who realized the agricultural potential of the springs. He bought several tracts of land for $500 in gold. Other entrepreneurs soon followed, including Francis Rooney, J.D. Martin, and Cesario Torres, founder of the Seven D Ranch. Gallagher established the town of St. Gall in 1868 on the site of the original fort. By 1871, St. Gall had grown to over 400 citizens. The Texas legislature established Pecos County that year, but the first elections were not held until 1872. George M. Fraser became the first county judge. St. Gall was designated the county seat, but the name never became popular. In an 1881 vote, the community became Fort Stockton. A large two-story courthouse, completed in 1884, was visible for miles.

Ranchers, farmers, and small businessmen immigrated to the frontier town seeking new opportunities. Several irrigation companies launched projects that expanded well into the 20th century. Herman Koehler, James Rooney, and Herman Butz opened saloons and mercantile businesses. Annie Frazier Johnson Riggs acquired the Koehler Hotel in 1903, and the Riggs Hotel was soon famous among area cowboys and ranchers for its hospitality. Organized religion arrived in 1877 with the founding of St. Joseph Catholic Church, where Fr. Jose Ferra served as the first priest. Anglos and Mexican Americans originally attended church together, but ethnic prejudice began to divide the congregation; Division Street, marking the dividing point between old St. Gall and the fort settlement, gradually became the de facto line of segregation. The paternalism toward "Mexicans" lasted into the second half of the 20th century, until finally broken down by the actions of Mexican American individuals and groups.

In the late 1800s, the building of railroads across West Texas, miles from Fort Stockton, isolated the frontier community. This remote location attracted a lawless element that eventually required intervention by the Texas Rangers. One notorious conflict between Sheriff Andrew Jackson Royal and Judge O.W. Williams and others ended with a shooting in the courthouse. The city retained its frontier character well beyond the turn of the century.

In 1910, new economic forces launched permanent change. Local businessmen raised $30,000 to help fund the extension of the Kansas City, Mexico & Orient Railroad to Fort Stockton as a stop on its route to Mexico and the Pacific. The railroad project sparked a building boom, with new stone banks and hotels on Main Street replacing the adobe and wood of earlier days. A few short years later, the discovery of vast oil resources in eastern Pecos County and the extension of US highways through West Texas further fueled the economic boom of Fort Stockton. World War II brought an additional boost when Gibbs Field, a flight training school, was established.

Cultural events grew in scale as well, as small social clubs gave way to school sports events and movie theaters. Comanche Springs, a popular swimming spot for decades, formed the basis for a uniquely Fort Stockton event. The Water Carnival began in 1936 with a bathing review, swim and diving events, band concerts, a parade, and the crowning of Sammie Lee Warnock as the first Miss Fort Stockton. Over the years, the event grew into a large-scale production that has continued to the present day.

In the 1950s, the waters of Comanche Springs began to fail (and eventually go dry), and the large irrigation projects ended. Fort Stockton sought new enterprises to diversify the economy. The discovery of large natural gas reserves augmented the continued development of oil fields. In 1954, the Fort Stockton Historical Society was founded to preserve the community's interesting history and to develop properties such as the Annie Riggs Hotel and the old military fort as tourist attractions. Today, a healthy mix of agriculture, oil and gas, small businesses, tourism, and renewable energy technologies, including wind turbines, sustain the West Texas town that remains an oasis for both citizens and visitors alike.

One

Claiming Comanche Springs

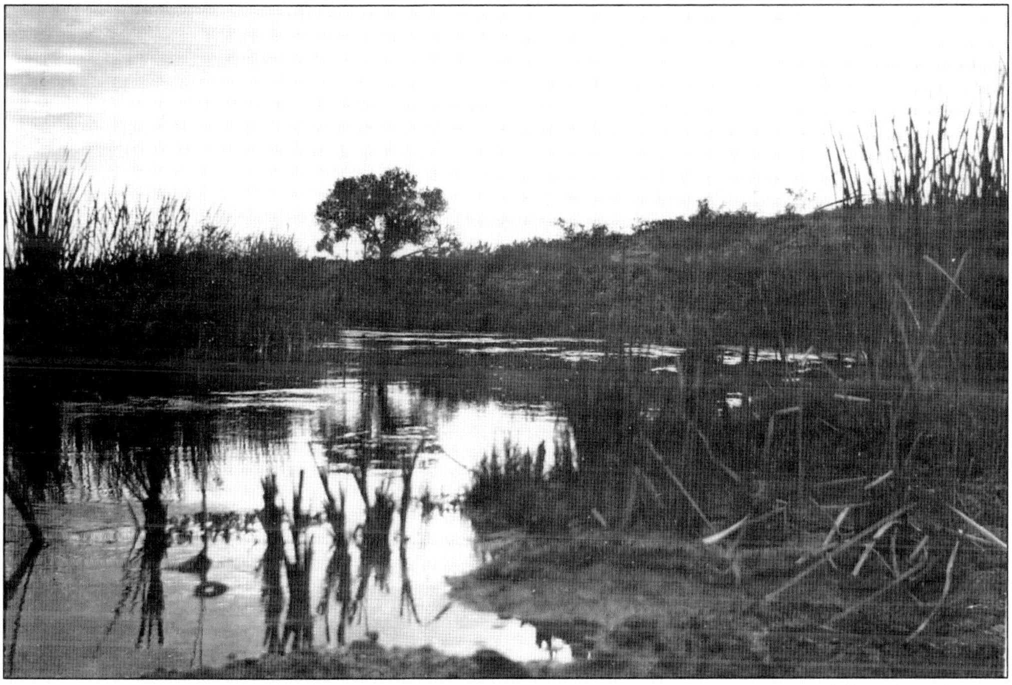

For centuries, Comanche Springs provided a crucial water source in the middle of arid West Texas. Control of this scarce resource was central to survival. The Comanche knew this, as did the soldiers who built the military post of Fort Stockton. From its beginning, the waters of Comanche Springs were a central feature defining life in Fort Stockton. This photograph from around 1900 captures a view along Comanche Creek.

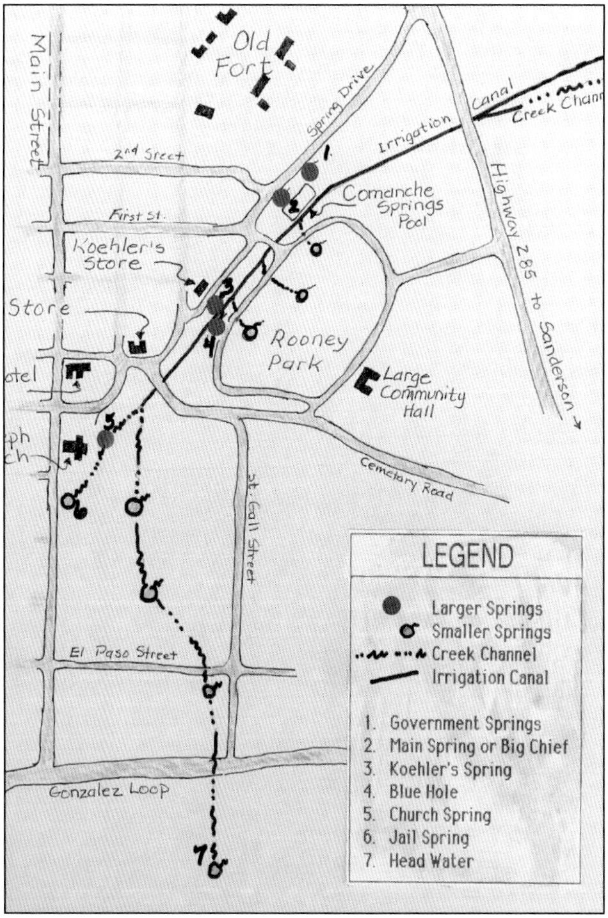

Historian Kenneth Neighbors asserted, "Springs are to plains as passes are to mountains." As this sketch illustrates, seven springs combined to form Comanche Creek, which flowed eastward into the Pecos River. Jose Policarpo Rodriguez, interpreter with the 1849 Whiting expedition, first christened them Comanche Springs because of the numerous deeply worn trails that converged here and then ran south, marking the path of the annual Comanche raids into Mexico.

The Stockton Plateau is a vast plain broken by steep-sided, flat-topped mesas. Several are defined by their distance from the springs, such as Five-Mile Mesa and Seven-Mile Mesa. Stone tools and ashes from Native American campsites remain in the shallow shelters along the rocky ledges. Early pioneers found Comanche graves on the mesa rims, where the view extends for miles. A handwritten note on this old postcard comments, "The dust is blowing awful here."

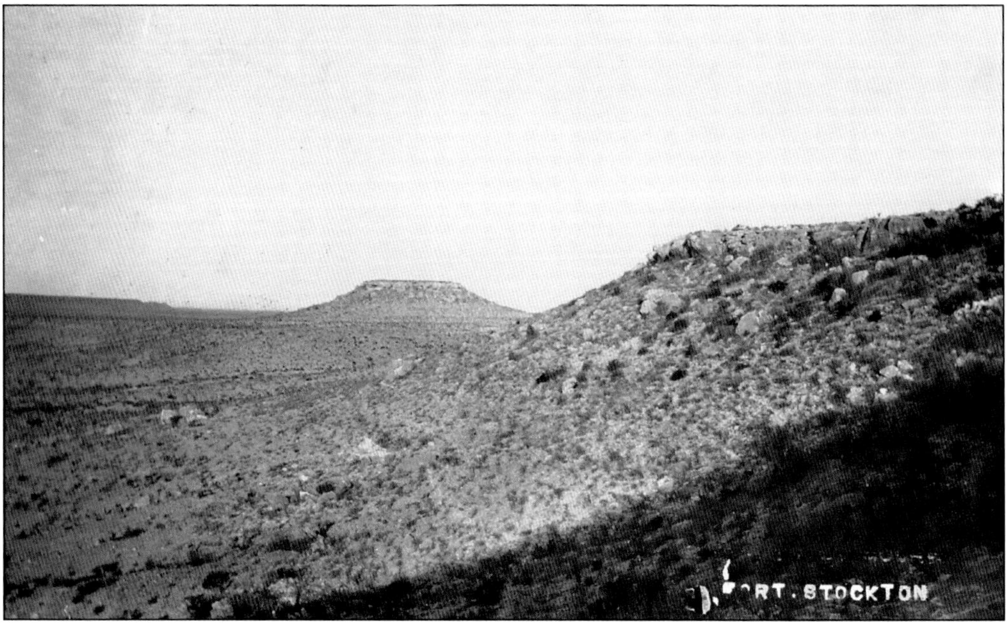

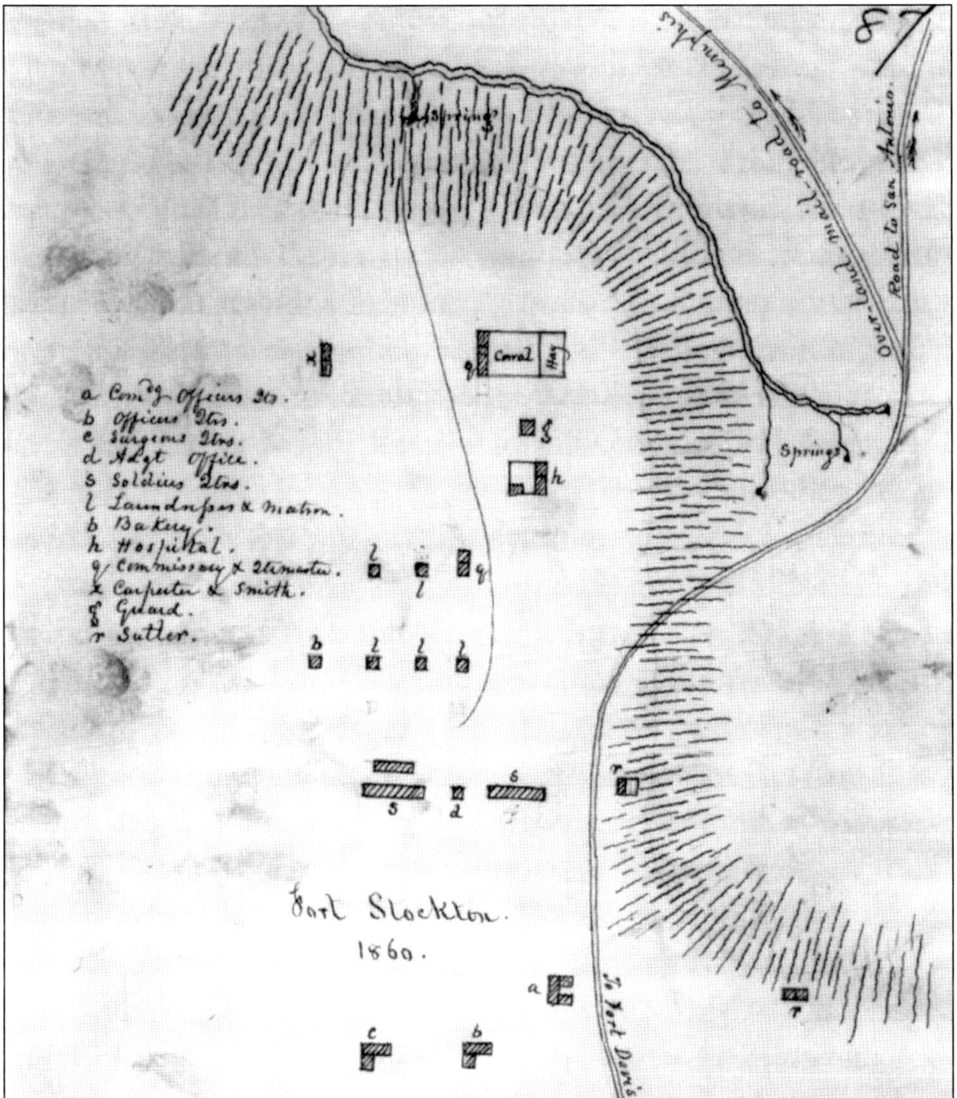

In April 1859, Company H, 1st United States Infantry, under the command of Capt. Stephen D. Carpenter, established Camp Stockton on the west bank of Comanche Creek. Adobe bricks and thatch for roofing offered the only local construction materials; wood or lumber were freighted in. The young post had a rocky start. An inspector found construction work poorly done and described discipline and instruction as "below mediocrity." Captain Carpenter worked hard to improve the situation. A year later, when this sketch was completed, Inspector J.F.K. Mansfield pronounced Fort Stockton one of the best built and arranged posts in the service. Texas seceded from the Union in 1861, and all federal troops left the state; Fort Stockton was abandoned in May of that year. The fort was occupied only briefly by Confederate forces. (Courtesy of the National Archives.)

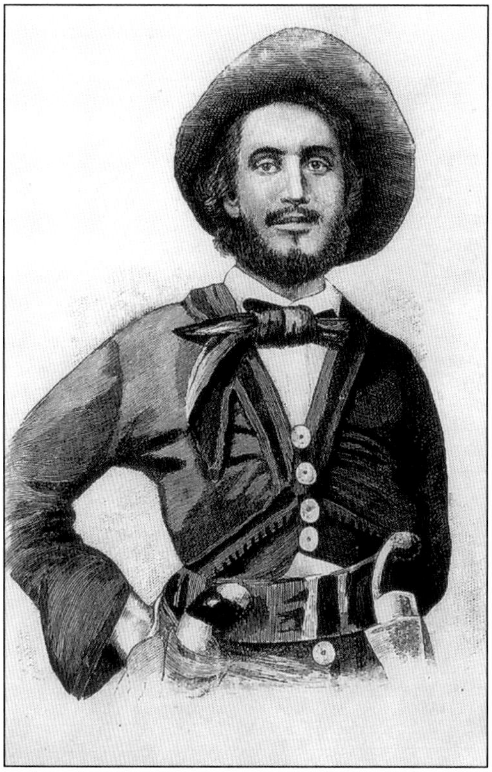

The most unusual event in the fort's short history was the camel experiment. In the late 1850s, former Navy man Edward Fitzgerald Beale (pictured here in an 1837 sketch) led expeditions that tested the feasibility of camels as pack animals in the Southwest. Beale submitted favorable reports, but the authorities remained unimpressed. In 1859, Lt. Edward Hartz, 8th Infantry, conducted several surveys into the mountains south of Fort Stockton using camels. The animals proved their worth in terrain so steep they had to climb on their heavily padded knees. (Courtesy of the US Naval History Center.)

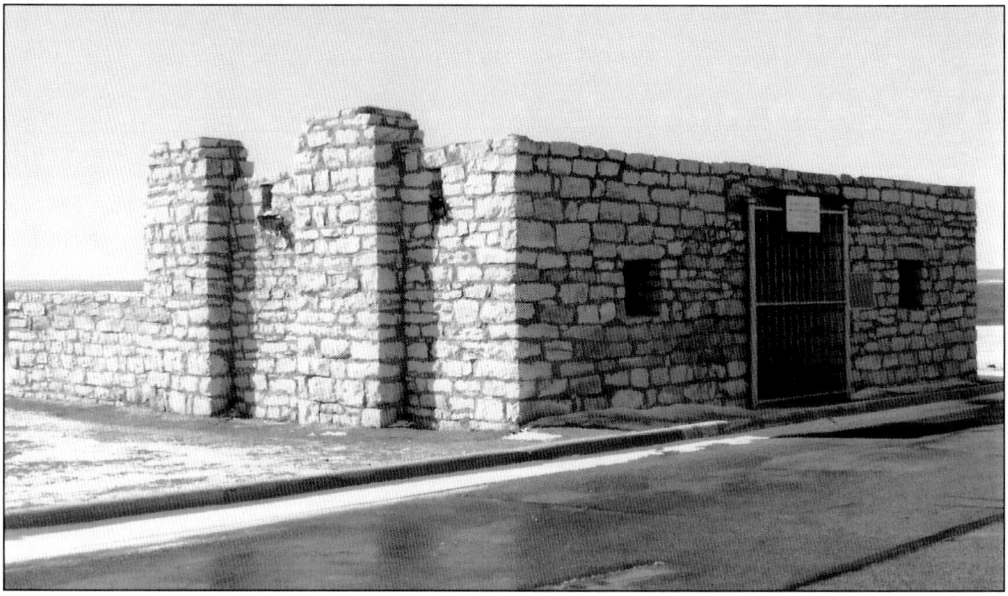

Fort Stockton helped protect several stage routes, including the San Antonio–San Diego stage mail line. In 1857, James E. Birch won the first contract for mail service from San Antonio to San Diego. The average trip took 38 days. The line was dubbed the "Jackass mail" because 100 miles of the Arizona desert were crossed on mules. In 1936, Roland Warnock supervised construction of this replica of the stage stop at Tunis Springs, east of Fort Stockton, by the Texas Highway Department, using stone from the original station. (Photograph by James Collett.)

Two

Defending the Texas Frontier

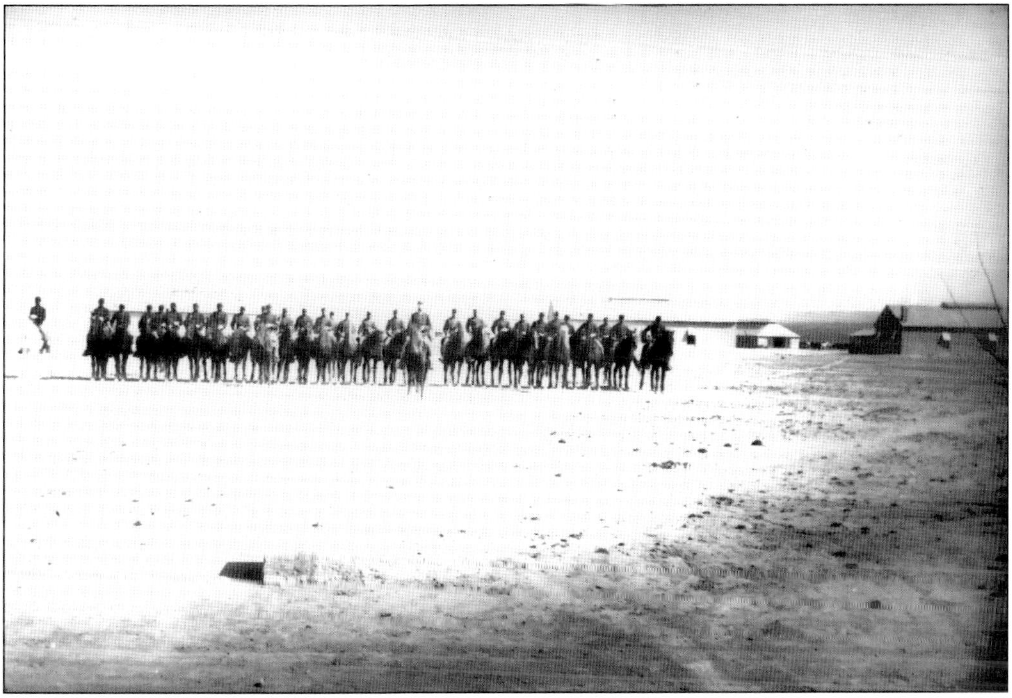

The US Army returned to Fort Stockton in July 1867. Their mission of frontier defense remained the same, but the troops were different. For nearly two decades, Fort Stockton was home to newly created cavalry and infantry regiments of African Americans, who became known as Buffalo Soldiers. Units like the 10th Cavalry (pictured in parade formation at Fort Stockton) faced Comanche and Apache and endured heat, cold, dust, and boredom.

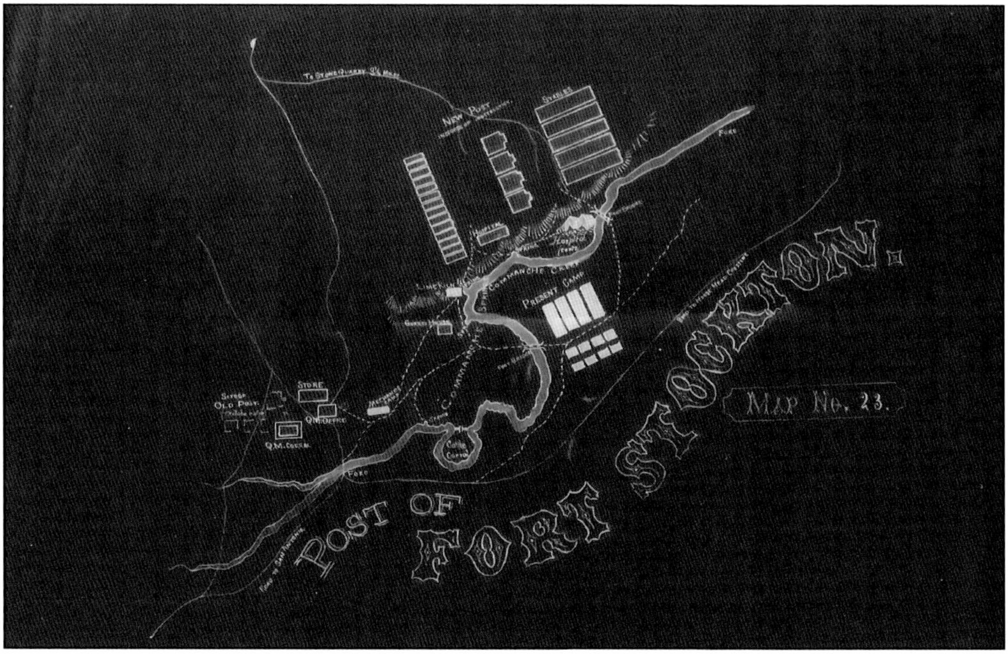

Col. Edward Hatch reestablished Fort Stockton with several companies of the 9th Cavalry, which consisted of black troops recruited in New Orleans. As this sketch map illustrates, the new post was a half-mile north of the first site. Mexican civilians were employed to make the adobe for the buildings. During Hatch's time at the fort, it served as the headquarters for the 9th Cavalry. (Courtesy of the National Archives.)

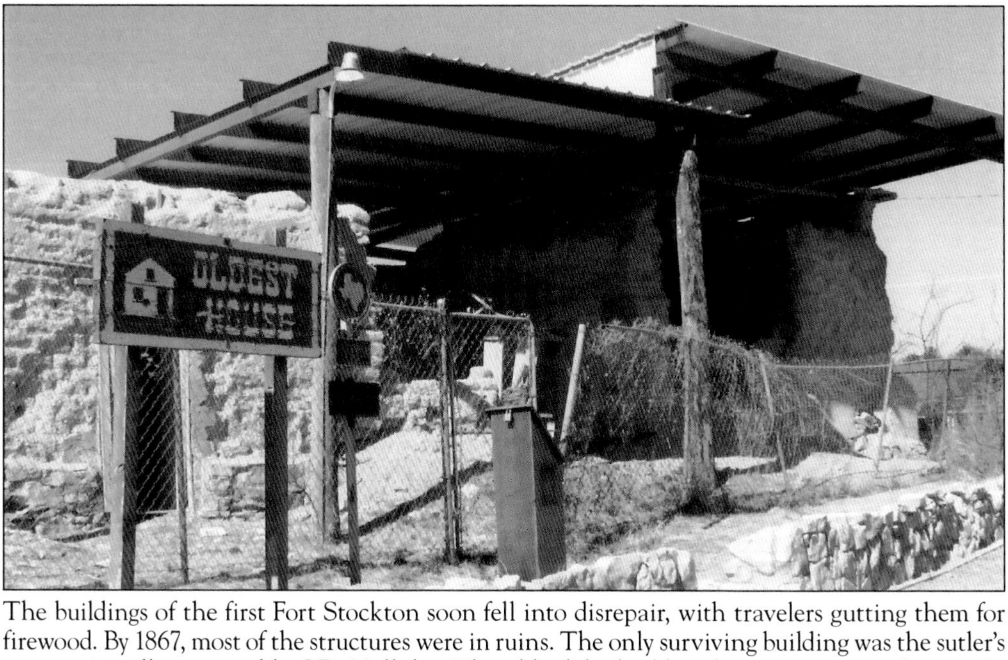

The buildings of the first Fort Stockton soon fell into disrepair, with travelers gutting them for firewood. By 1867, most of the structures were in ruins. The only surviving building was the sutler's store, originally operated by J.D. Holliday. The old adobe building became a private home. At various times, the Sosa, Piña, and Ramos families lived there. Now known as the Oldest House, its crumbling walls have attracted a collection of ghost stories.

Capt. William George Wedemeyer produced an invaluable written and visual record of the postwar fort. Wedemeyer, a captain in the 16th Infantry, served at the post from 1883 until its abandonment in 1886. He continued a journal started during his service in the Civil War. He also began to take photographs with equipment he purchased shortly before coming to the fort. Wedemeyer continued his journals and photographs throughout his career. He retired as a major in 1891.

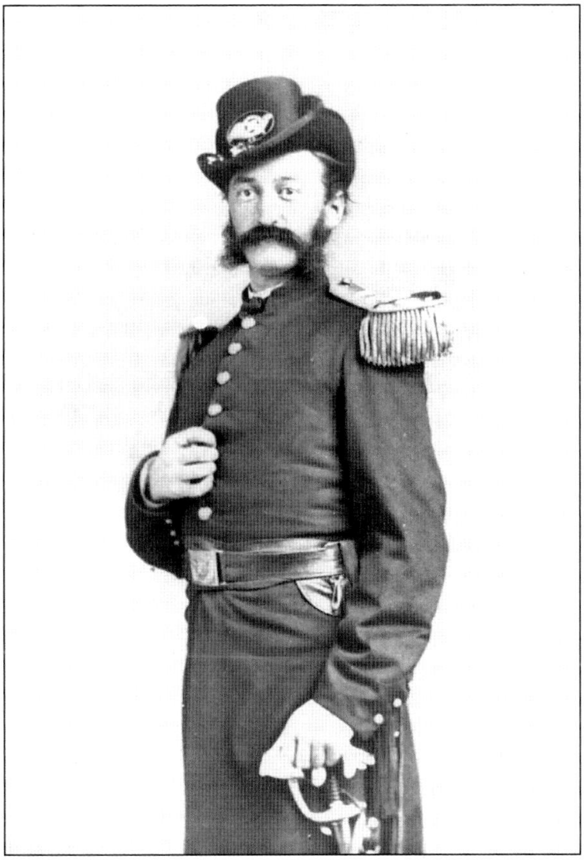

By the time this 1884 photograph of 10th Cavalry troops leaving on patrol was taken, clashes with Indians in Texas had virtually ceased. However, the 1870s were marked by repeated attacks by various Indian bands on stages, isolated travelers, and even larger freight wagon trains. The troops had little success against these attacks, as the Indians could vanish into the vast territory, and the poorly fed military ponies had little stamina with which to pursue them.

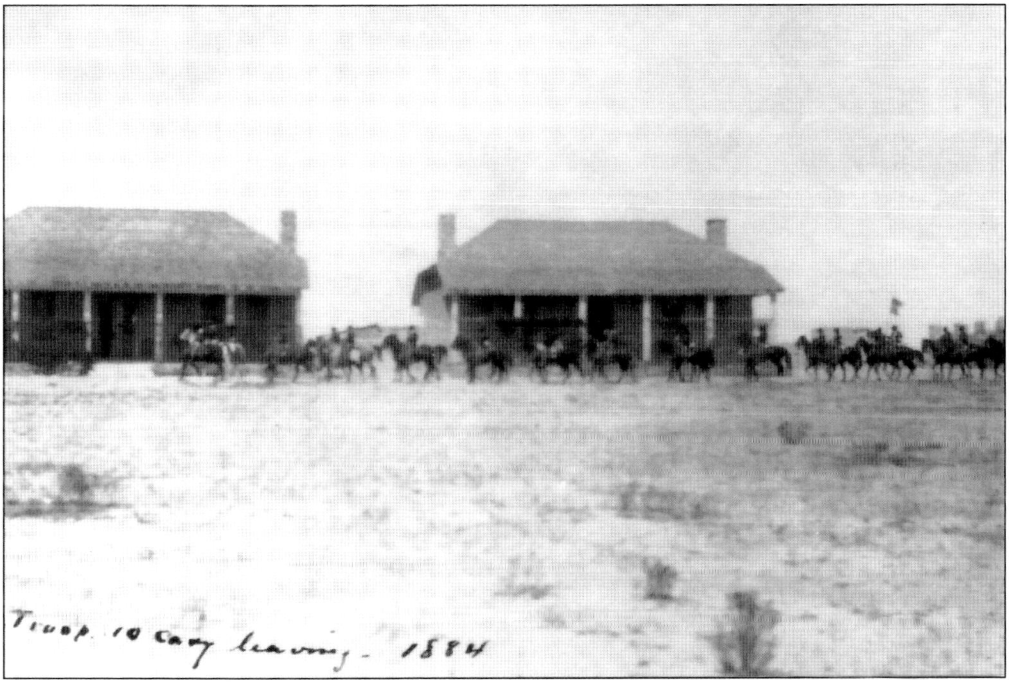

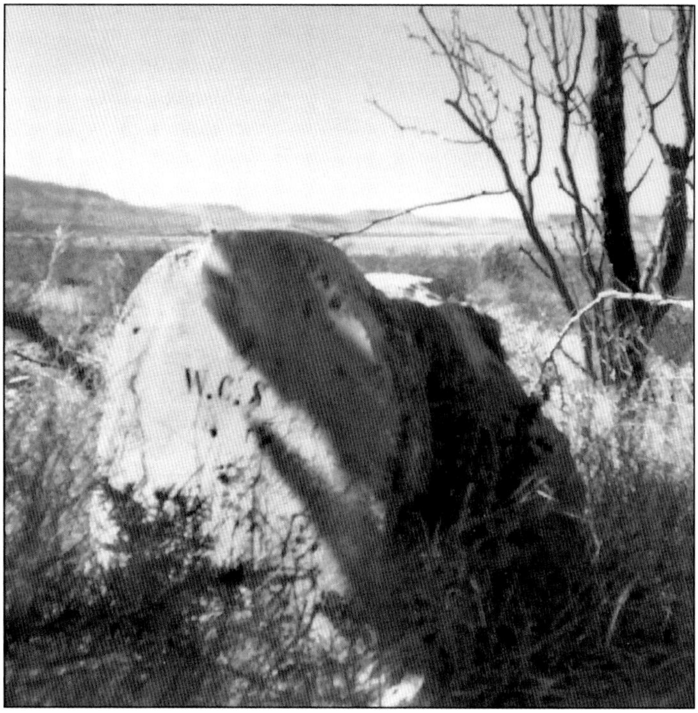

The newly formed Buffalo Soldiers sought opportunities to prove their worth as fighters. In December 1867, while camped in the ruins of Fort Lancaster 80 miles to the east, Company K, 9th Infantry from Fort Stockton was attacked by a large party of Indians and renegades. The troops successfully repulsed several assaults and suffered only three casualties, which occurred when Indians killed the horse guards and stole over 30 horses. The lonely grave of guard William Sharpe is all that marks this important battle site. (Photograph by James Collett.)

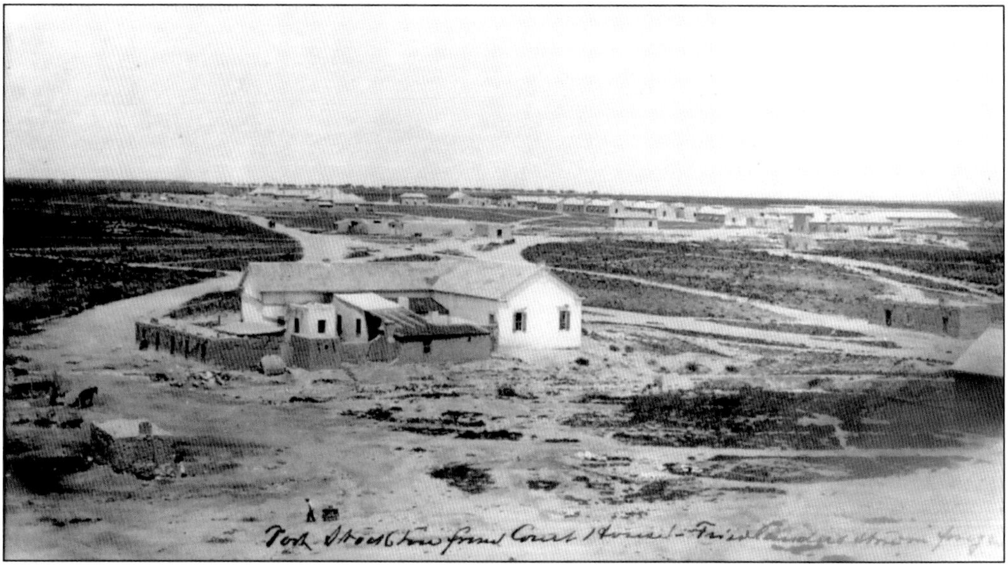

In 1884, Captain Wedemeyer photographed the fort from atop the Pecos County courthouse. The officers' quarters are in the background behind the store of post trader Joseph Friedlander. The barracks are across the parade ground, the guardhouse is just right of center, and the hospital is on the right. Most structures were adobe, constructed on foundations of stone quarried from nearby mesas. Shingled roofs and other wood had to be freighted 400 miles from San Antonio. (Courtesy of Nita Stewart Haley Memorial Library.)

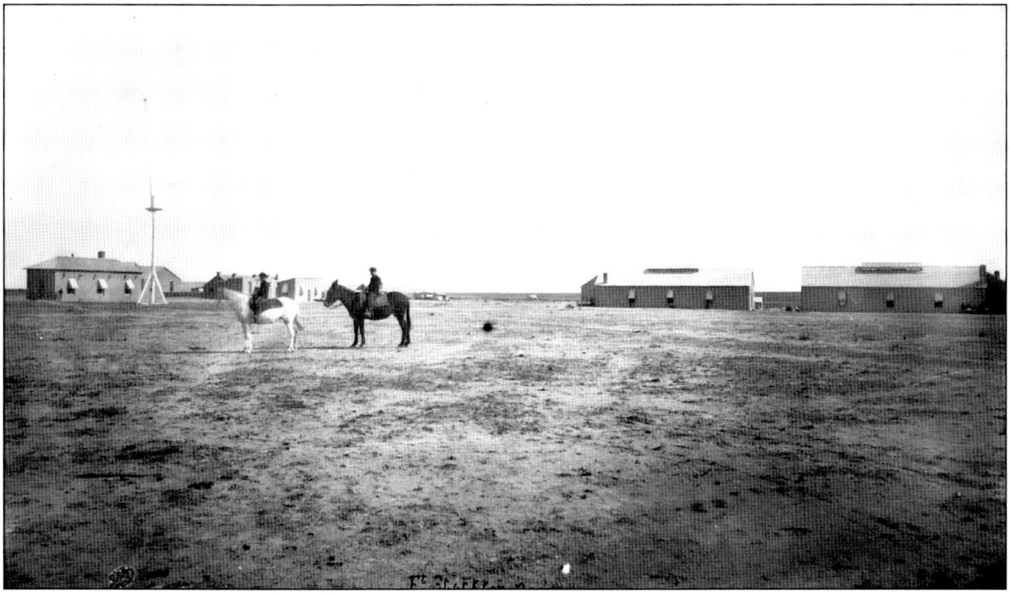

In this view from the north end of the parade ground, the quartermaster building is behind the flagpole. Two of the four barracks along the eastern side of the parade ground are on the right. Measuring 80 by 24 feet, each could accommodate a full company. During these years, units serving at the fort included the 9th and 10th Cavalry and the 16th, 24th, and 25th Infantry. Seven-Mile Mesa is visible in the background.

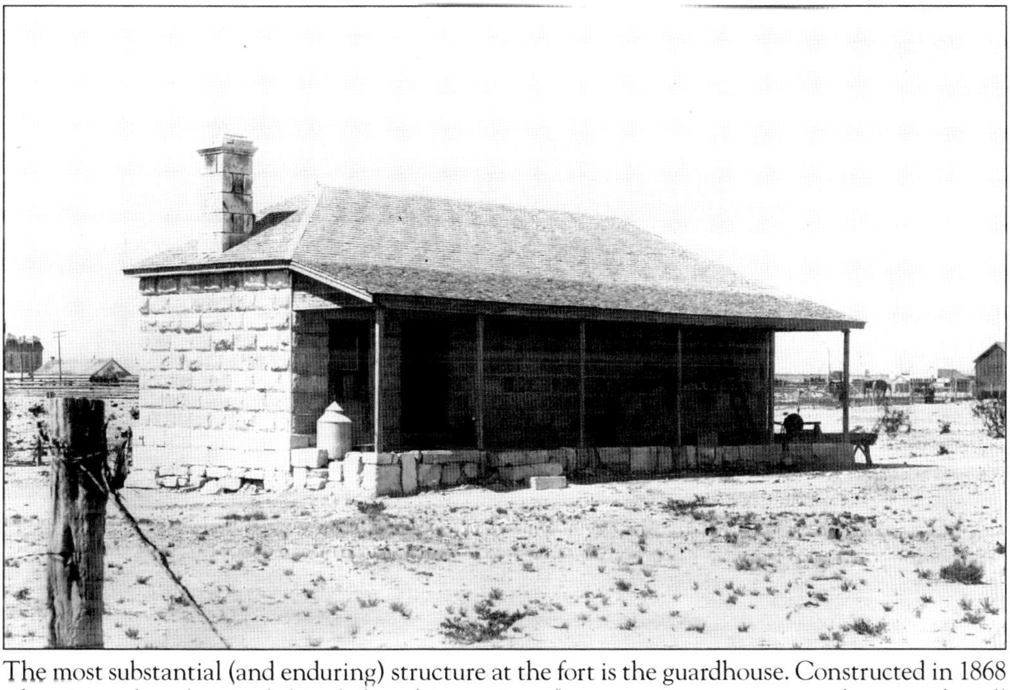

The most substantial (and enduring) structure at the fort is the guardhouse. Constructed in 1868 of native rock and a wood-shingled roof, it consists of two sparse rooms—a guardroom and a cell with arm and leg shackles. The Army inspector general noted, "The cell is not heated except by the exhaled air of its occupants." At times, as many as 15 prisoners were crowded into the guardhouse. (Courtesy of Mart Adams.)

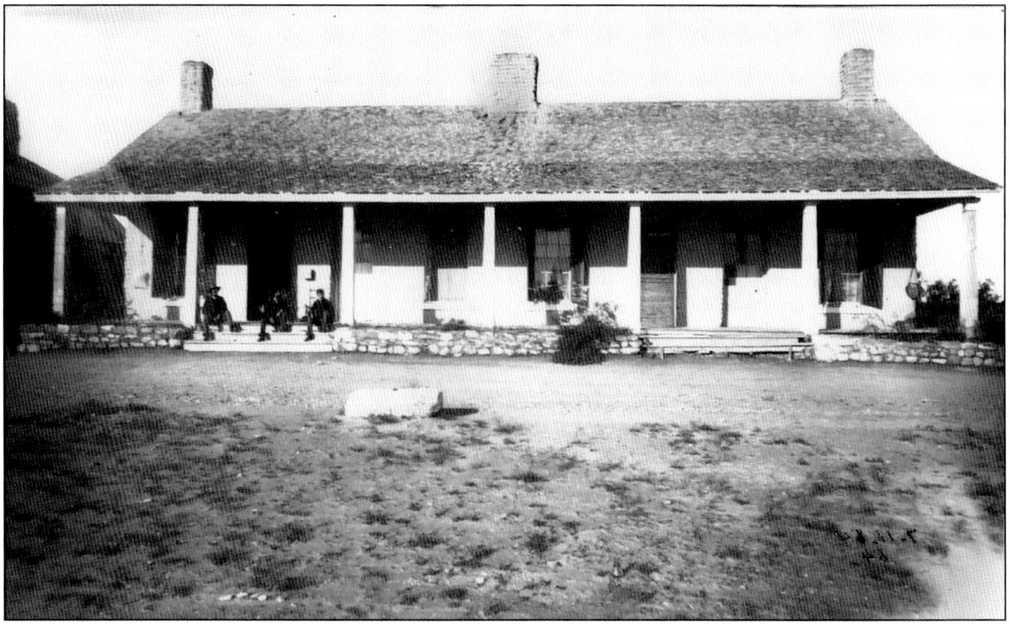

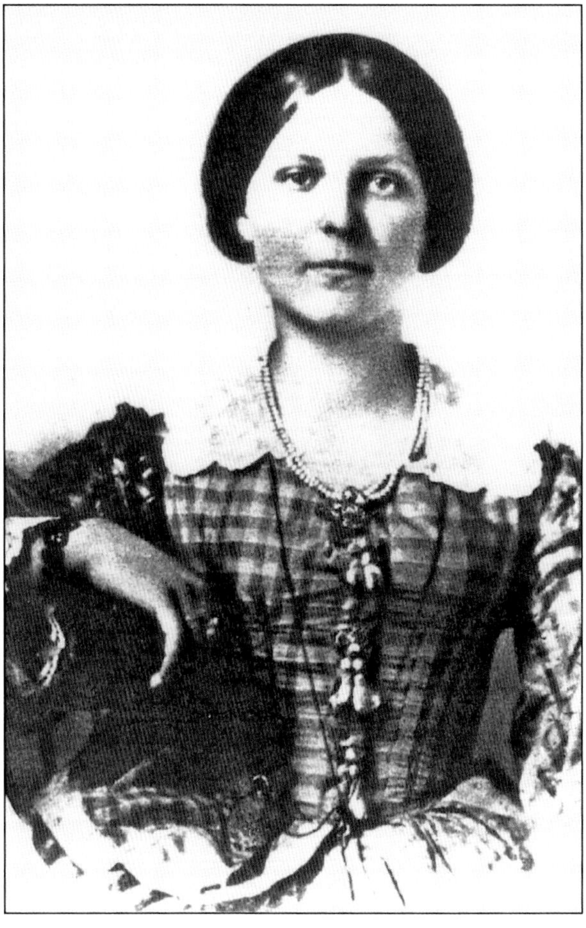

The five officers' quarters west of the parade ground were one-story adobe buildings with shingled roofs, front porches, and wood floors. Rooms were 15 by 18 feet with 14-foot ceilings. Captain Wedemeyer was not impressed with the accommodations. "As no repairs have been made, they are getting worse." By 1884, the Indian threat was largely eliminated, and closing the post was a regular discussion with the Army.

Life at the fort was difficult for women, even officers' wives. Captain Wedemeyer's wife, Ado (pictured here when younger), found life quite different from assignments back east. In one instance, a rabid coyote wandered into her sitting room. Wedemeyer remarked on how even basic staples were limited. "There are but four chickens in the country, and the eggs are so scarce that the Mexicans bring them in three at a time, for which they ask 25¢."

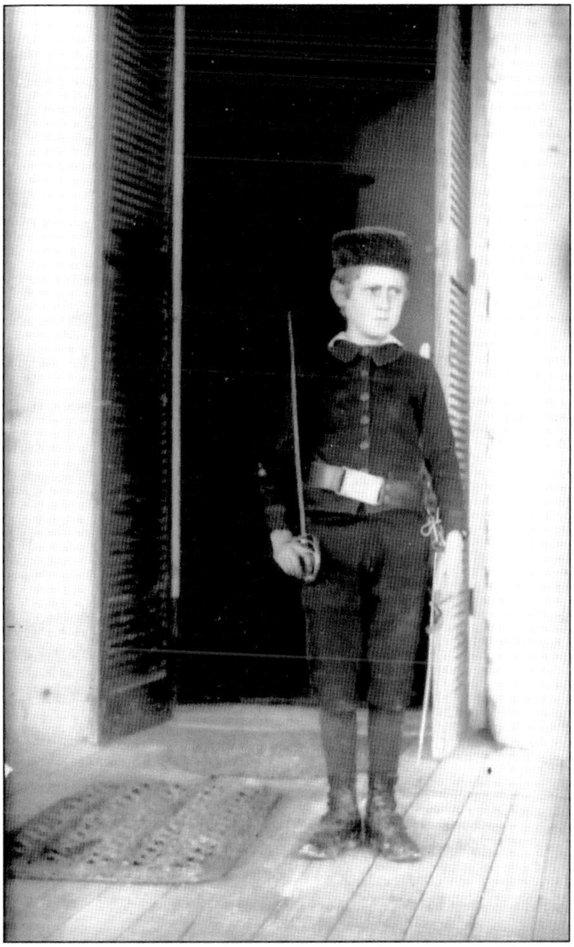

Otto, the Wedemeyers' son, lived with them at the post during these years. In this photograph, he poses solemnly in his soldier uniform. An archeological excavation conducted years later uncovered a small metal soldier among the stones that once held up the front porch of an officer's quarters.

Otto shared the fort with several other children: Colonel Wade's son John and Maj. Horace Jewett's daughters Hattie and Lizzie, as well as the captain's dog Punch. This may be Otto and Punch, though no details on individuals are provided. Otto once accompanied his father on a march to Pecos Falls, northeast of the fort. Wedemeyer also took him duck hunting at Leon Springs, west of the fort.

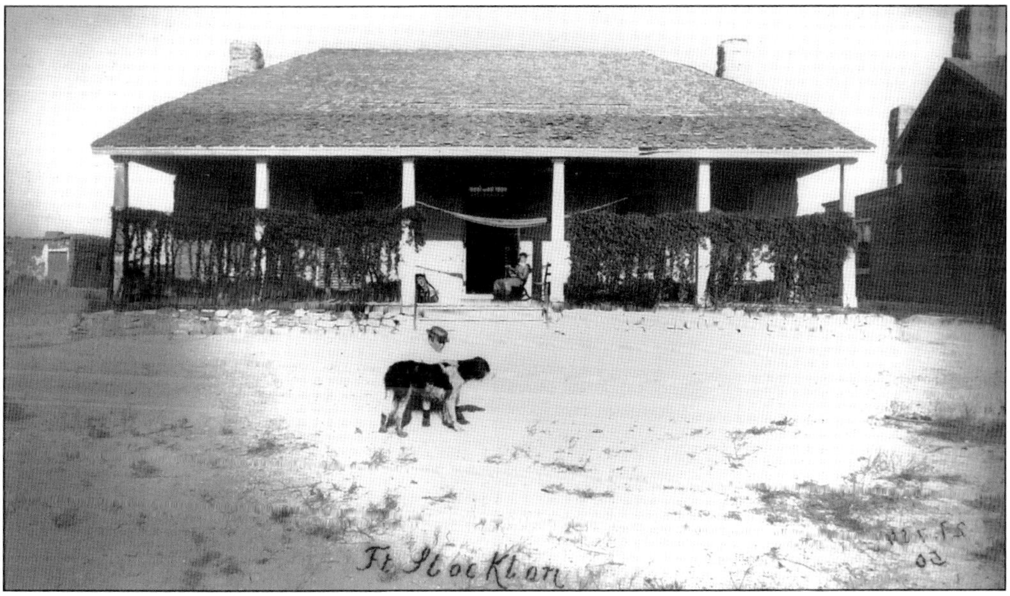

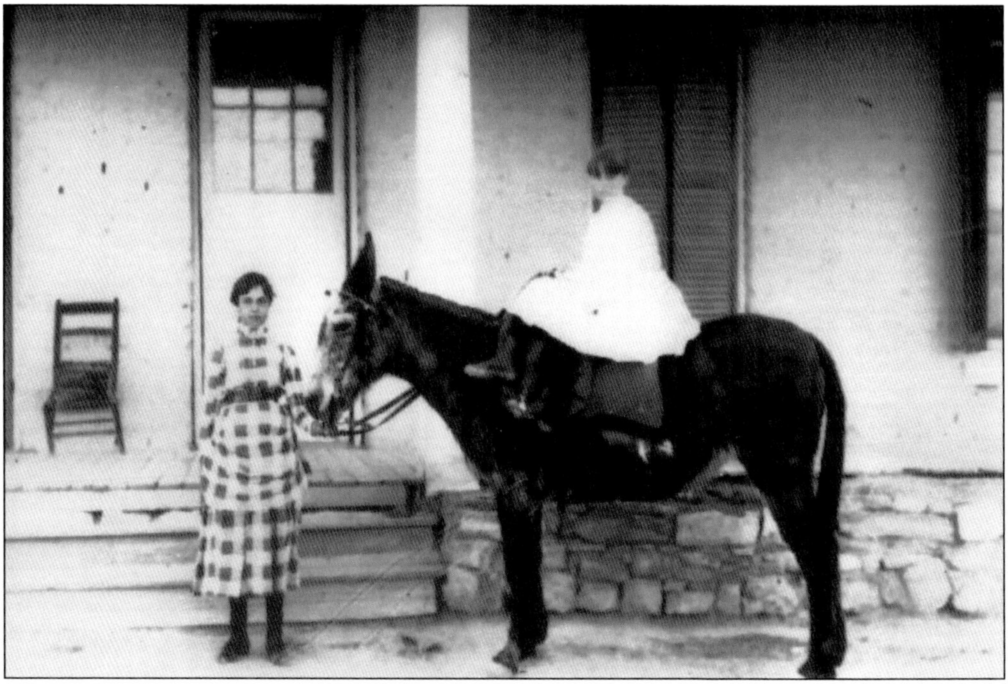

Children at the fort seemed to have generally enjoyed life there. Captain Wedemeyer wrote, "Capt. Keyes and Lt. Cooper have families here, and their girls are good playmates for Della. They have an old burro, and the girls get on him until nothing can be seen of the burro except his ears. Then the old gray back gets tired and he dumps the crowd and runs for the stable."

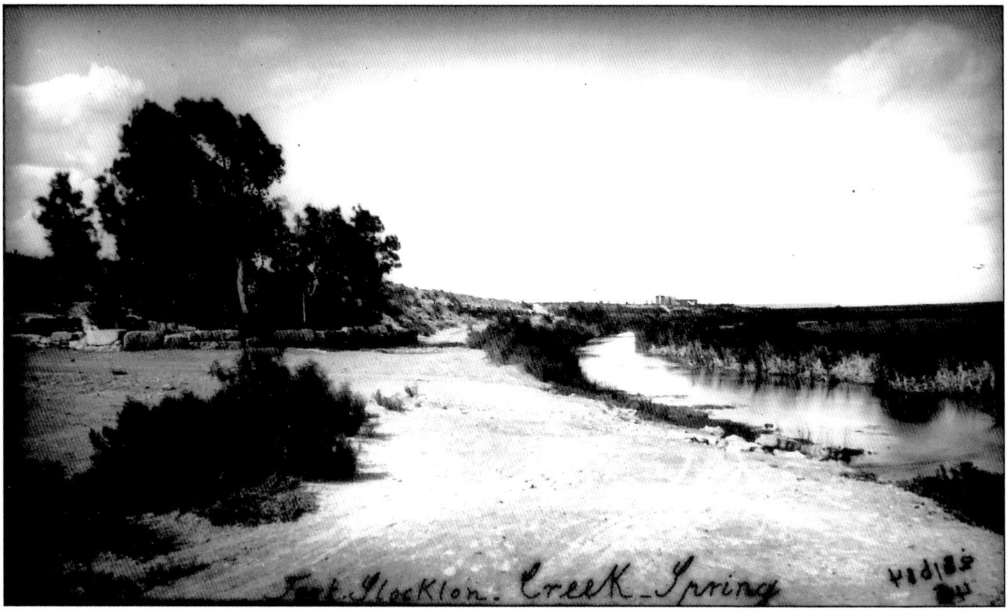

Of Comanche Springs, Captain Wedemeyer wrote, "The water is considerably impregnated with alkali and not pleasant, though one becomes accustomed to it. The creek at the post is twenty-five feet wide and six feet deep and the current is quite rapid." In Wedemeyer's photograph (perhaps the earliest of the springs), the post hospital is visible on the creek bank just right of center.

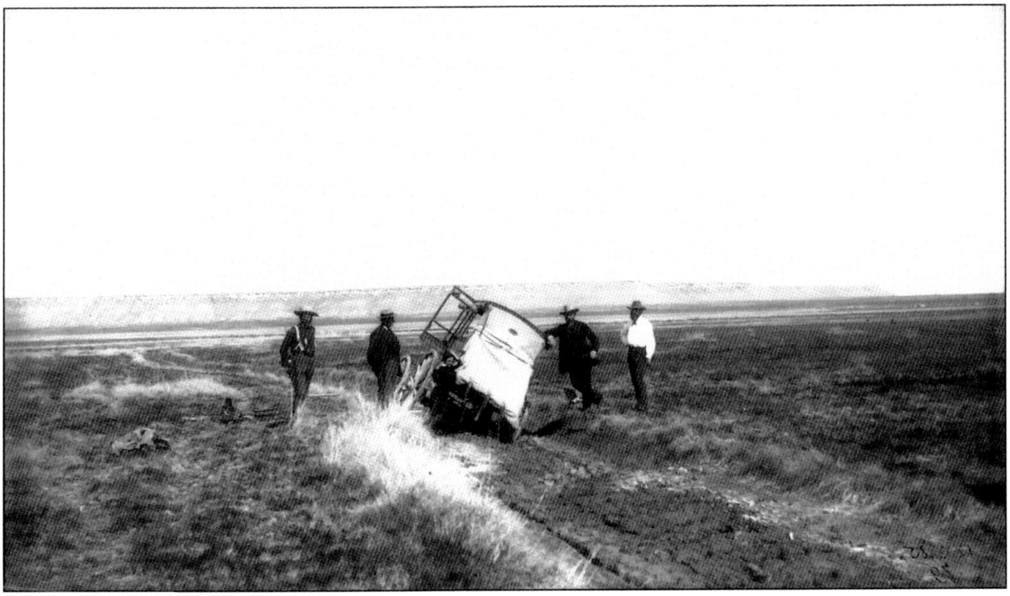

Here, the stage has broken down on the Old Main Road north of Seven-Mile Mesa. Pictured from left to right are Capt. William Wedemeyer, Maj. Horace Jewett, Wedemeyer's son Otto, Frederick Young, and Dr. Tesson. Wedemeyer encountered several Texas commanders during his tour of duty and was not hesitant to include his views of them. Of Col. Benjamin Grierson, 10th Cavalry, he wrote, "He is a great talker and full of himself and his works."

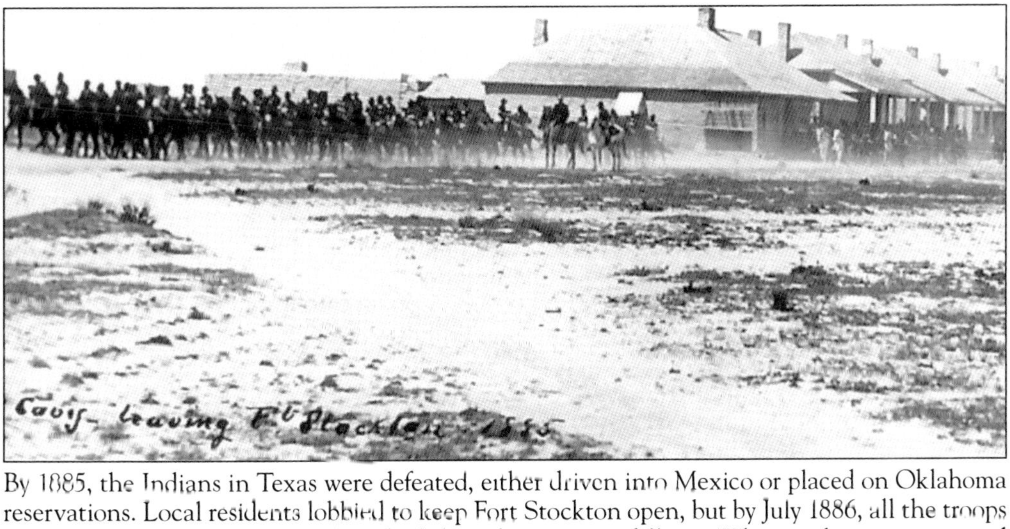

By 1885, the Indians in Texas were defeated, either driven into Mexico or placed on Oklahoma reservations. Local residents lobbied to keep Fort Stockton open, but by July 1886, all the troops were gone. One resident later described their departure as follows. "The cavalry were mounted and the infantry riding in wagons and hacks along the western portion of the trail, heading into the sunset with a shroud of dust boiling up into the sky."

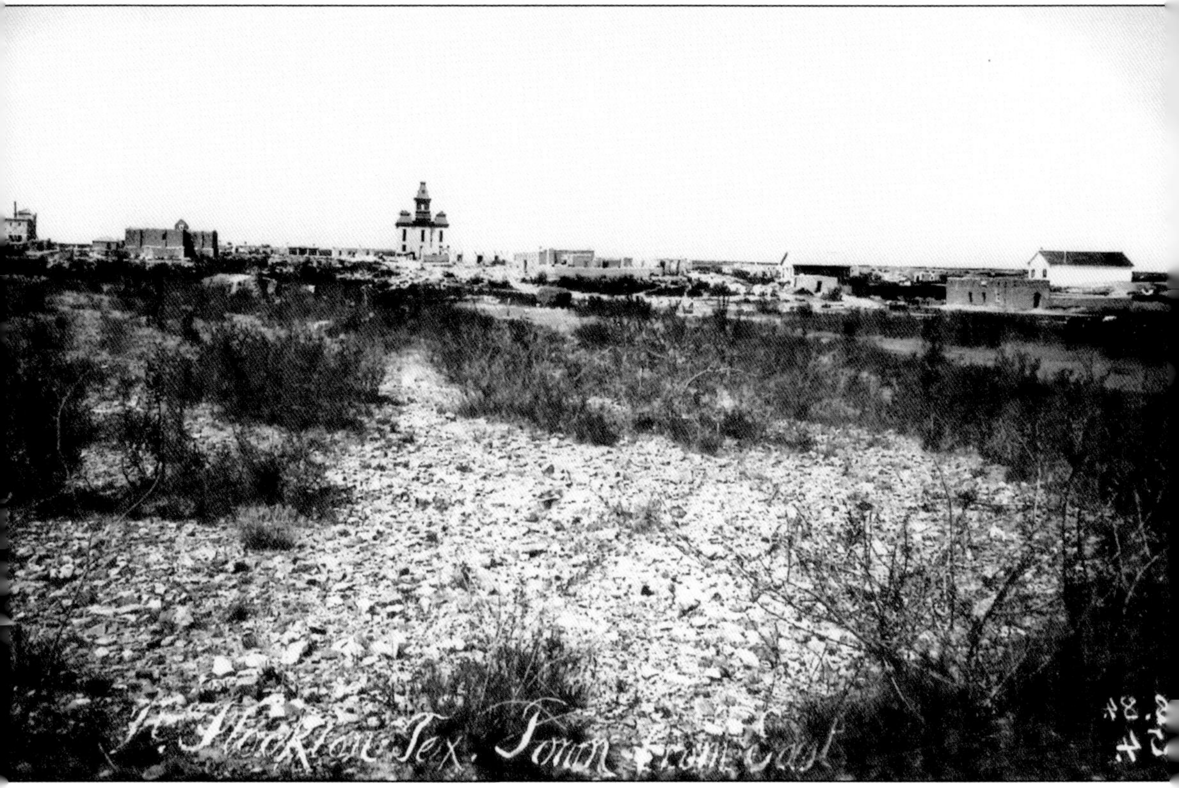

Captain Wedemeyer also photographed the small community that had grown up alongside the post. The new Pecos County Courthouse (center) dominates the skyline, surrounded by a scattering of adobe buildings. The departure of troops marked the end of the post of Fort Stockton era, but another era had already begun. The citizens of the town of Fort Stockton faced the challenge of a different kind of survival in this isolated region.

Three

Establishing Pecos County

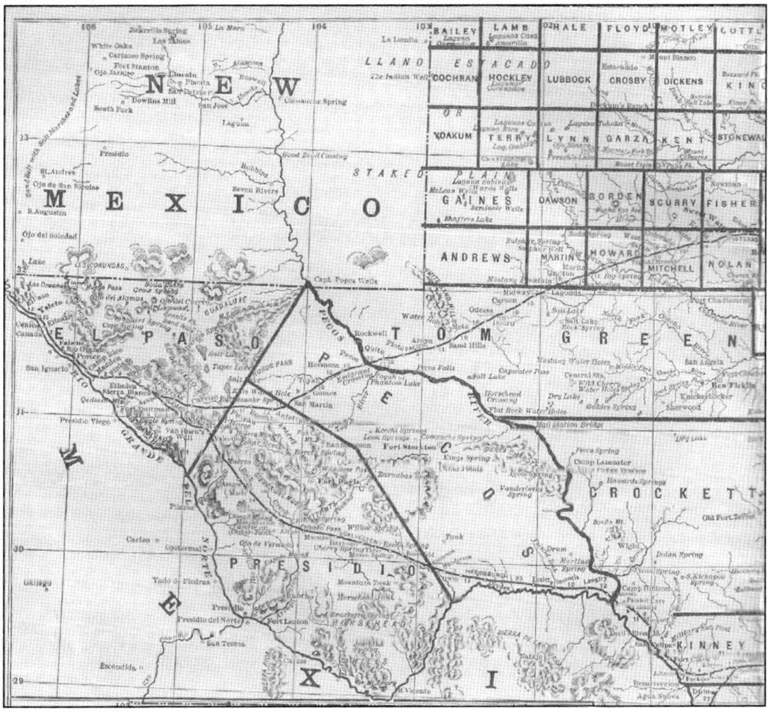

The Texas Legislature created Pecos County in 1871. Its 12,000 square miles included all the western bank of the Pecos River in Texas. Over the next three decades, the residents of Pecos County struggled to establish law and order within this frontier domain. This map dates from around 1883.

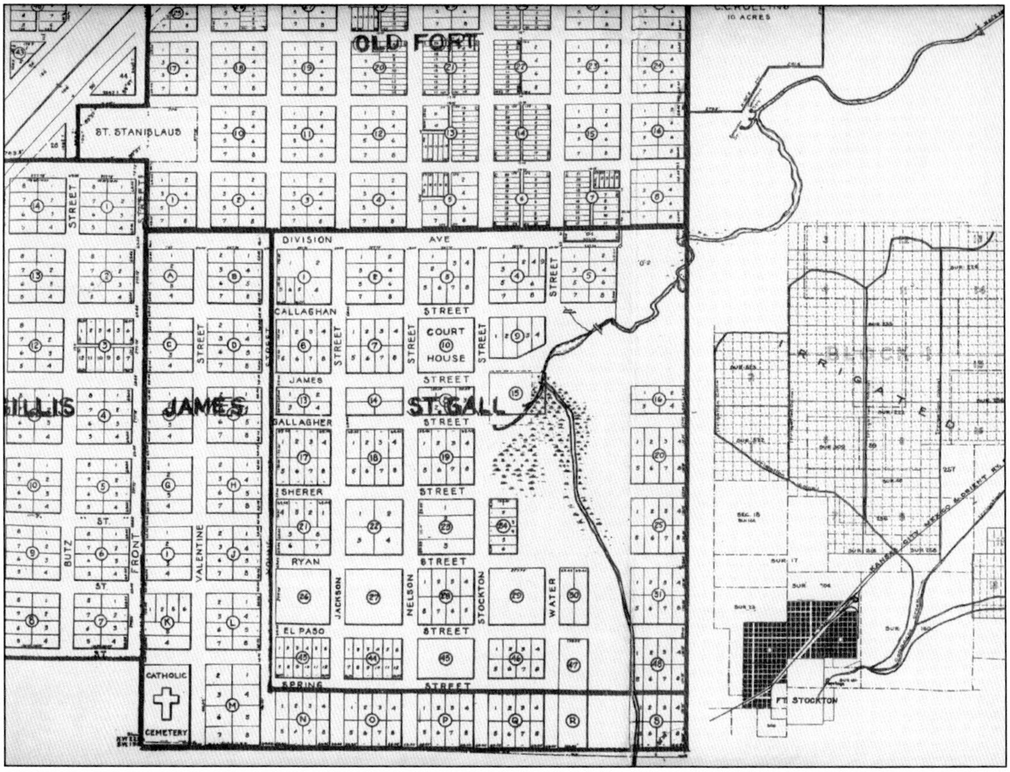

Peter Gallagher, an Irish businessman from San Antonio, purchased several tracts in 1868, including Comanche Springs and the land occupied by the fort. He donated 160 acres for a townsite named St. Gall. The name never became popular, and in 1881, Fort Stockton became the town's official name. This 1969 plat includes the original St. Gall. Division Avenue would later become the unofficial dividing line between Anglo Fort Stockton and the "Mexican" town.

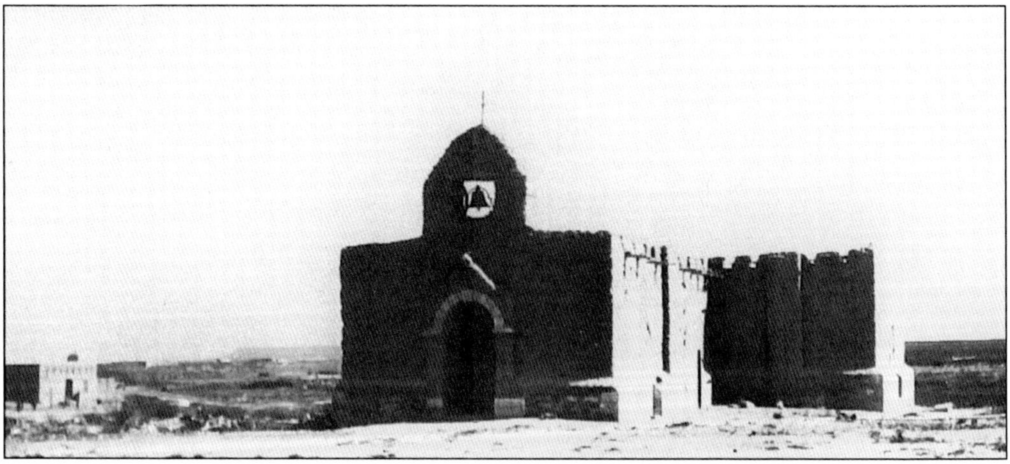

Peter Gallagher, a Catholic, also donated three acres for a church in 1871. Fort Stockton became part of a mission area, served from Fort Davis, that covered five counties. Work on St. Joseph Catholic Church began in 1876, when Fr. Joseph Hoban recorded the first baptismal records. The original adobe structure had a stone foundation three feet high; lumber for the church was freighted in from San Antonio.

On March 9, 1872, officials for Pecos County were elected by 386 voters. These included Andrew Loomis, sheriff; Edward Bates, district clerk; Jacob Jacobs, treasurer; and F.W. Young, surveyor. Also elected were justices of the peace George M. Frazier (precinct one), Cesario Torres (precinct two), Francis Rooney (precinct three), and Hopolito Carrasco (precinct four). The district clerk's office served as the courthouse. In 1877, a contract for a two-story jail (pictured) was awarded for $1,725.

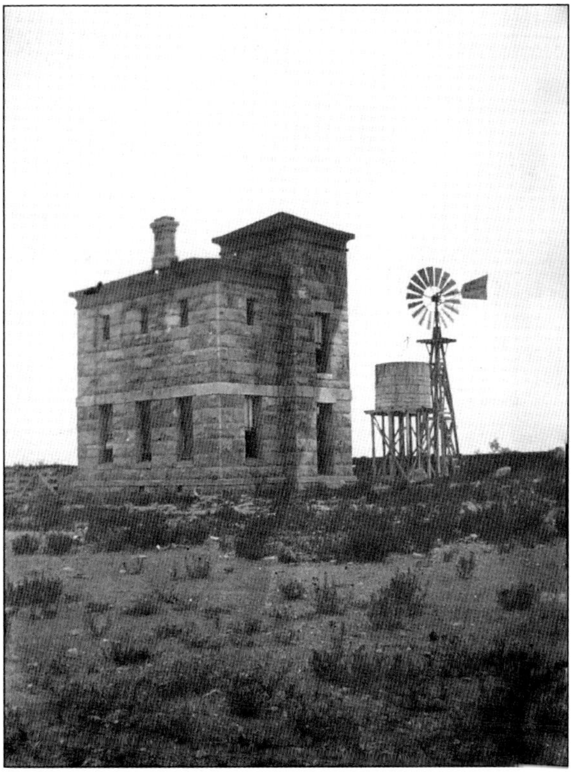

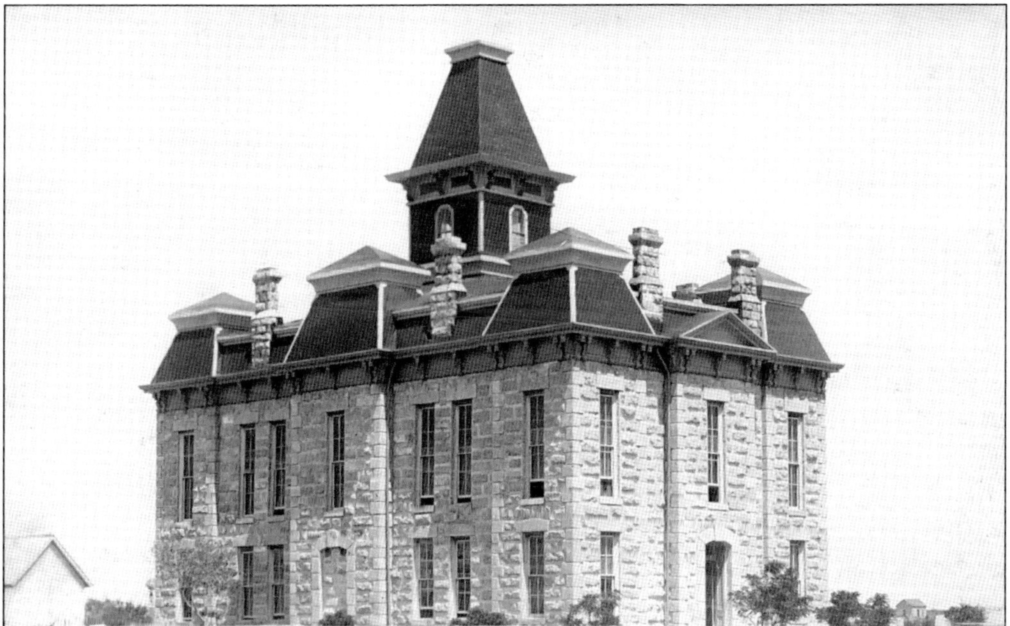

By 1882, county commissioners were prepared to build a courthouse. M.F. Corbett, businessman and former post trader, sold the block for the courthouse for one dollar. J.M. Archer won the construction contract for $10,000. The two-story rock building was completed in 1886. In 1883, Reeves County was created from the northern end of Pecos County, with Pecos as the county seat.

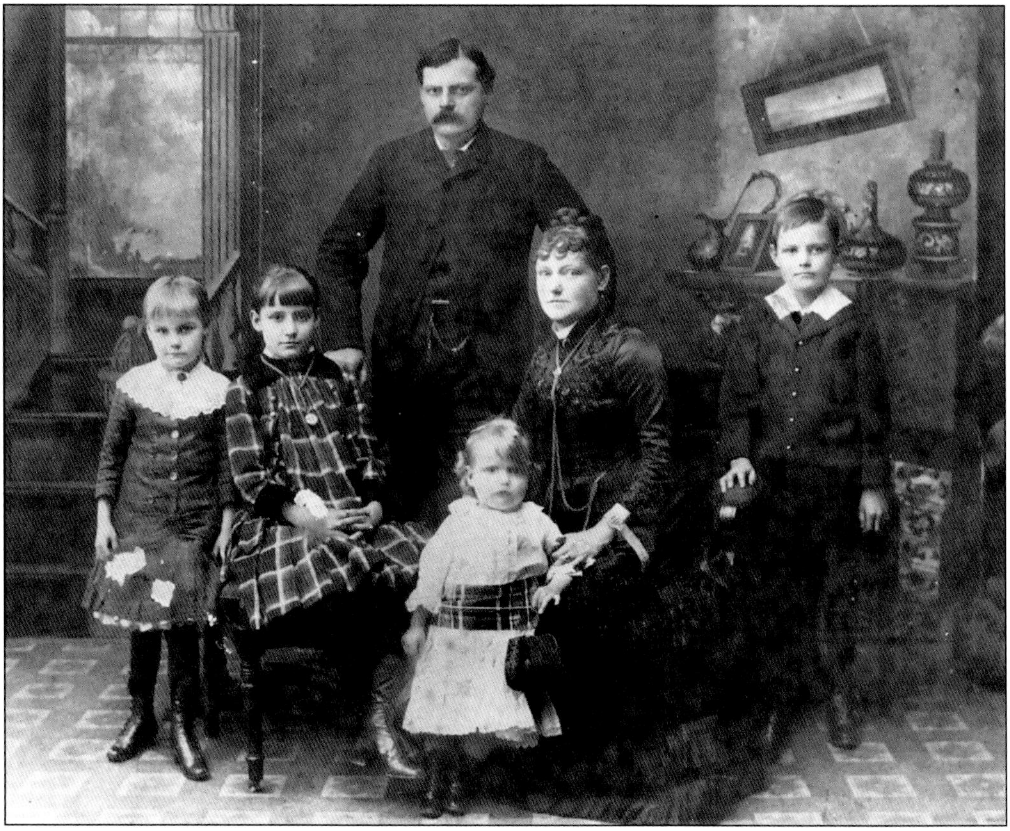

Frederick William Jung, a German immigrant, anglicized his name by changing it to Young when he came to San Antonio. After serving in the Union army as a musician, Young relocated to Fort Stockton around 1870, acquiring the job of post trader. Young and his wife, Matilda Sophia Loeper Young, pose with four of their children. The youngsters in this image are, from left to right, Aileen Maxon, Eloise Courtny, Lilian McKay, and Andrew Hart. All of the middle names were taken from officers from the fort.

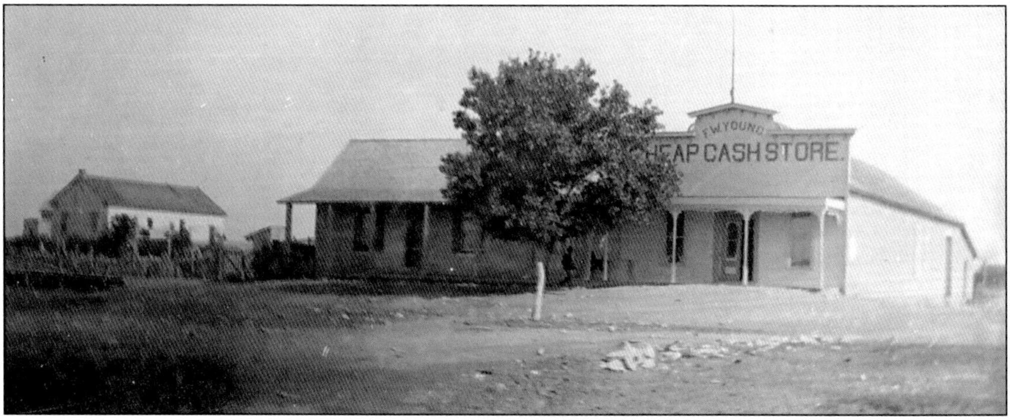

In 1876, Young opened a mercantile store (pictured) that was among the first businesses in the community. Captain Wedemeyer, who had known Young in the service, had little faith in him. "He is a poor businessman. At present, things do not look very prosperous." Wedemeyer reported Young gave a "hop" (dance) when he opened for business.

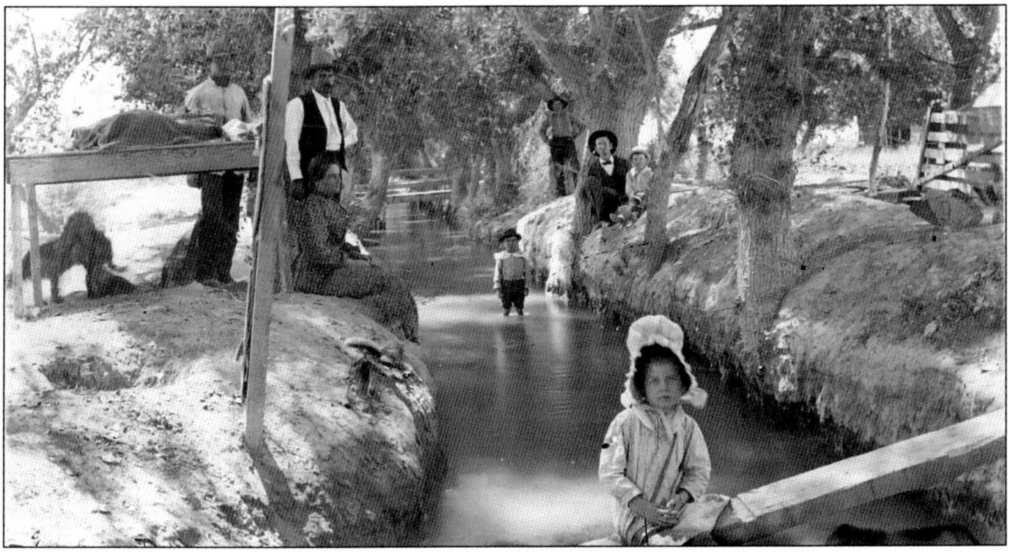

Cesario Torres acquired land along Comanche Creek east of Fort Stockton in 1869. Torres, his brother, and his father-in-law, Felix Garza, dug a large irrigation ditch with wooden shovels. They maintained the ditch for 10 years, earning 37 sections of land from the state of Texas. The large cottonwood trees growing along the ditch later became a source of recreation for family outings. This is illustrated in this photograph from around 1900 of an unidentified group enjoying the area.

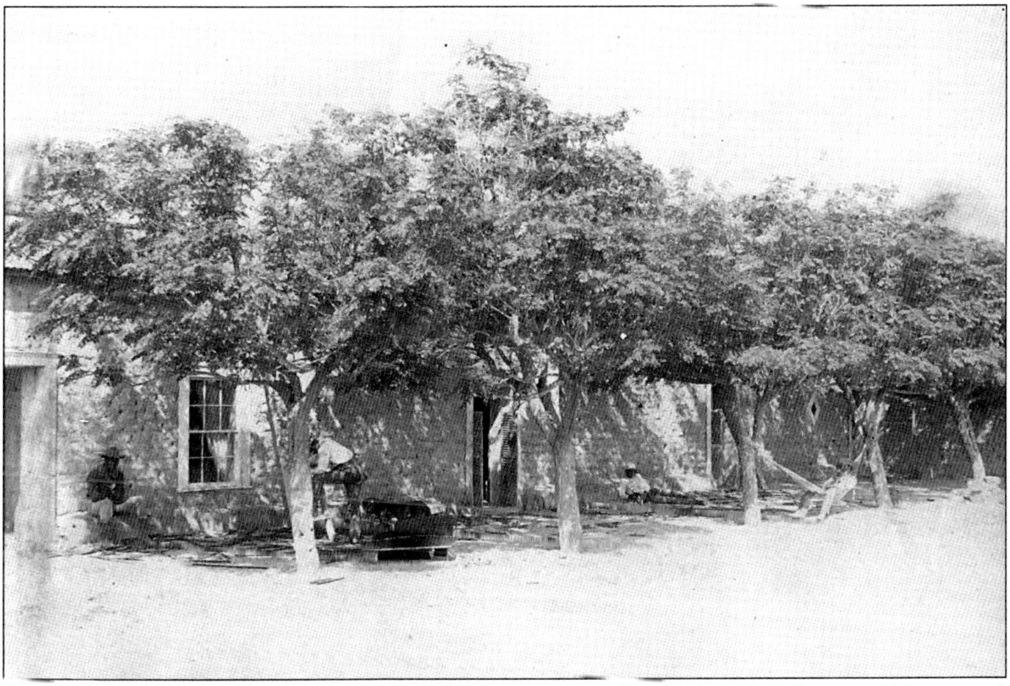

Torres established the Seven-d ranch (headquarters pictured), which included over 1,000 irrigated acres. The ranch was named for the brand, which was a figure "7" connected to a small letter "d." The Seven-d was a profitable enterprise for Torres, with over 40 families working on his farms. In addition to farming, the Seven-d became one of the first cattle ranches in the county.

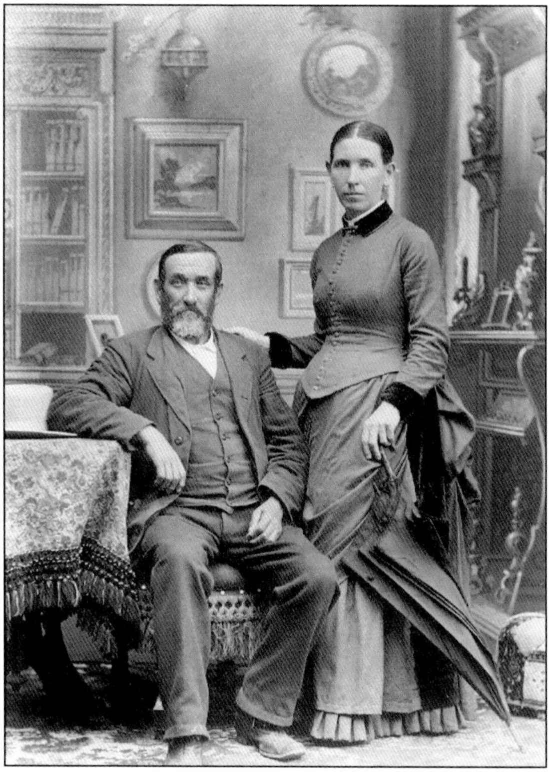

Francis Rooney and his wife, Jane, both Irish immigrants, began moving their cattle to Fort Stockton from Sabinal, Texas, in 1870. Rooney lost much of his original herd to a violent Indian attack near the Pecos River. He persisted and was among the first to bring cattle to Pecos County. With only a small adobe house, Rooney began farming and ranching near San Pedro Springs, six miles to the north.

Like Torres, Rooney developed irrigation canals on his property. He was the first in the county to use barbed wire to manage his cattle. Rooney also imported cottonwood and willow trees by oxcart from Presidio, Texas, to plant along the canals. These groves became popular sites for community holiday picnics, such as the one pictured on the cover. Here, wagons gather for another event in the shade of Rooney's trees.

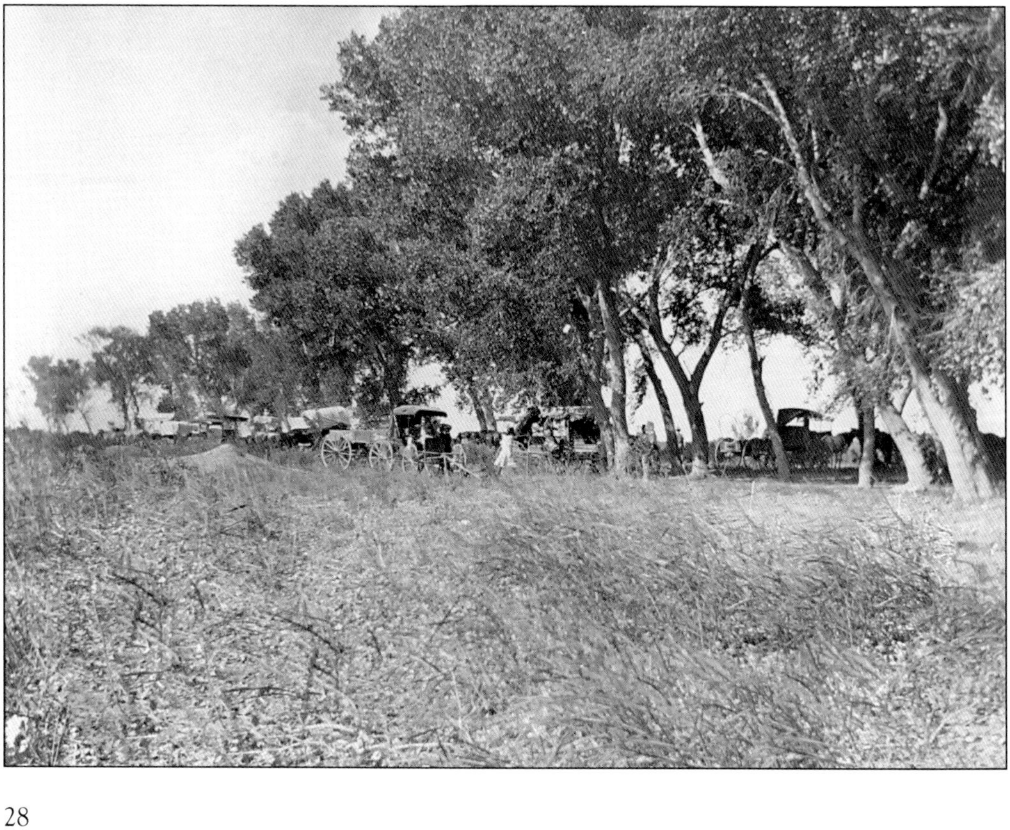

George M. Frazier, who freighted on the Chihuahua Trail, brought his family to Fort Stockton in 1869. He ranched in the Leon Valley west of Fort Stockton and later helped develop irrigation projects there. Frazier also had a home in Fort Stockton for his wife, May, and their seven children. In 1872, he became the first county judge for Pecos County, serving until 1884.

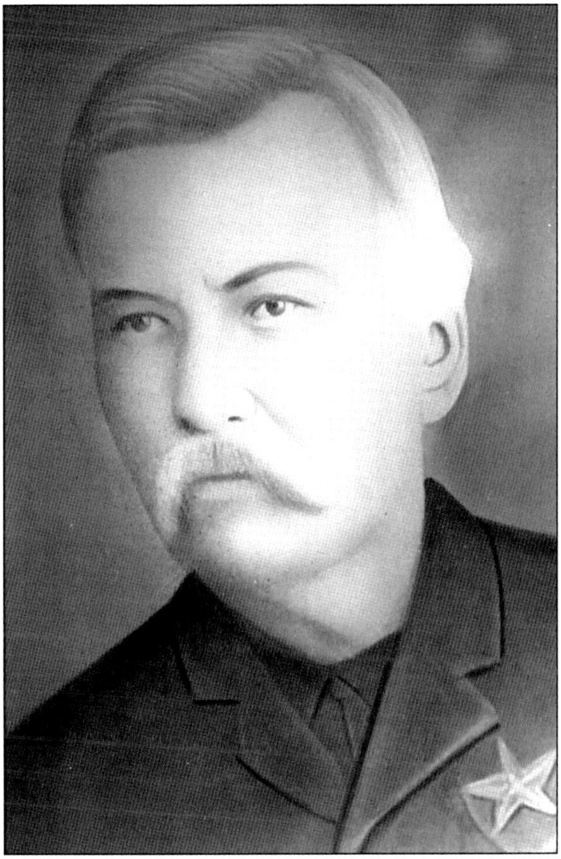

By 1883, two railroad lines crossed Pecos County, neither passing near Fort Stockton (see map on page 23). The San Antonio–San Diego Mail (page 12) ceased operations in 1881. Then, only wagon roads with difficult and dangerous crossings, like this one on the Pecos River near Sheffield (pictured around 1890), ran to Fort Stockton. (Courtesy of Texas State Library and Archives Commission.)

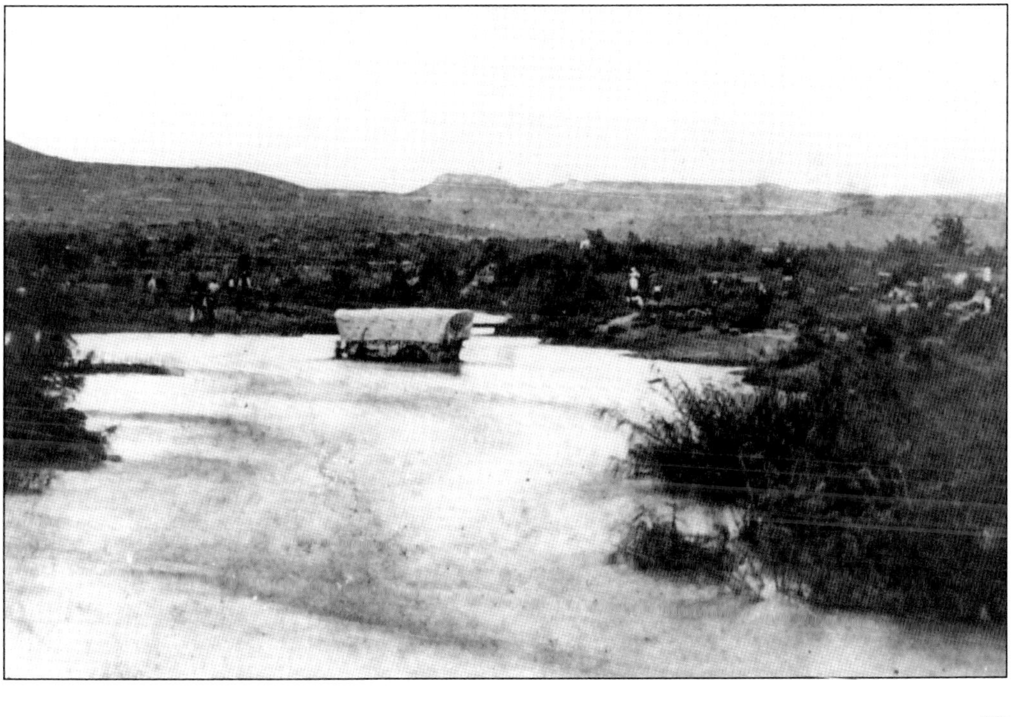

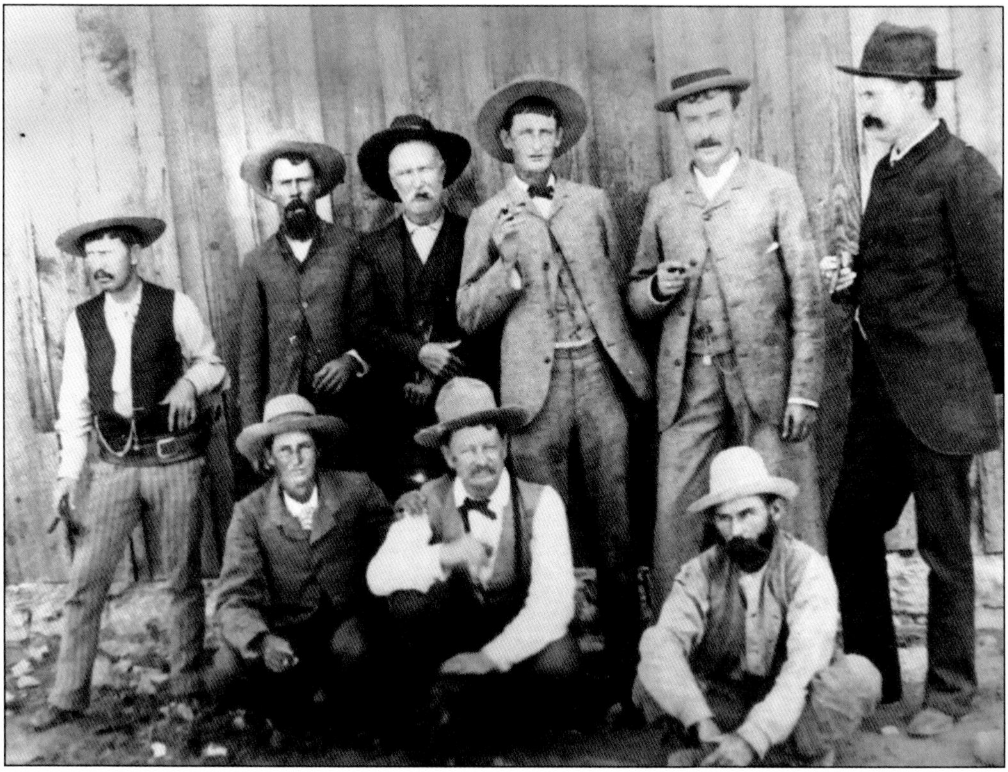

The Texas & Pacific Railroad spurred growth around the town of Pecos. This led to the creation of Reeves County from northern Pecos County in 1883, and Pecos became the county seat in 1884. Fort Stockton leaders divided over the formation of Reeves County. This 1883 photograph in Pecos includes, from left to right, (seated) Lee Heard, Herman Koehler, and unidentified; (standing) Bud Frazier, Tom White, George M. Frazier, Allen Heard, John Rooney, and Tom Babb.

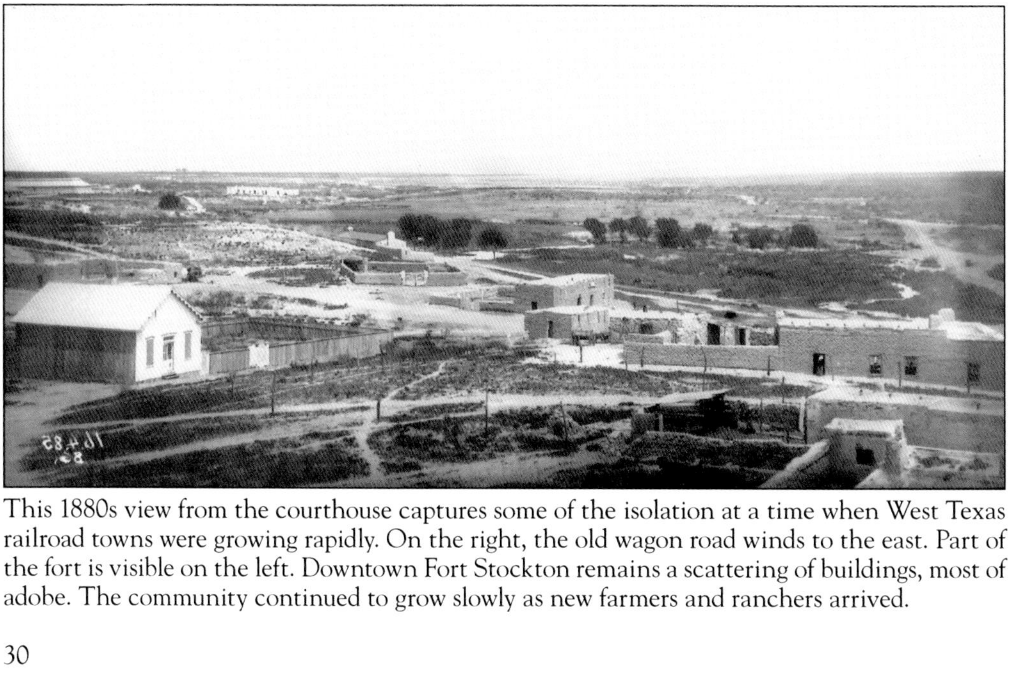

This 1880s view from the courthouse captures some of the isolation at a time when West Texas railroad towns were growing rapidly. On the right, the old wagon road winds to the east. Part of the fort is visible on the left. Downtown Fort Stockton remains a scattering of buildings, most of adobe. The community continued to grow slowly as new farmers and ranchers arrived.

In 1875, the Texas Legislature enacted a law authorizing grants of land to builders of "canals and ditches for the purpose of irrigation and navigation." To qualify, a minimum of three miles had to be completed. This is the charter of the Garza Irrigation and Manufacturing Company, established with $10,000 investment capital for a term of 50 years. By the end of the year, five other irrigation companies had been established in Pecos County.

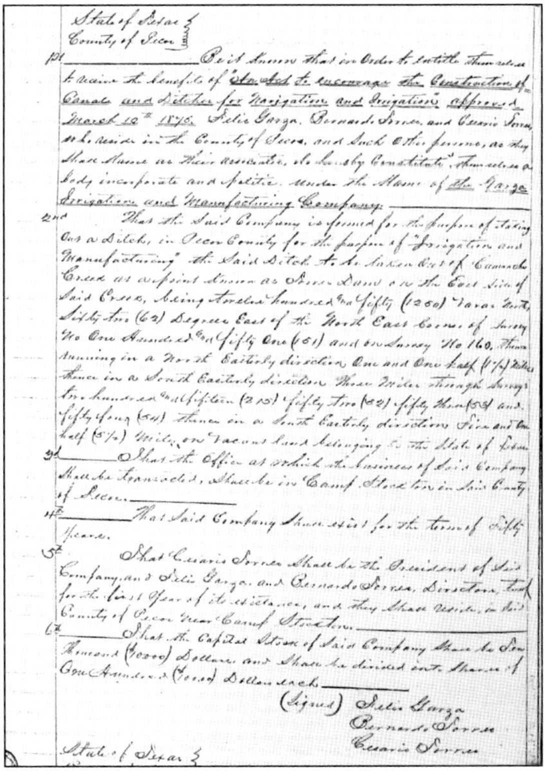

State of Texas }
County of Pecos }

1st ____ Be it known that in Order to entitle themselves to receive the benefits of "An Act to encourage the Construction of Canals and Ditches for Navigation and Irrigation" approved March 10th 1875. Felis Garza, Bernardo Torres and Cesario Torres who reside in the County of Pecos, and such other persons, as they shall name as their associates, do hereby Constitute themselves a body incorporate and politic, under the Name of the Garza Irrigation and Manufacturing Company.

2nd That the said Company is formed for the purpose of taking Out a Ditch, in Pecos County for the purpose of "Irrigation and Manufacturing" the said Ditch to be taken Out of Comanche Creek at a point known as Torres Dam on the East side of said Creek, being twelve hundred and fifty (1250) Varas North Sixty two (62) Degrees East of the North East Corner of Survey No One Hundred and fifty One (151) and on Survey No 160. thence running in a North Easterly direction One and One half (1½) Miles thence in a South Easterly direction Three Miles through Surveys two hundred and fifteen (215) fifty two (52) fifty three (53) and fifty four (54) thence in a South Easterly direction Five and One half (5½) Miles on vacant land belonging to the State of Texas

3d ____ That the Office at which the business of said Company shall be transacted, shall be in Camp Stockton in said County of Pecos.

4th ____ That said Company shall exist for the term of Fifty Years.

5th That Cesario Torres shall be the President of said Company, and Felis Garza and Bernardo Torres, Directors, [illegible] for the first Year of its existance, and they shall reside in said County of Pecos near Camp Stockton.

6th ____ That the Capital Stock of said Company shall be Ten Thousand (10000) Dollars and shall be divided into shares of One Hundred (100) Dollars each.

(Signed) Felis Garza
Bernardo Torres
Cesario Torres

State of Texas }

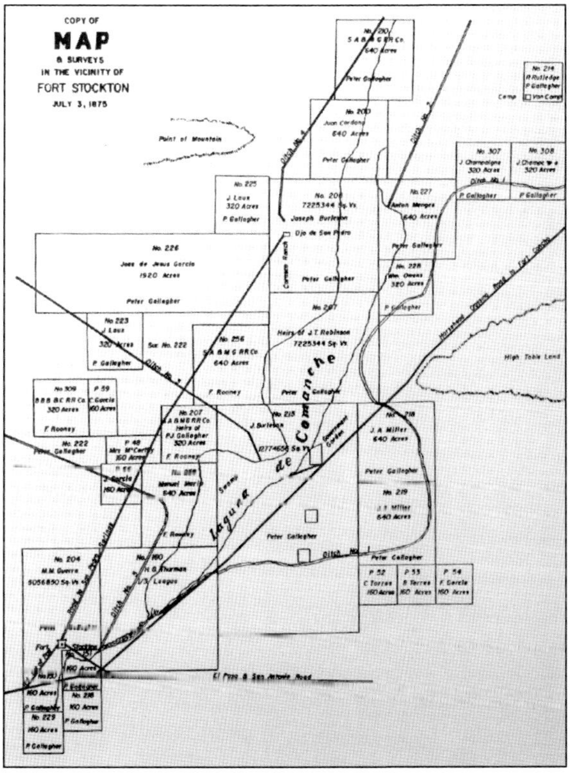

Torres, Gallagher, and Rooney all developed ditches for their irrigation companies. The area downstream from Fort Stockton became known as the "Irrigated Lands." The growing farm region attracted both permanent and seasonal workers. This 1875 map shows the different grants and who their owners were, as well as the five major irrigation ditches. At times, lengthy legal disputes arose over the water rights of these different owners.

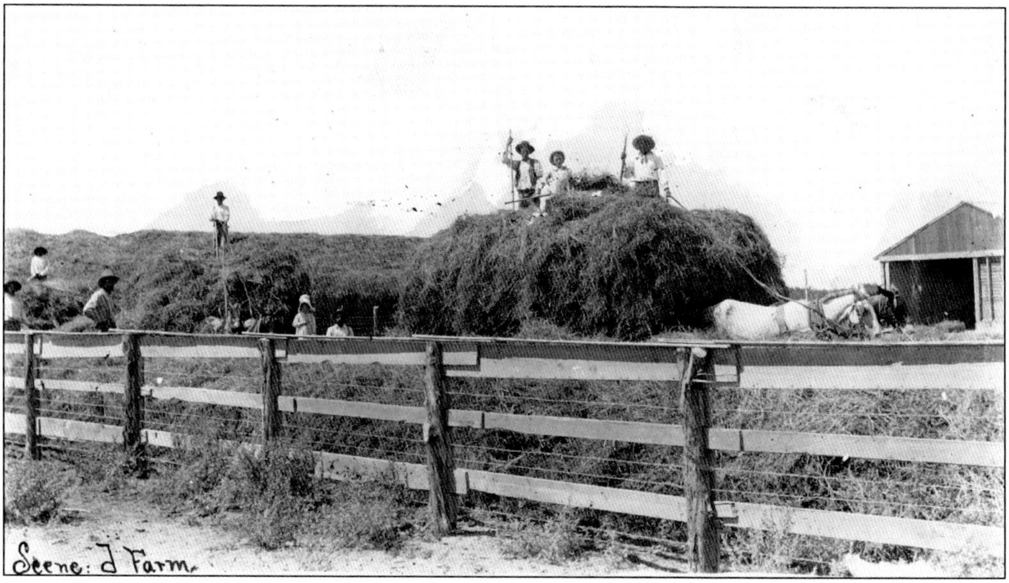

Crops grown on the irrigated lands included corn, oats, and hay, all of which could be sold locally for feed. Several farms, including the Seven-d, produced large crops of alfalfa hay (pictured). Much of the work was done by hand, and crops were transported by wagons. The posts of Fort Stockton and Fort Davis provided good markets until they closed. Hay also became a feed supplement for local cattle.

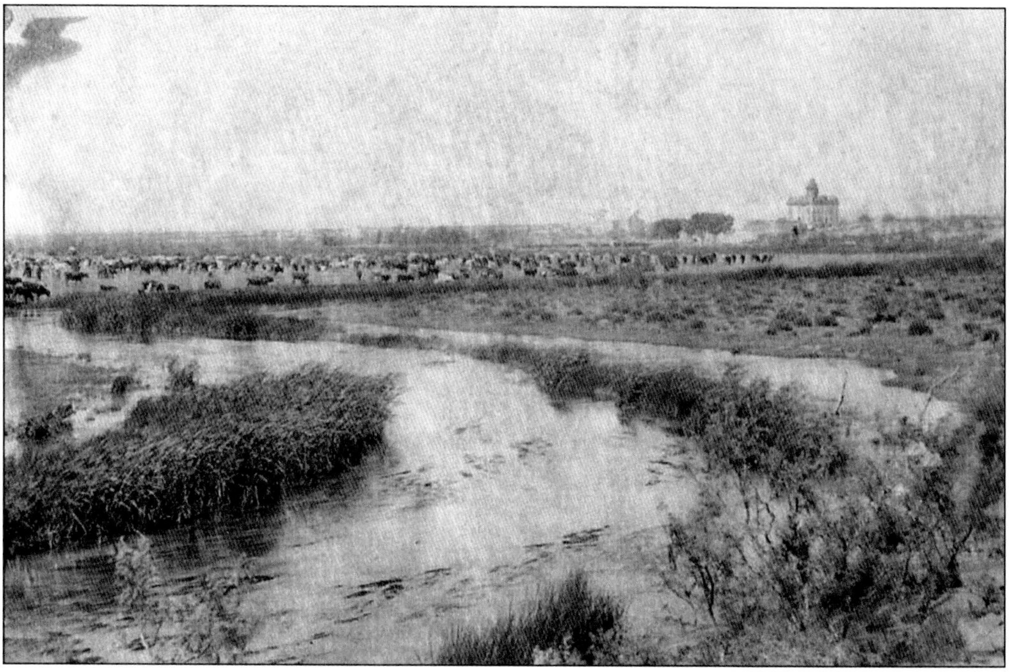

Captain Wedemeyer commented, "I do not think I ever was in a country where beef was as poor [in taste] as it is here." He admitted that cattle in the area "thrive well, notwithstanding the poor quality of feed." As the area of irrigated land expanded, the cattle business and the beef flavor improved. In this photograph from around 1900, cattle graze along Comanche Creek. The Pecos County courthouse is in the background.

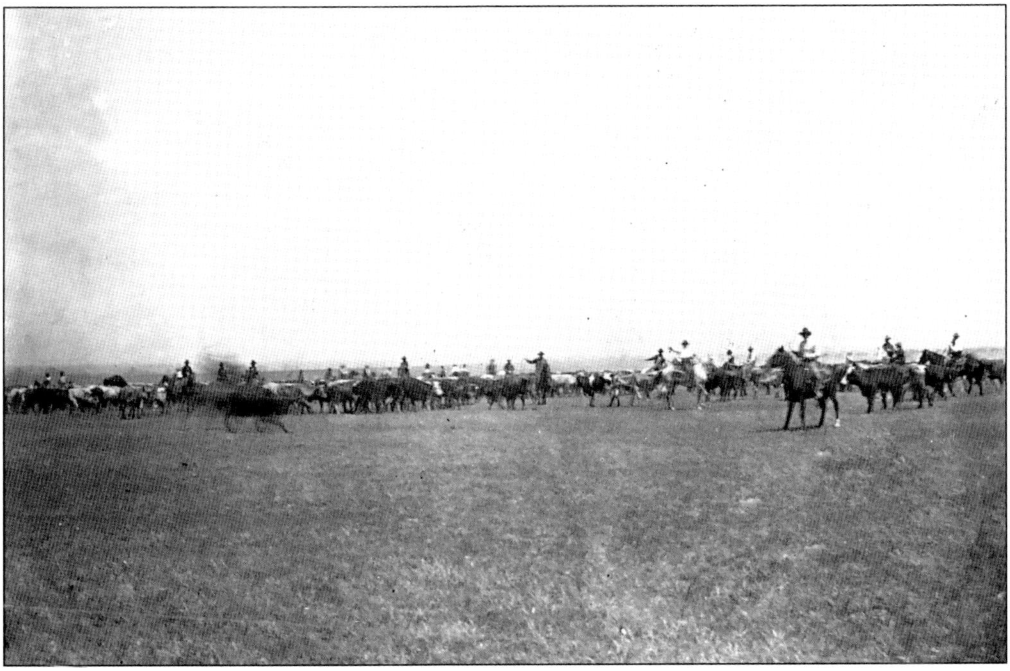

In 1886, Cesario Torres sold his Seven-d Ranch to Jesse H. Presnall and Hart Mussey. In 1883, Presnall and Mussey had purchased the land on which the military post was located. Hart drove a large herd of cattle to the ranch from their Muleshoe Ranch near Sheffield. This undated photograph (with the caption "One herd after separating") captures the look of a drive like Mussey's.

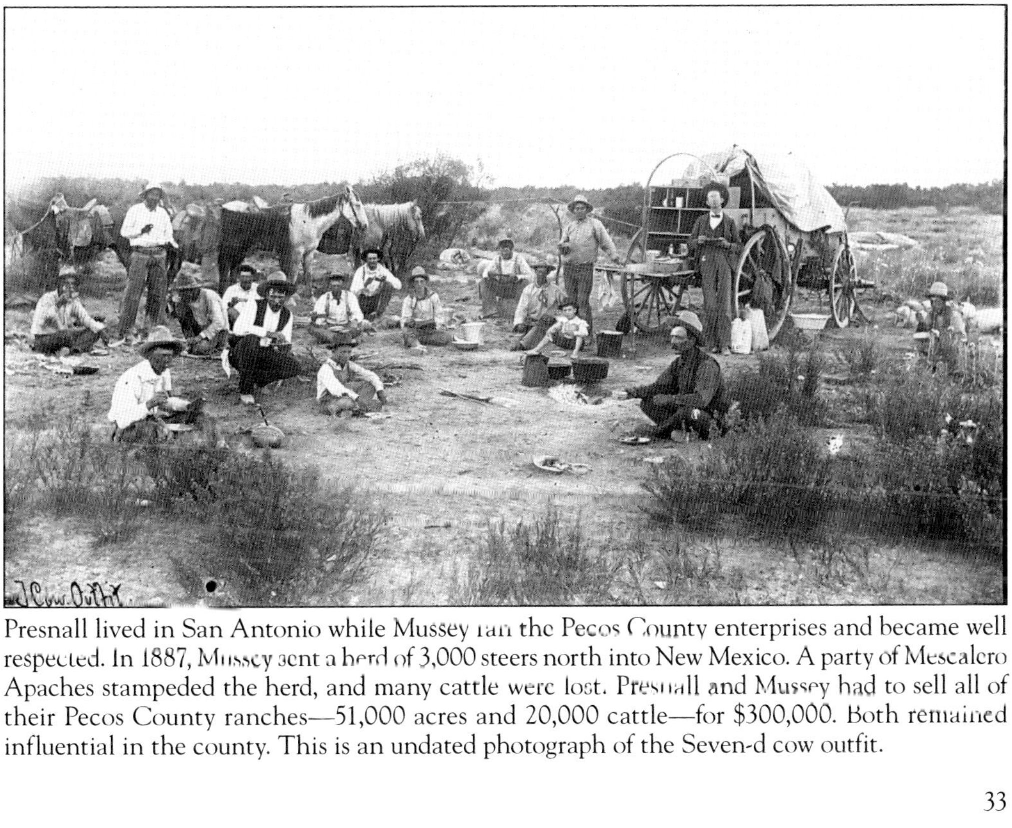

Presnall lived in San Antonio while Mussey ran the Pecos County enterprises and became well respected. In 1887, Mussey sent a herd of 3,000 steers north into New Mexico. A party of Mescalero Apaches stampeded the herd, and many cattle were lost. Presnall and Mussey had to sell all of their Pecos County ranches—51,000 acres and 20,000 cattle—for $300,000. Both remained influential in the county. This is an undated photograph of the Seven-d cow outfit.

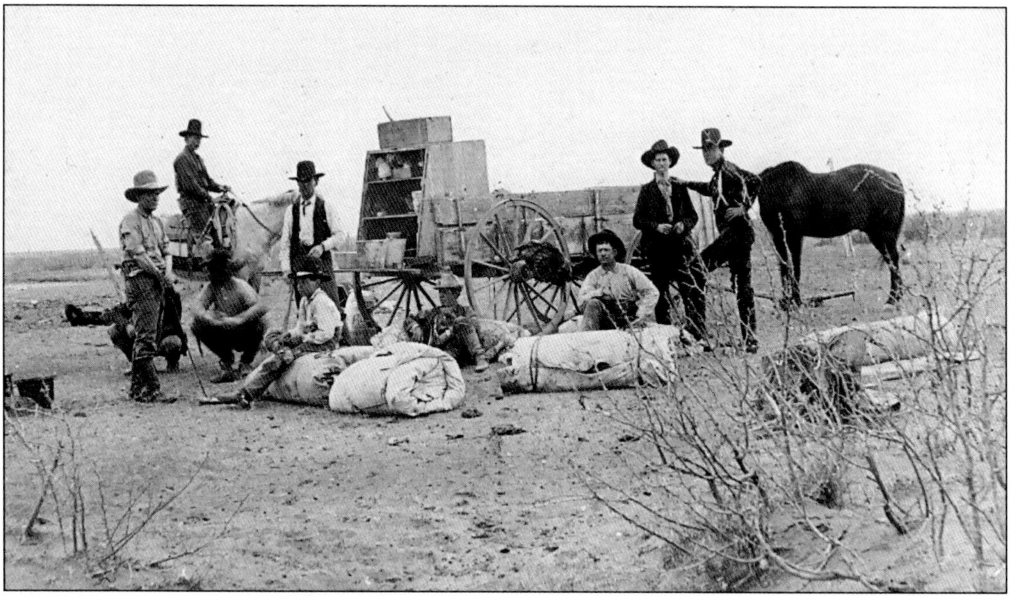

James Dunn Houston, another early cattleman, grazed herds along the Pecos River as early as 1871. Houston partnered with cattle baron George W. Littlefield to drive herds north to market and later purchased ranches in Pecos County. The cowboys in this photograph of Houston's outfit include Morgan Livingston, Jim Livingston, Shipton Parke, Bob Anderson, Ike T. Hock, Hiram Stephenson, and Tom Cope. The era of large cattle companies using the open range was short-lived.

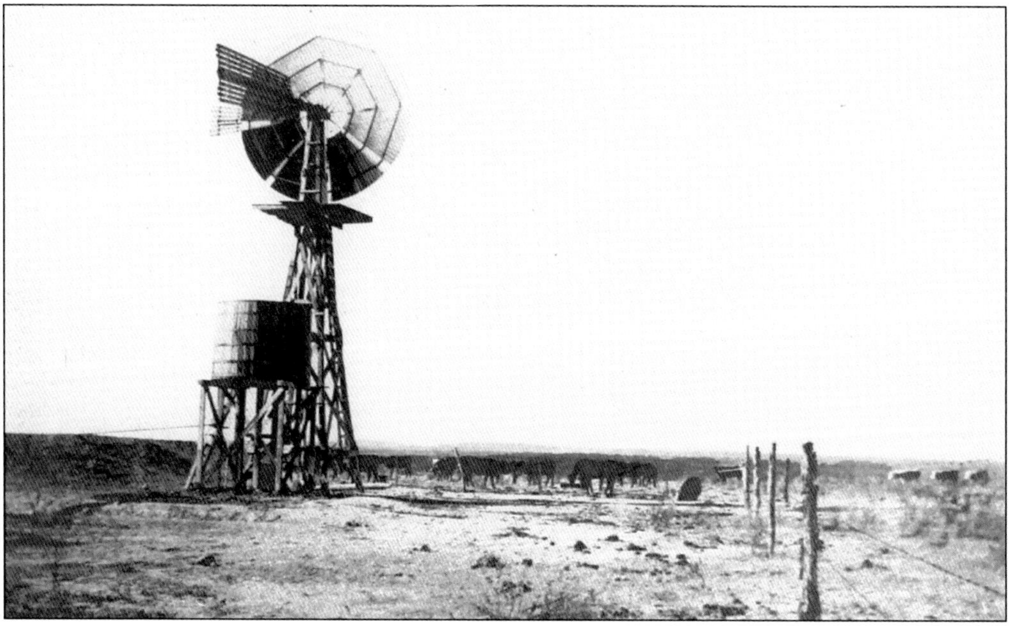

The Western Union Beef Company, which purchased the Seven-d, had 300 men on the payroll and sent several herds up the trail annually. However, more open range was claimed each year; farmers and sheep men began fencing their acreage. By 1877, the Seven-d was putting up its own fences. This Eclipse windmill and fence on the Rooney property illustrate the importance of land management in this arid region.

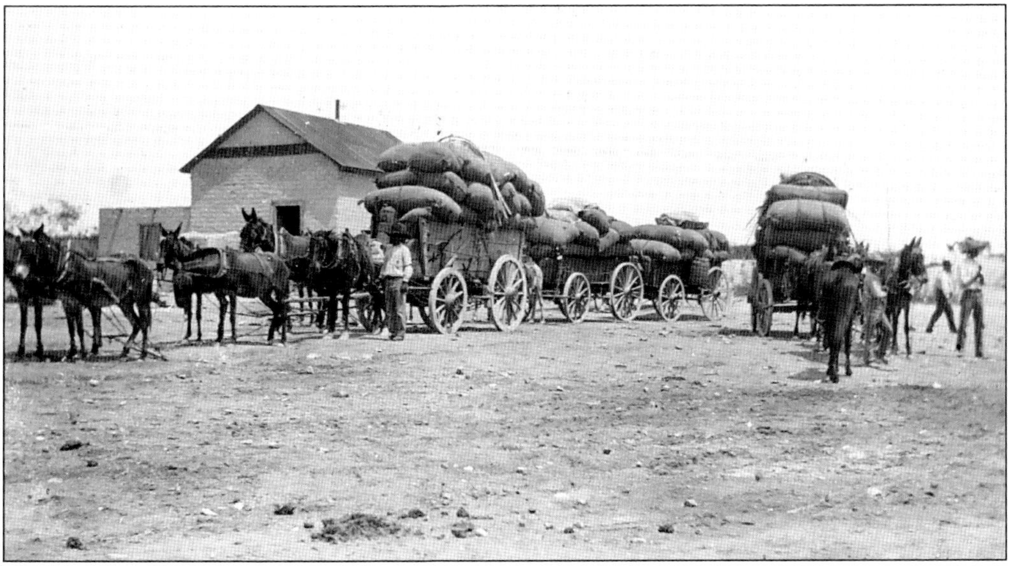

In 1881, Charles Downie drove a flock of sheep to his land in southern Pecos County. Other sheep men soon followed. Mexican herders watched the sheep by day and herded them into rock corrals at night. Frictions with cattlemen developed, but no serious violence ensued. Downie hired Mexicans to shear at 1.5¢ per sheep. Wool was hauled to market in freight wagons such as these. Pecos County became a major wool producer.

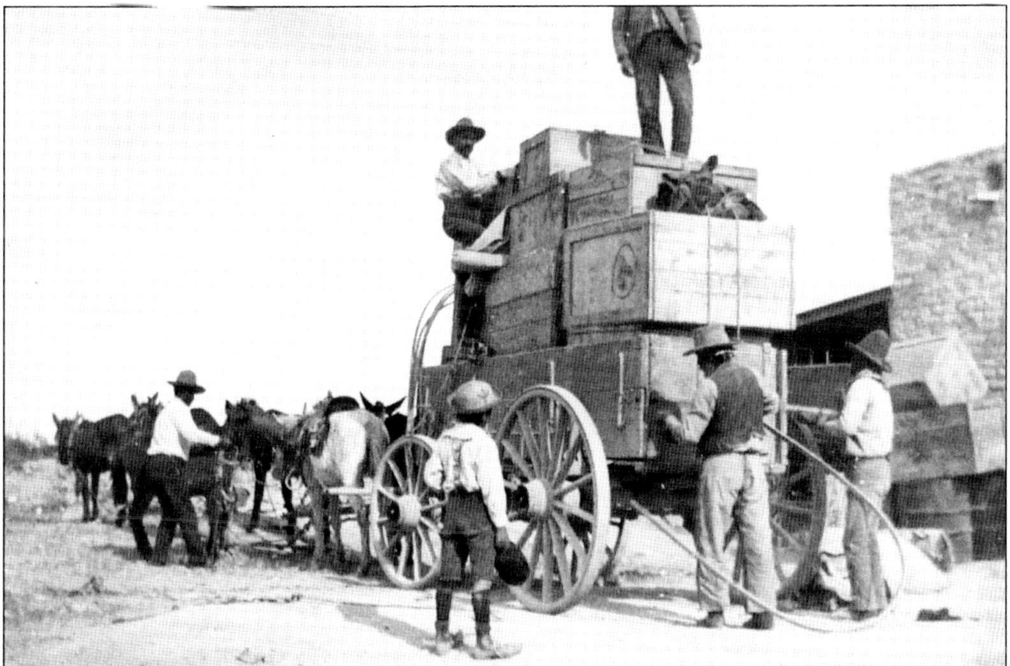

With no railroads, Fort Stockton remained dependent on wagon and stage transportation. Haymond, on the Southern Pacific Railroad (see page 23), became Fort Stockton's first major railroad connection, with freight and stage lines carrying people, goods, and mail. In 1904, Fort Stockton shifted its railroad connection to Monahans on the Texas Pacific. This photograph shows what would have been a familiar scene.

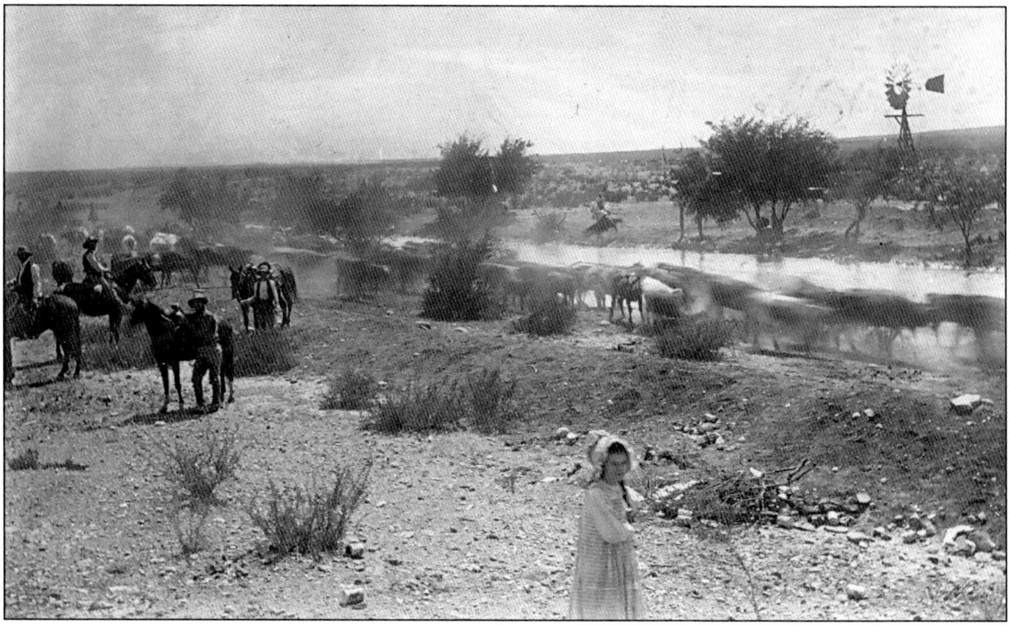

As open range disappeared, the ranching frontier moved westward. In 1886, widow Hannah Riggs and several of her children established ranches in western Pecos County and adjacent Jeff Davis County. This 1898 roundup took place on the ranch of Hannah's son Tom. The girl in the photograph is Myrtle Johnson, daughter of Tom and his wife, Mary Jane.

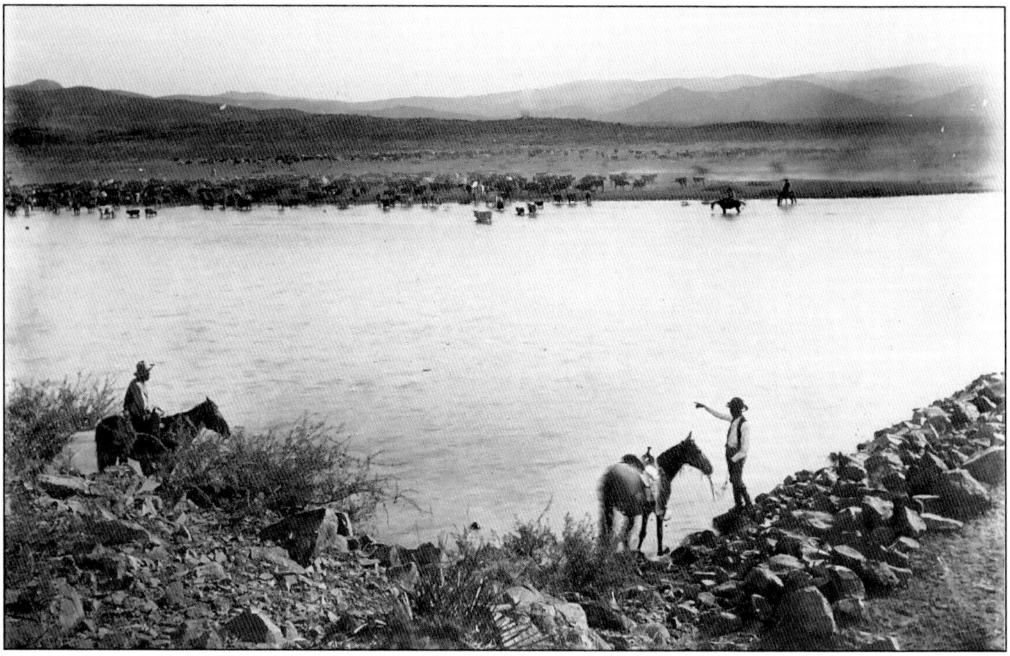

Tom Riggs's brother Richard ranched on the northeast side of the Barrilla Mountains in Jeff Davis County. Richard "Dick" Riggs and several brothers were on their way to Arizona to join other family members when Dick rode into the Davis Mountains and found much of the land unoccupied. In this 1898 photograph, Dick Riggs (holding his horse's reins) and foreman Ed Suckler (at left on horseback) oversee a roundup.

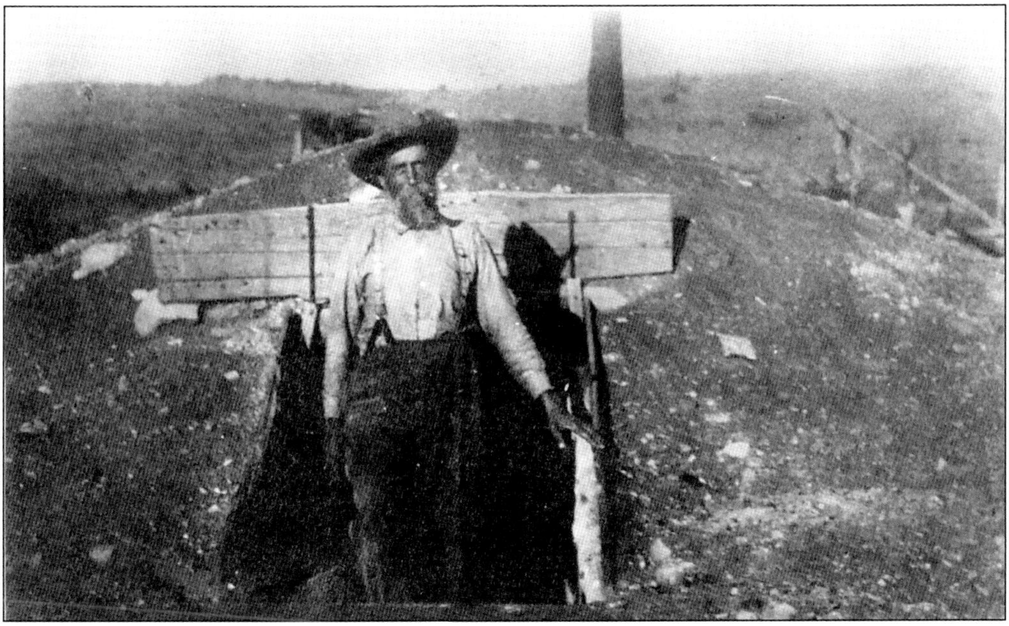

Ranching remained a difficult and isolated life. James Wade (pictured) came to Pecos County in 1890, settling on Independence Creek in southeastern Pecos County. The 60-mile trips to Fort Stockton by wagon for supplies were rare. When a flood in 1905 destroyed the Wade homestead, he moved his cattle and horse-breaking operation west to the Glass Mountains south of Fort Stockton, where he constructed this dugout.

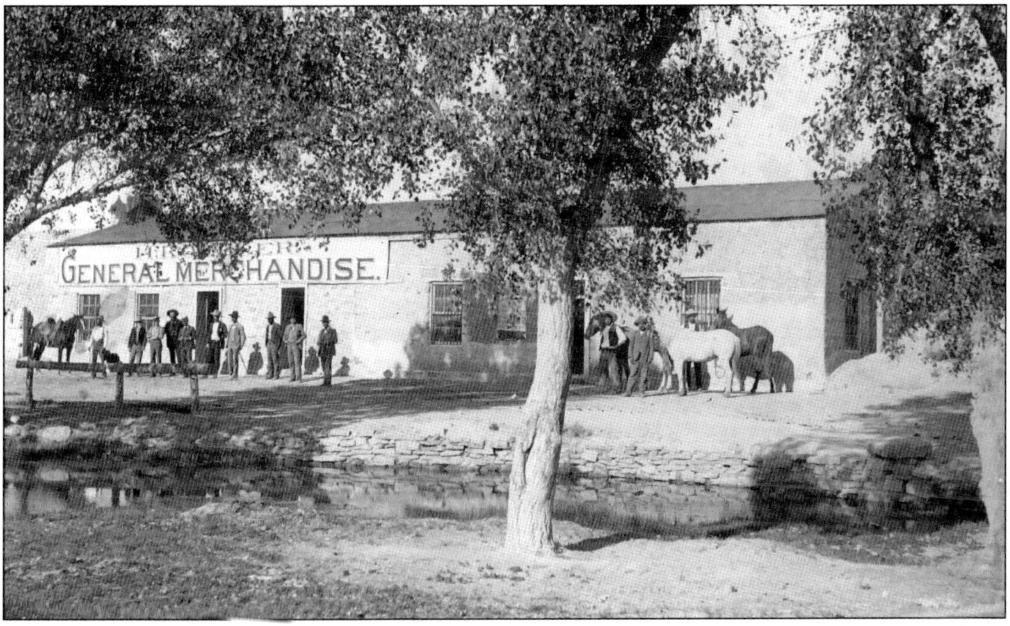

When in Fort Stockton, cattlemen and sheep men often frequented different businesses, which therefore shared the trade. Competing with Young's store (page 26) was the nearby establishment of Herman Koehler, first constructed by Peter Gallagher. One end of the building contained the store. The other end was a saloon and billiard hall. Koehler's also functioned as an impromptu hotel, with travelers and drunks bedding down in quilts on the floor.

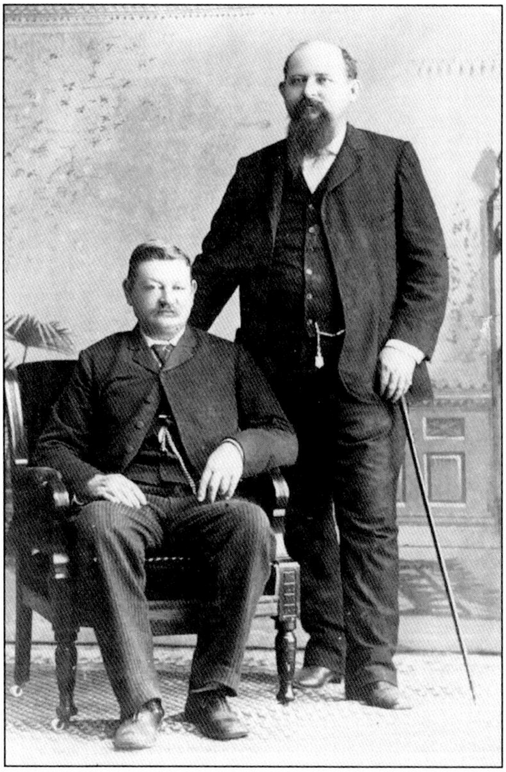

Herman Koehler (seated) was a German immigrant from San Antonio who became a clerk in M.F. Corbett's general merchandise store. Koehler purchased the store in 1882. He clearly marked his prices and met complaints with the comment, "By God don't take it." Koehler had a generous nature and never turned away the poor, the needy, or cowboys short of cash.

By the time of this 1890 photograph, Fort Stockton's population was around 250. Most citizens worked hard to survive on a frontier still lacking many basic amenities. Desperados, such as the Jesse Evans Gang, operated in the Trans-Pecos country (the vast triangle of Texas west of the Pecos River) but avoided the towns. Koehler's saloon (pictured) sometimes became the site for drunken disputes, but most ended without major bloodshed. However, events would soon bring several men into deadly clashes.

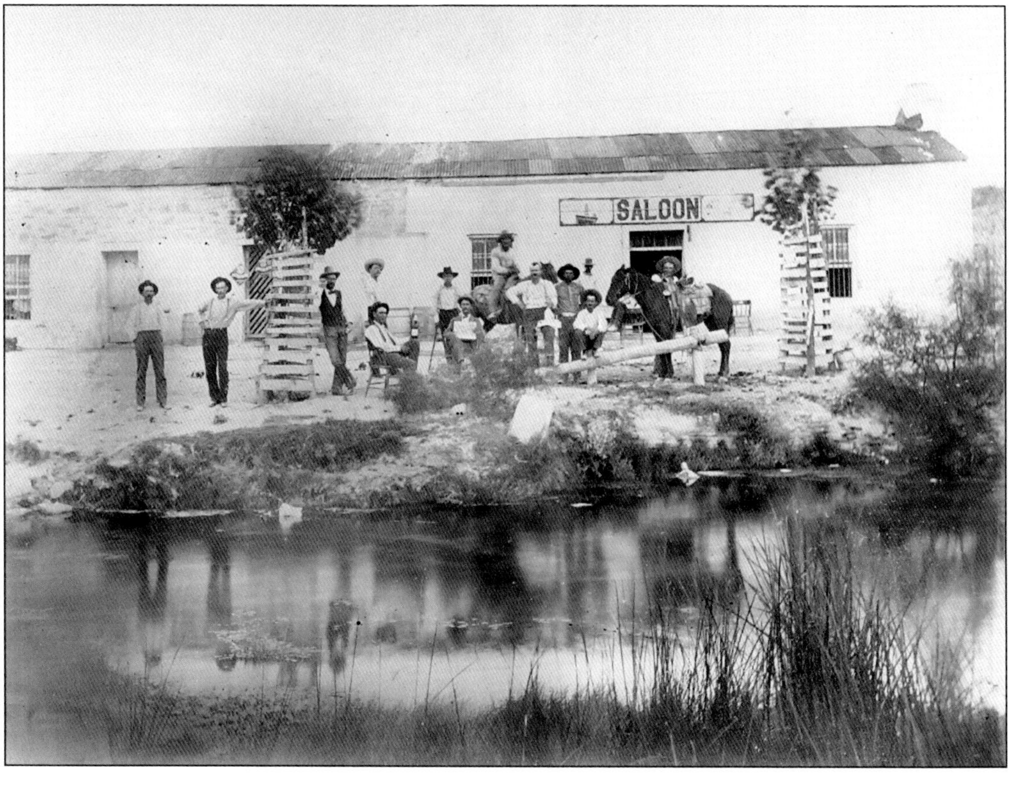

Oscar Waldo Williams, seeking a more arid climate for his health, moved to Fort Stockton in 1884 to become the deputy county surveyor for Pecos County. Williams mapped the last large unsurveyed tract in the county in 1885. The following year, he was elected county judge, serving until 1898. Elected again in 1890, Williams served until 1900.

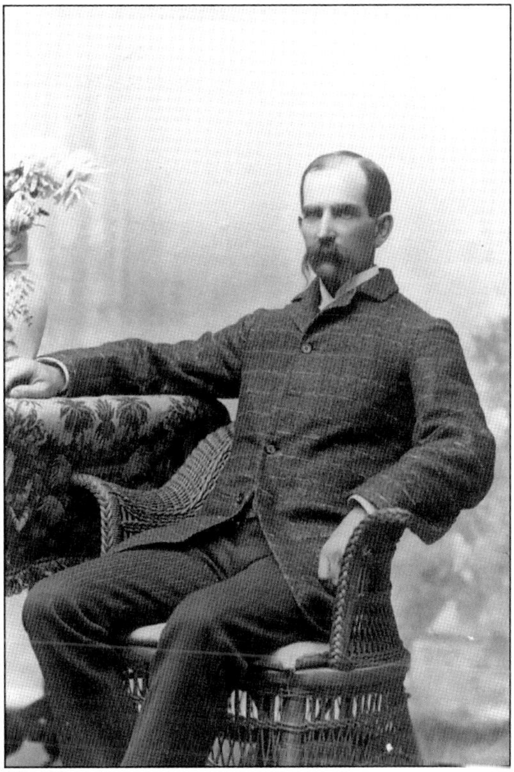

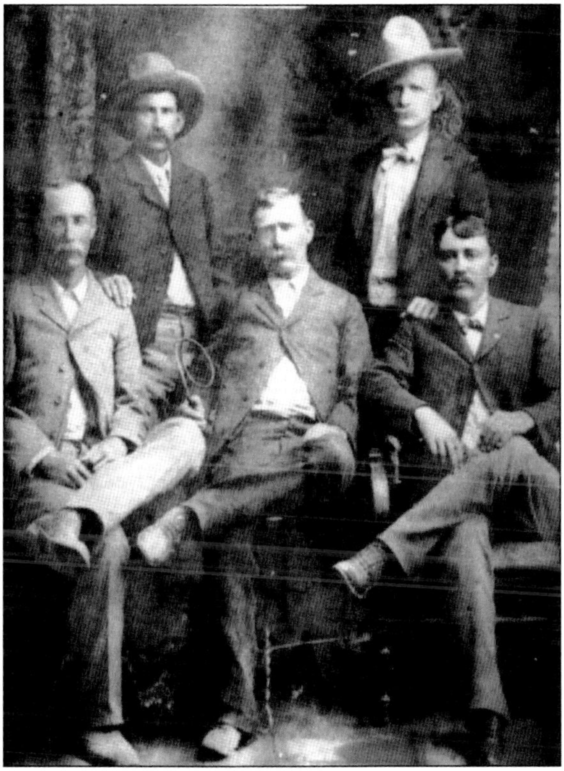

Barney Riggs joined his family (page 36) in Pecos County in 1888. Convicted of murder in Arizona in 1887 and given a life sentence in Yuma Prison, during a riot, Riggs rescued prison superintendent Thomas Gates and was given a pardon on condition that he leave the territory and never return. In 1891, Riggs married Annie Frazier Johnson, becoming her second husband. Pictured are, from left to right, (first row) Moye Grinder, Barney Riggs, and John Chalk; (second row) Tom Riggs and Lon (Stump) Robbins.

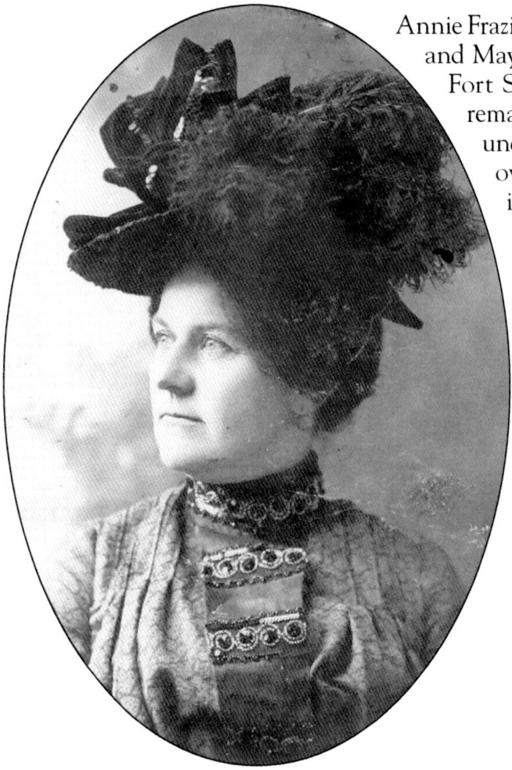

Annie Frazier was the eldest daughter of Judge George Frazier and May Frazier (page 29). When her family moved to Fort Stockton from New Mexico in 1869, the area remained a contested frontier. That same year, troops under Col. Ranald Mackenzie fought a battle with over 100 Lipan and Mescalero Apache Indians in southern Pecos County. The Frazier family prospered in the young county. In 1877, Annie married James Johnson.

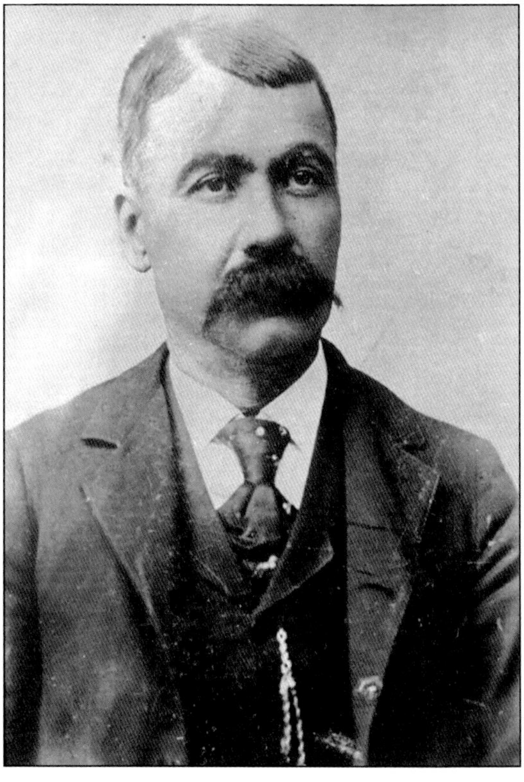

James Johnson was one of eight individuals listed as a stockman in the 1880 census. In February 1876, Johnson had been elected Pecos County sheriff. Johnson only served until June, when he resigned. The following January, he was appointed county treasurer. He was to be paid on a commission basis, and he served in that office until 1886. Johnson was Annie Frazier's first husband. Annie ran the Johnson Hotel, a popular boardinghouse, during their marriage.

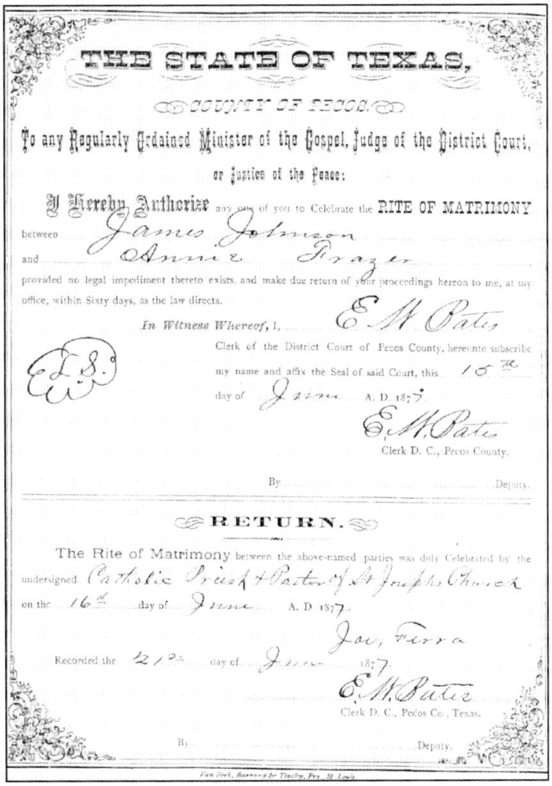
THE STATE OF TEXAS,

COUNTY OF PECOS.

To any Regularly Ordained Minister of the Gospel, Judge of the District Court, or Justice of the Peace:

I Hereby Authorize any one of you to Celebrate the RITE OF MATRIMONY between James Johnson and Annie Frazer provided no legal impediment thereto exists, and make due return of your proceedings hereon to me, at my office, within Sixty days, as the law directs.

In Witness Whereof, I, E. M. Pate Clerk of the District Court of Pecos County, hereunto subscribe my name and affix the Seal of said Court, this 15th day of June A. D. 1877.

E. M. Pate
Clerk D. C., Pecos County.

By .... Deputy.

RETURN.

The Rite of Matrimony between the above-named parties was duly Celebrated by the undersigned Catholic Priest & Pastor of St Joseph's Church on the 16th day of June A. D 1877.

Jos. Ferra

Recorded the 21st day of June 1877.

E. M. Pate
Clerk D. C., Pecos Co., Texas.

By .... Deputy.

Van Beek, Barnard & Tinsley, Prs., St. Louis

Fr. Jose Ferra united James Johnson and Annie Frazier in marriage on June 16, 1877. St. Joseph's was still only partly complete at the time, and Father Ferra served the parish from Fort Davis. The couple had six children, but the marriage was not a happy one. Despite her strong Catholic faith, Annie eventually divorced Johnson, who drank and treated her poorly.

Andrew Jackson Royal purchased the Leon Ranch west of Fort Stockton in 1889 and moved his family from Junction, Texas, where some accounts claim he murdered a man. In May 1892, Royal killed Apolinar Mendoza, his Mexican hired hand, with a shotgun, outside the Koehler Saloon. O.W. Williams served as foreman of the grand jury investigating the incident. Royal was not indicted, but this began Royal's conflicts with Williams.

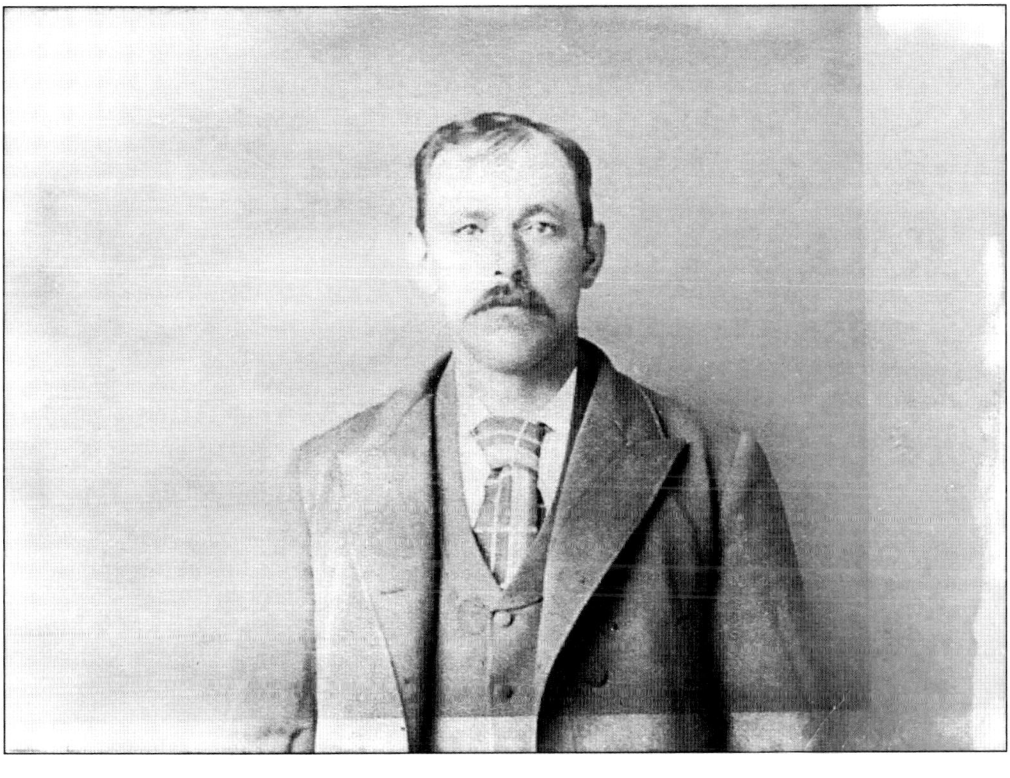

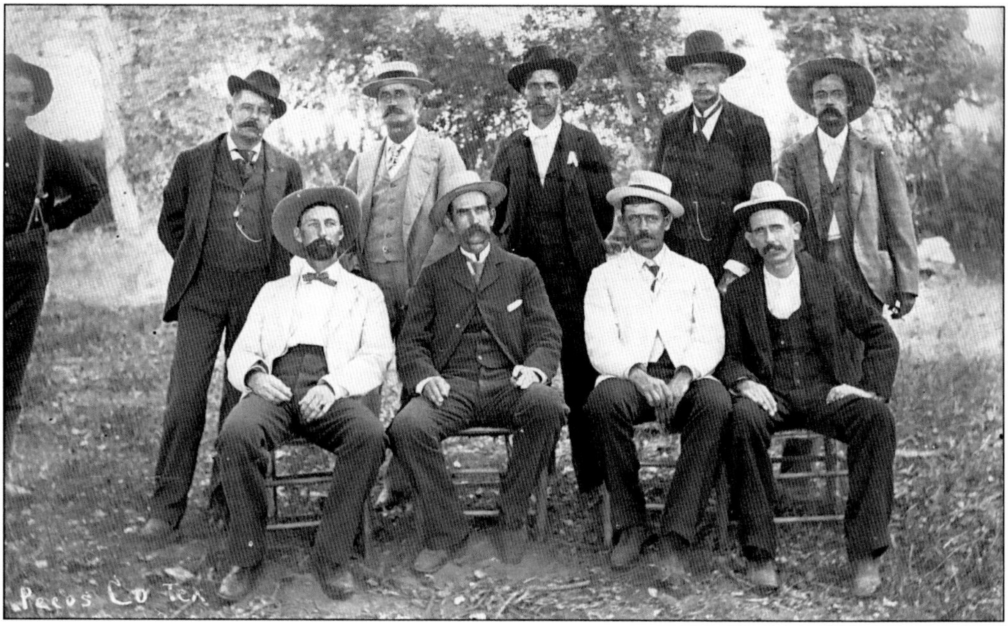

Royal became embroiled with several other individuals, including Morgan Livingston, Shipton Parke, and Frank and James Rooney. Several involved in the conflicts are included in this July 4, 1898, photograph of Pecos County officials. Pictured are, from left to right, (first row) John M. Odom, treasurer; O.W. Williams, judge; Frank Rooney, clerk; and James Rooney, commissioner; (second row) George Hawthorne, commissioner; Morgan Livingston, commissioner; W.P. Ratchford, surveyor; Tom J. Ray, commissioner; and W.C. Crosby, deputy sheriff.

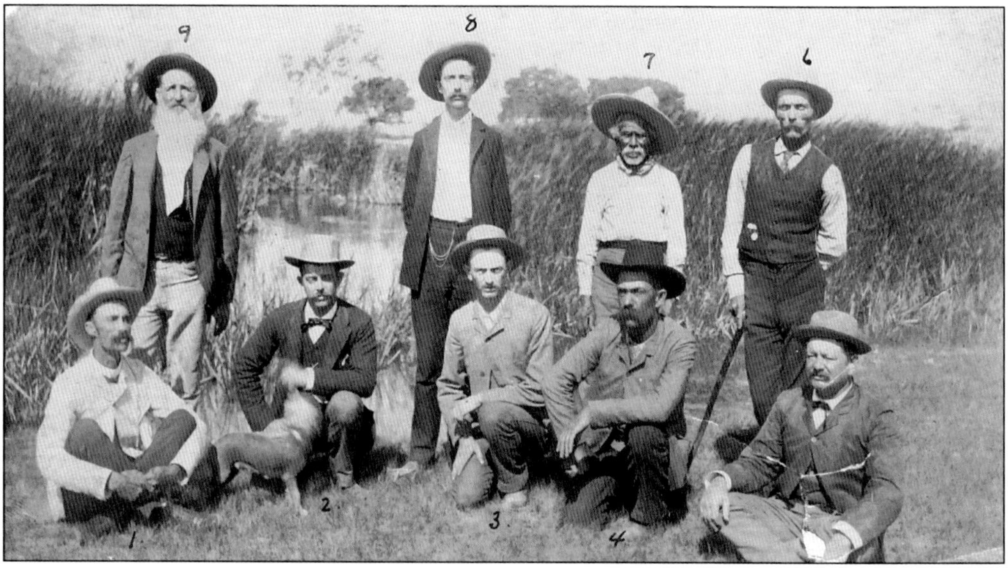

Royal became county sheriff in 1894, and Williams became county judge. Over the next two years, the feud between them grew increasingly bitter. Accounts vary. Royal was either a legalized bully or a tough frontier lawman. Both sides called for the Texas Rangers. The town became an armed camp. This group includes, from left to right, (seated) Hart Mussey, Charley Wilson, George Hawthorne, Reuben Mussey, and Herman Koehler; (standing) John Edgar, Andrew Jackson Royal, Jesus Jaramilla, and W.P. Matthews.

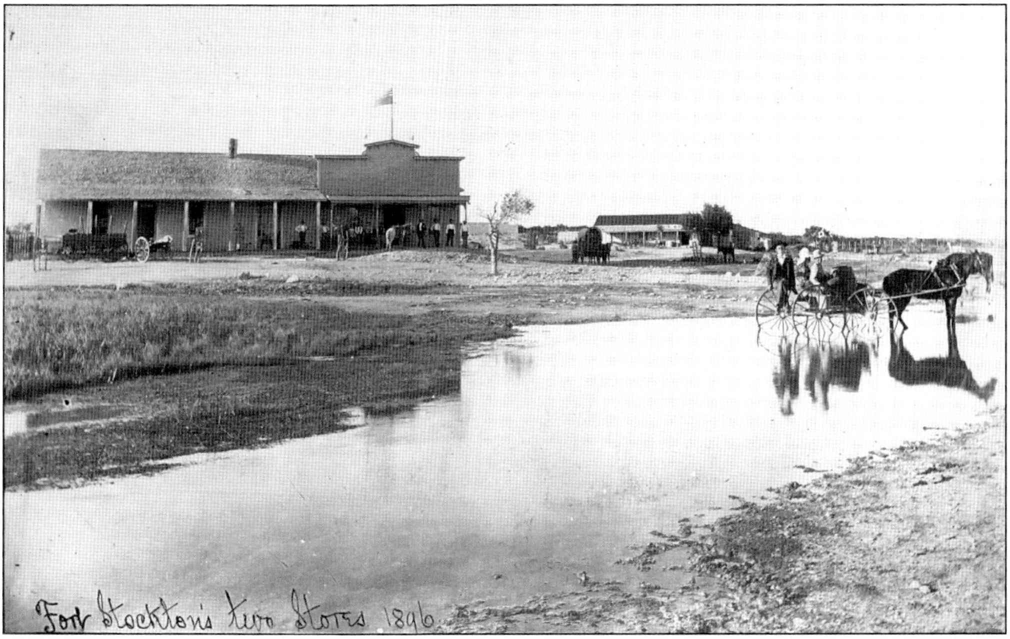

The death of Herman Koehler in July 1894 added to the tension. Royal claimed Koehler owed him money and that he had won Koehler's saloon in a card game. Williams appointed Francis Rooney to manage Koehler's estate. Rooney denied Royal's claims, further angering the sheriff. Koehler's nephew Herman H. Butz came from New Braunfels to help settle his uncle's estate. In this 1896 photograph, Koehler's saloon is on the right and Young's mercantile store is on the left.

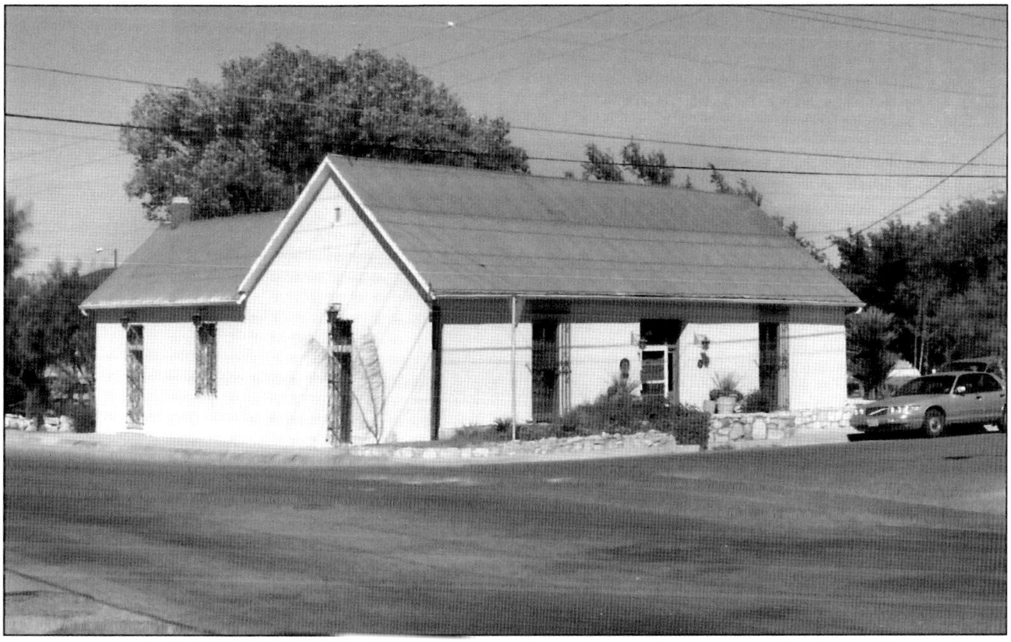

Royal acquired the Grey Mule Saloon (pictured here) as a direct challenge to Koehler's. He employed Barney Riggs (page 39) as a special deputy sheriff, having known him when both were in Junction. After a shootout with James and Frank Rooney at Koehler's, Royal began constructing an adobe wall around the Grey Mule. A maze of legal charges and claims entangled all participants.

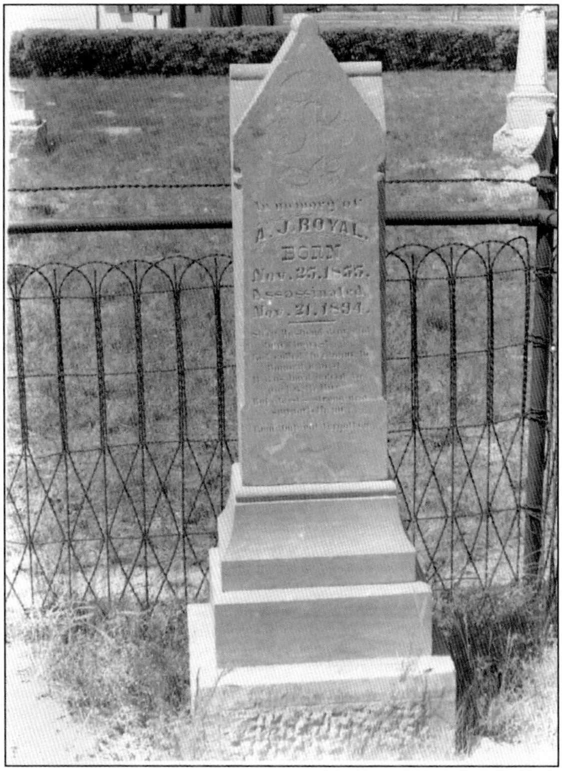

The feud ended abruptly in November 1894. Royal lost his bid for reelection as sheriff. While seated in his former office in the courthouse, he was killed by a shotgun blast. No one was ever charged with his murder. Since that time, various theories have been proposed regarding the identity of his killer. Royal's wife, Naomi, had the word "assassinated" placed on his tombstone (seen here) in the Old Fort Cemetery.

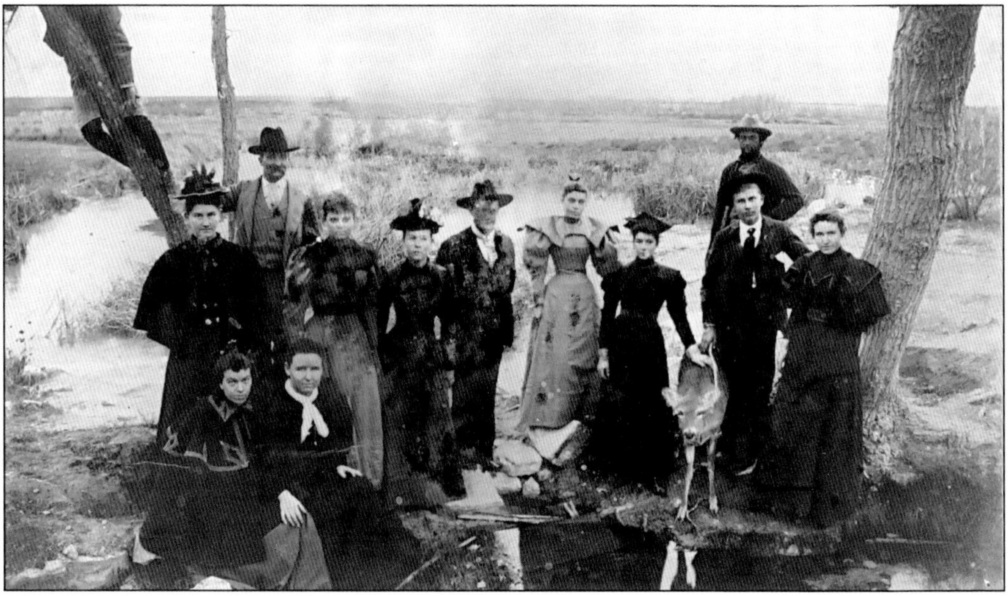

With Royal's death, tensions eased. Friends could enjoy a pleasant outing at Government Spring in 1896. Pictured are, from left to right, Willie Rooney (in tree) Emma Shelton Parke (Shipton's wife), Mary Rooney Richardson (seated), Jim Livingston (Morgan's brother), Emma Butz (seated), Mary Jane Lemons-Mansfield, Lizzie Teel-Talmon, Andrew Young, Mimie Shelton (Emma Parke's sister), Ophelia Crosby-Stephenson (beside deer), Herman Butz (with tie), W.C. Crosby, and Agnes Rooney.

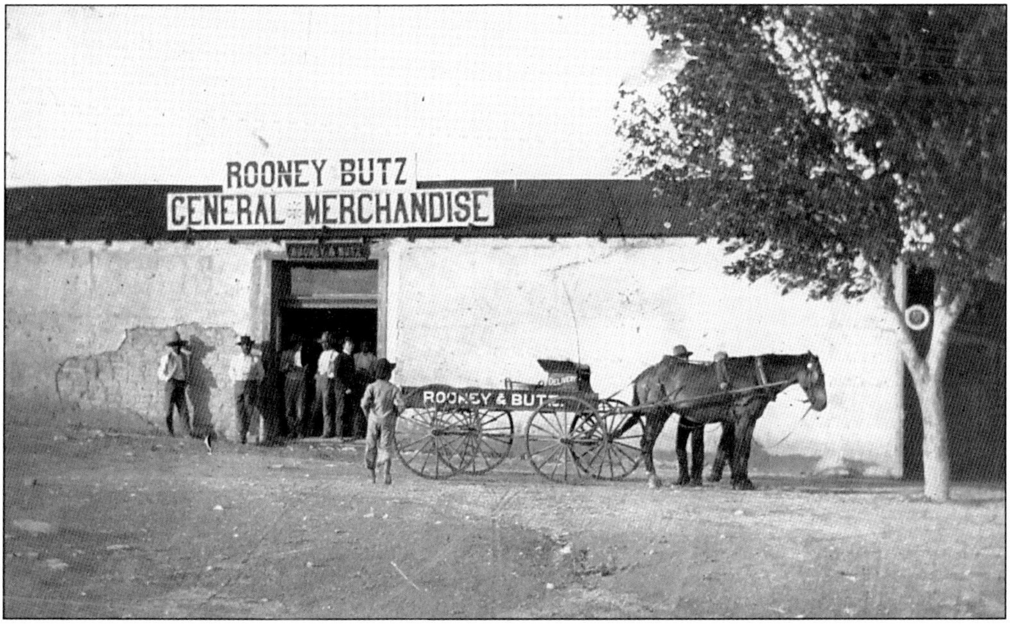

Herman H. Butz came to Fort Stockton as a young man of 17. He first worked as a clerk for George Hawthorne, who purchased his uncle's store. In 1894, Butz, with his partner James Rooney, purchased the Hawthorne store and renamed it the Rooney and Butz Store (pictured). In 1898, Herman married Agnes Rooney, daughter of Francis Rooney and sister of James Rooney.

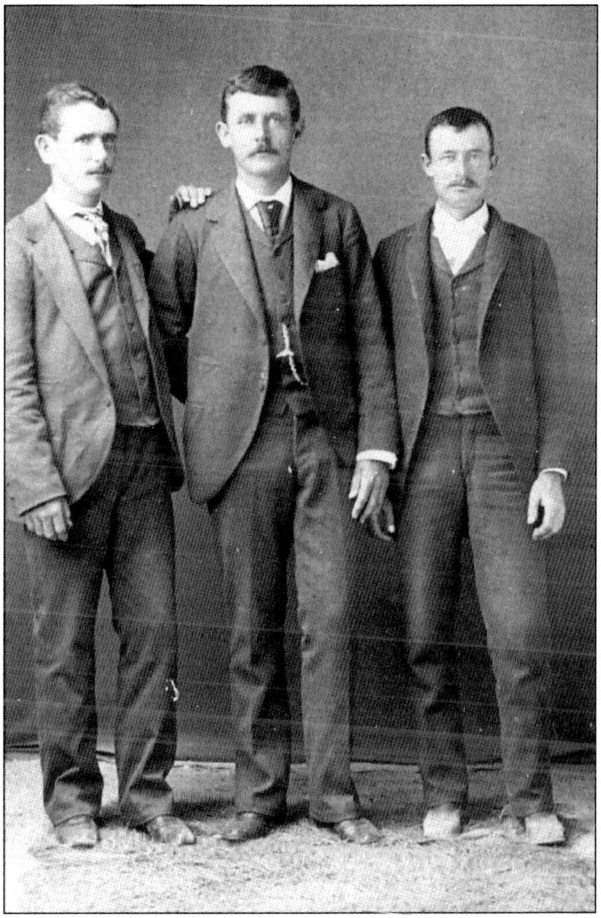

Francis Rooney (page 28) had prospered at San Pedro Spring on what came to be known as the old Rooney Farm and later as the Irrigated Farms. Rooney also pioneered the use of an irrigation dam on the Pecos River, with a project near Imperial, Texas. He passed his pioneering spirit to his sons, James (left) and Frank (center), and his nephew Francis (right).

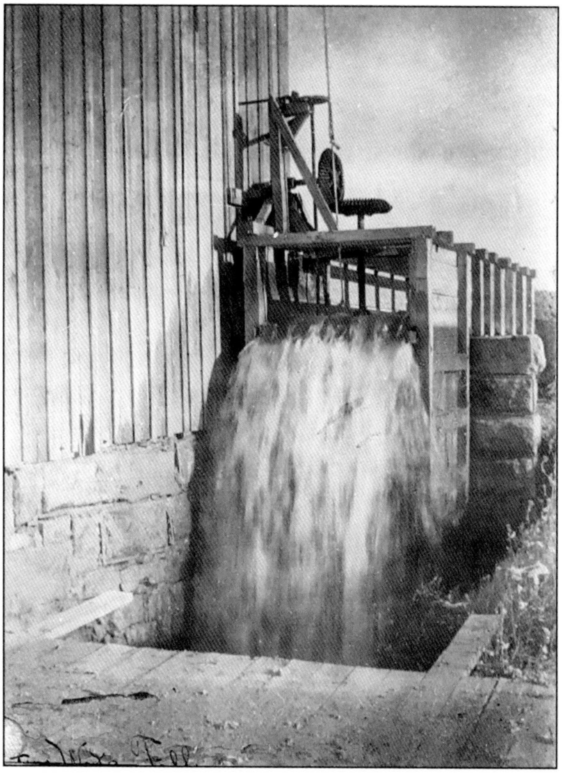

In 1897, Mexican tenants on the Rooney Farm made the first awkward efforts at planting 250 acres of cotton. To gin the cotton, James Rooney and Herman Butz had a second-hand gin shipped by rail to Haymond on the Southern Pacific and, in an arduous journey, hauled by wagon to Fort Stockton. A 10-foot waterfall, using water from a canal, powered the gin, which is pictured here.

Cotton was carried to a press and tamped by foot. A screw press produced the bales. Each bale required two hours to gin, and 141 bales were ginned the first year. Frank James placed a letter inside the first bale. Months later, he received a reply from England. Cotton cultivation spread to other irrigated areas. The gin (pictured) operated until 1908, when the Rooney Farm was sold to the Fort Stockton Irrigated Lands.

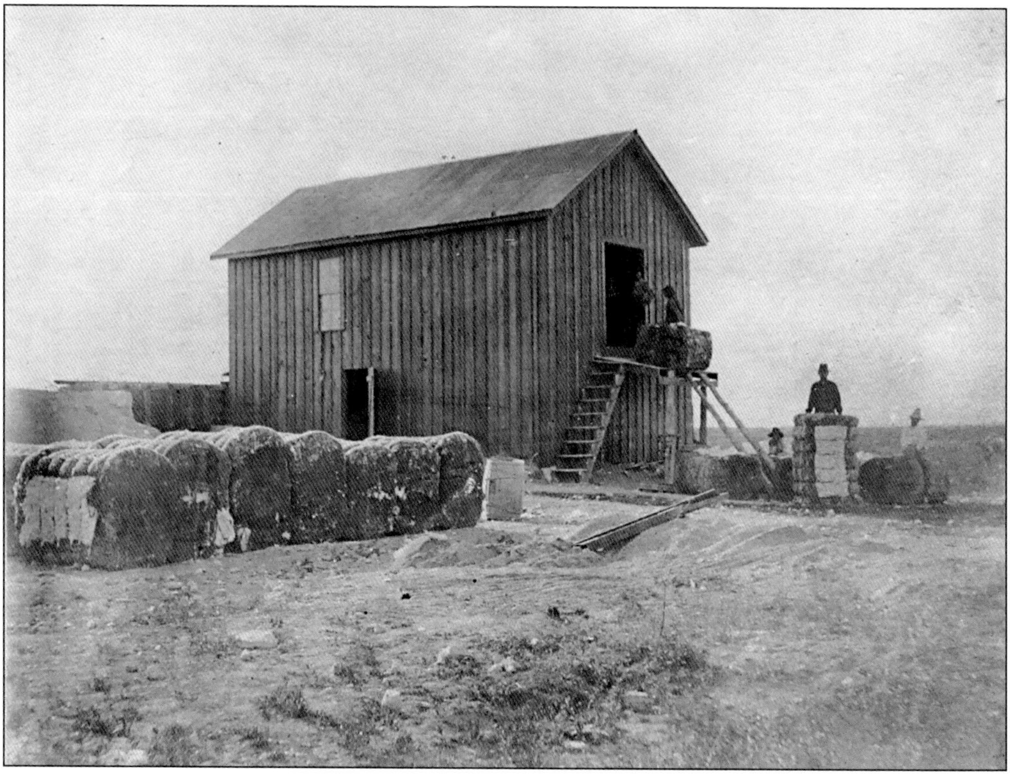

May Sanders was born in McCulloch County, Texas, in 1878. She moved with her family to Fort Stockton, where her father ran sheep south of town for several years before moving to New Mexico. When his father died in 1889, 18-year-old Frank Rooney took over the family farm. In 1896, Frank, the cattleman's son, married May, the sheepherder's daughter, at Hope, New Mexico, and brought her back to Texas.

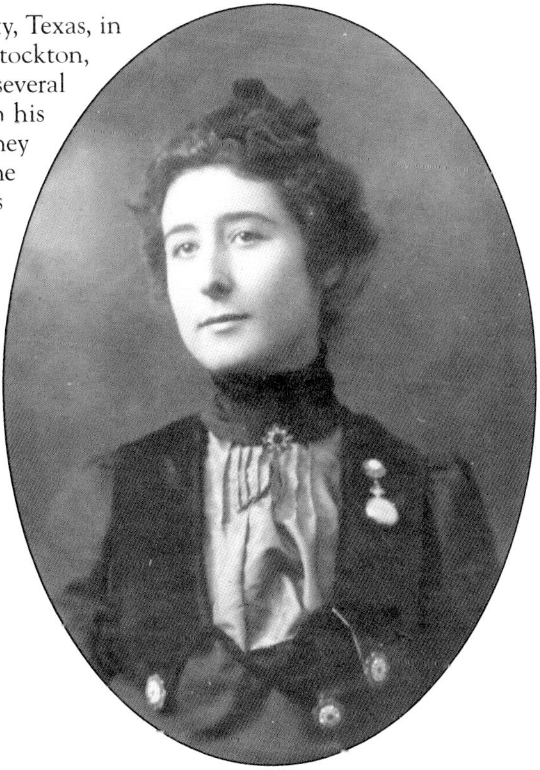

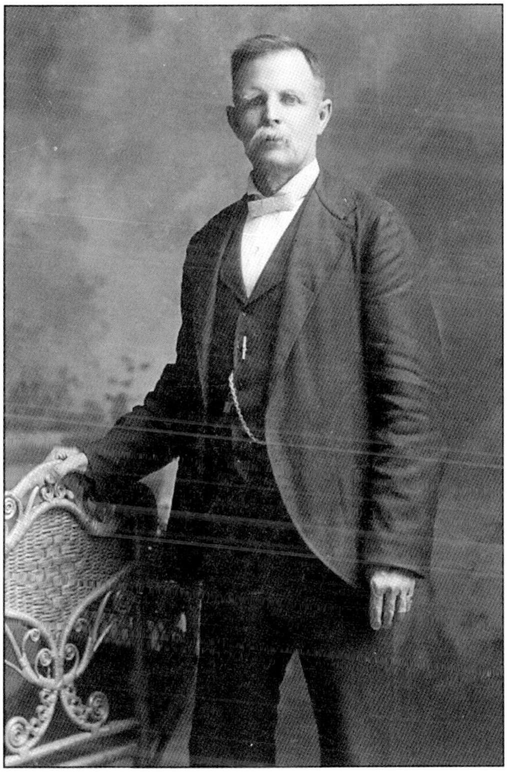

Shipton Parke came to Pecos County in 1887 as a cowboy for the Dunn Houston outfit (page 34). After several years on the N.A. Ranch in northern Pecos County, Parke formed a partnership with James and John Livingston that resulted in the Seven Bar Ranch. In 1896, Shipton married Emma Shelton in the old fort guardhouse. In 1899, when the partnership dissolved, the Seven Bar became the Parke Ranch.

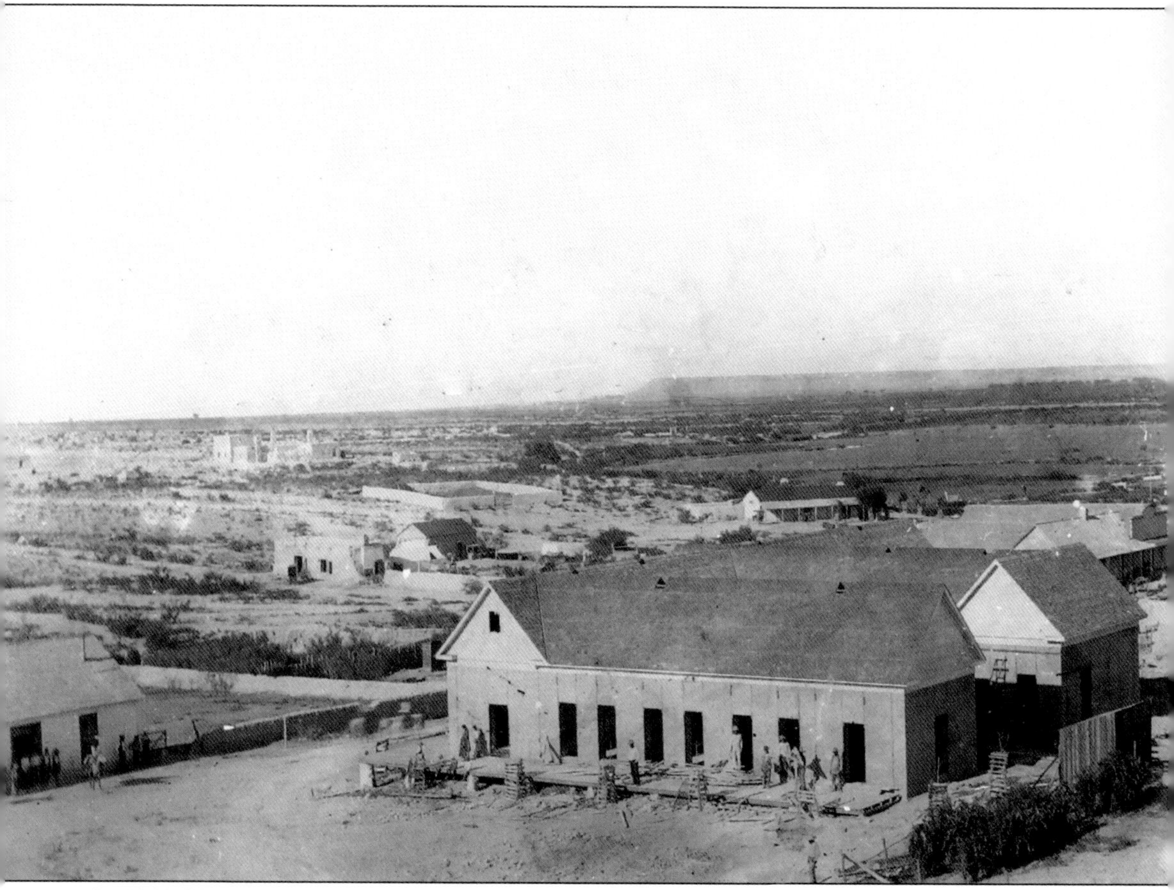

In 1900, Herman Butz, James Rooney, Ike Hock, R.B. Neighbors, and Jim and Morgan Livingston formed the Fort Stockton Hotel Company and purchased the land on the corner of Division and Main Streets for $100. They began construction of a large adobe building named, in honor of Herman Koehler, the Koehler Hotel. It was a one-story adobe building of 13 rooms, each 14 feet square with 10-foot ceilings. In this photograph, the Koehler is under construction. To the left of the hotel is the Grey Mule Saloon, including the adobe wall started by Andrew Royal during the feud. On the right behind the hotel is the Young Store, and in the center behind the hotel is the Rooney-Butz Store. In the background, just left of center, are the ruins of the fort hospital. Soon after its completion, Annie Riggs (page 40) leased the hotel and began operating it.

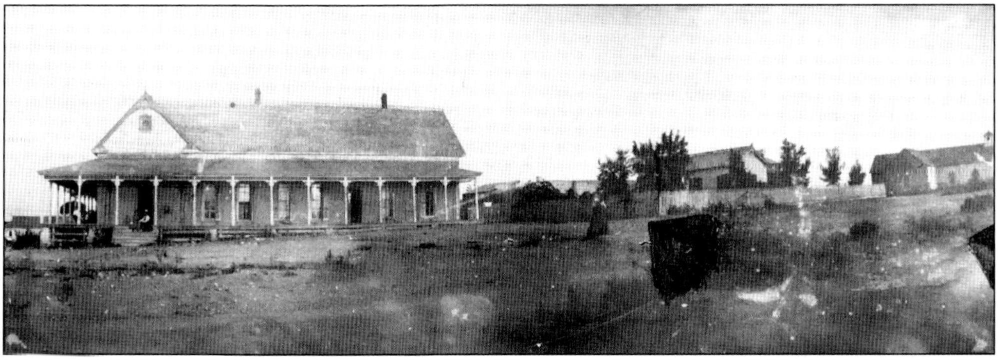

The Koehler had nine guestrooms, a kitchen, a parlor, a dining room, and a lobby. There were no lavatories or bathtubs, as the city had no water system. Coal oil lamps provided light, and wood stoves, fueled with mesquite roots, were used for cooking and heating. The hotel is pictured on the left. Next door is the home of Herman Butz (with fence). On the far right is Saint Joseph Catholic Church.

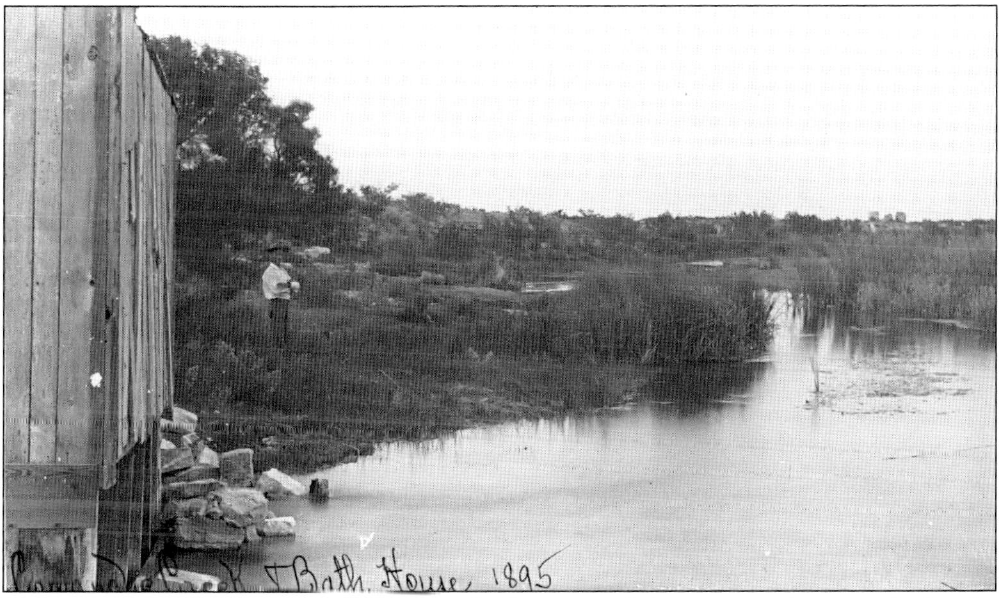

Those desiring a bath had to walk down to the Rooney and Butz Store and request the key for the wooden bathhouse, pictured in 1895, on Comanche Creek. Traveling salesmen and lawyers might find conditions primitive. For cowboys, this was almost luxurious. Fort Stockton acquired a water system in 1910.

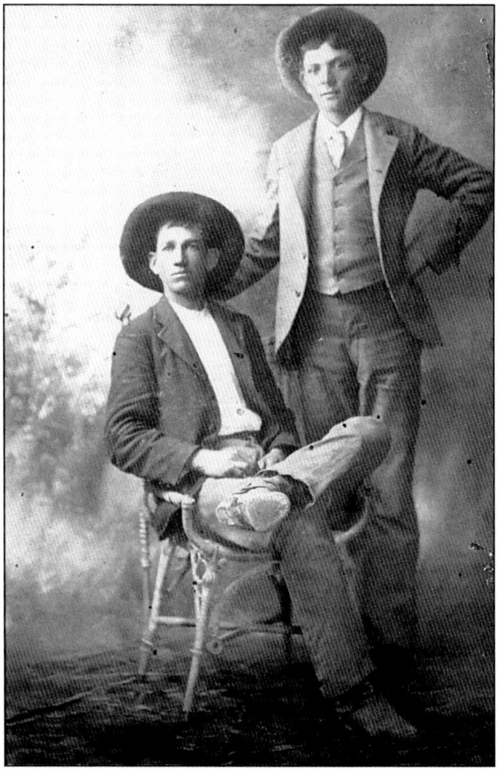

Annie Frazier (Johnson's) second marriage to husband Barney Riggs (page 39) was difficult, abusive, and dangerous. Barney survived the Royal feud but became connected with another dispute in Pecos. This one involved Bud Frazier (page30), Annie's brother and Barney's brother-in-law, who was the Reeves County sheriff. This feud also ended in bloodshed. In 1901, Annie divorced Barney, but she remained close to Earl, Barney's child from an earlier marriage. Earl Riggs (seated, with friend Hays Moore) was fond of Annie.

In 1896, Jim Miller, notorious gunman and associate of outlaw John Wesley Hardin, shot Sheriff Bud Frazier in a planned murder. Miller next issued threats against Barney Riggs. Barney carried his family to relatives, Annie riding with a shotgun in her lap, and then traveled to Pecos. On October 3, in the Johnson and Heard Saloon (pictured), Riggs killed two of Miller's gang, shooting both in the head. Miller fled the area, and Riggs was tried and acquitted.

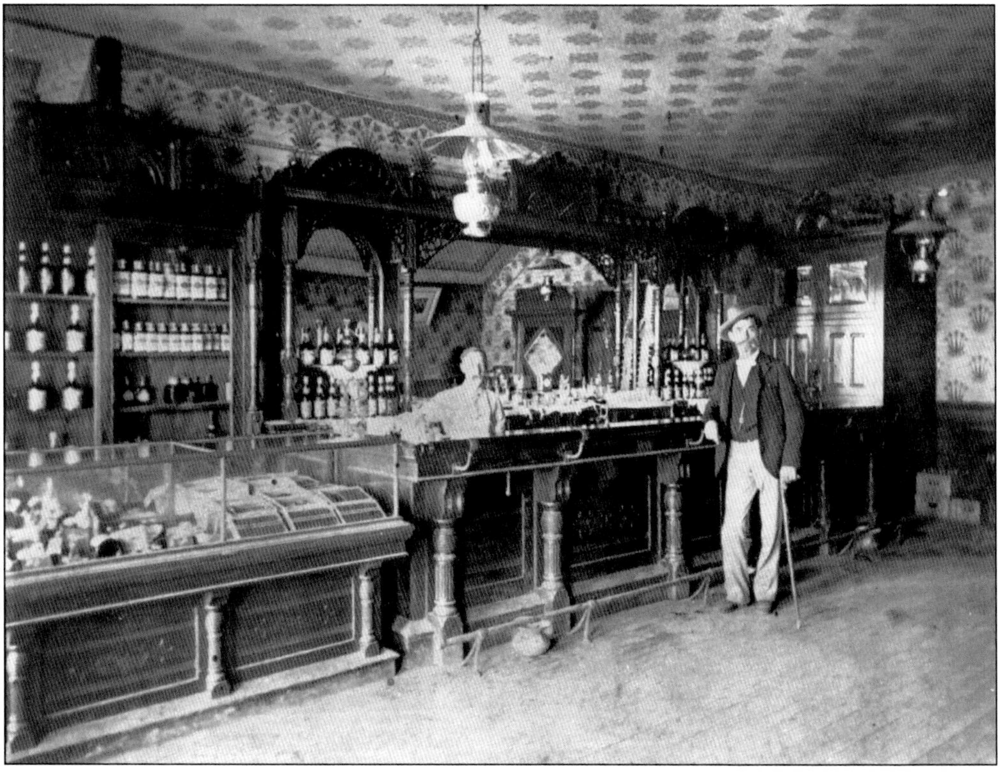

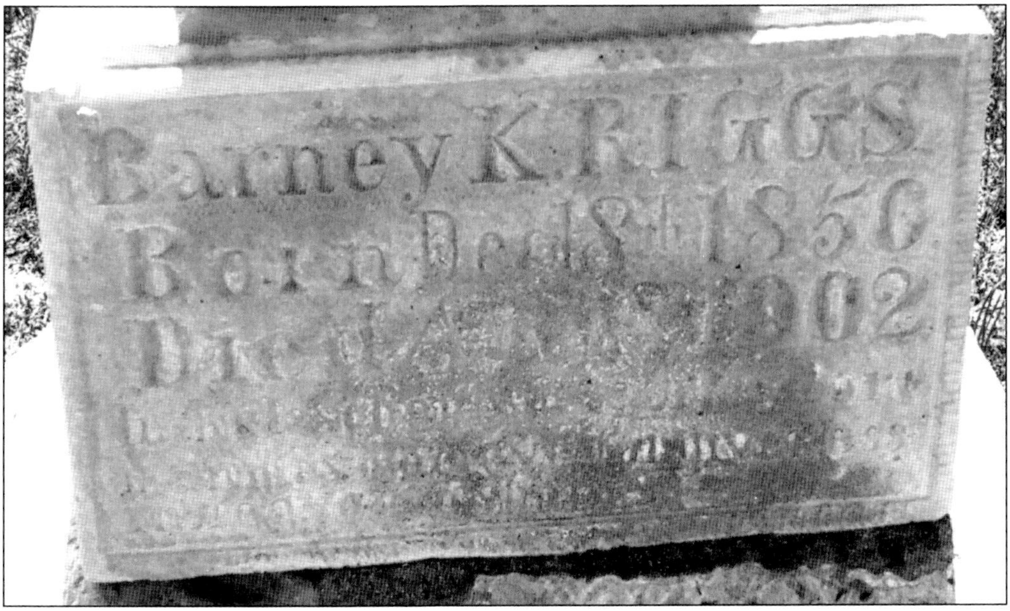

Barney Riggs met a violent end. In 1902, Buck Chadborn, divorce administrator for his mother-in-law, Annie Riggs, was helping obtain her settlement property, including 40 horses and her piano. Barney was uncooperative. He cursed Buck, striking him with a cane. On April 8, outside the Pena home, Buck shot Barney, mistakenly thinking he was reaching for a gun. Barney was carried to the Koehler Hotel, where he died. Barney's grave (pictured) is in the Old Fort Cemetery.

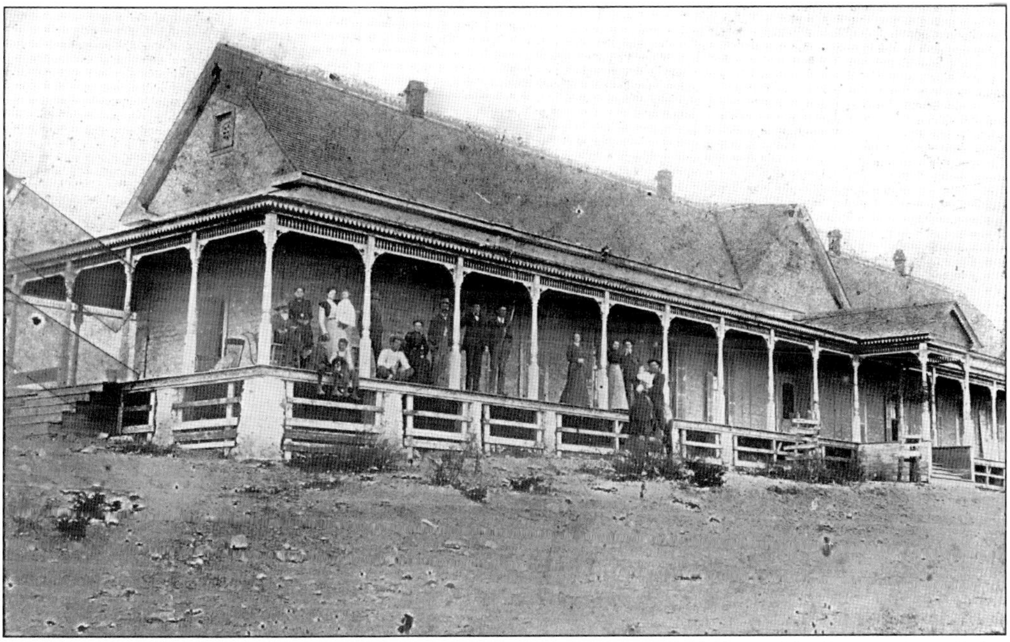

After her second husband's demise, Annie Riggs never remarried. In 1903, she purchased the Koehler Hotel for $4,750, spent $100 to refurnish it, and renamed it the Riggs Hotel. Residents included cowboys, traveling salesmen, lawyers and jurors in for court, and married couples. This group on the hotel porch includes Charles A. Crosby (far left, with beard), who was in the office with A.J. Royal when he was killed.

RIGGS HOTEL

Mrs. Anna Riggs, Prop.

1. Guests without baggage must pay in advance.
2. No account carried longer than one week.
3. All boisterous and profane language strictly forbidden.
4. All drinking or gambling in rooms strictly forbidden.
5. Please do not spit or throw ashes or matches on the floor.
6. Guests wishing early calls must notify clerk before retiring
7. And damage to furniture, other than ordinary wear, will be charged to occupants of rooms.
8. Guests must refrain from all singing or loud talking after reasonable hours for retiring.
9. Persons engaging rooms will be charged for same from time rooms are placed at their disposal whether occupied or not.
10. Please extinguish lights on leaving rooms or retiring. Extra charge for burning lights unnecessarily.
11. It is expected that parents will exercise proper care over children and not allow them to make a playground of halls and parlors.
12. Money, jewels and valuables must be left with clerk in office, otherwise proprietor will not be responsible for any loss.

MEALS A LA CARTE FROM 6:00 A. M. TO 10:30 P. M.

The Riggs Hotel became famous among area cowboys and ranchers for its hospitality and the meals prepared by Annie and her daughter Eva. Annie, however, expected guests to behave with decorum. Her rules (pictured) were posted for all to see. Annie carried a pistol in the pocket of her apron. If any of her male residents drank too much and became rowdy, she pulled her pistol and invited them to leave.

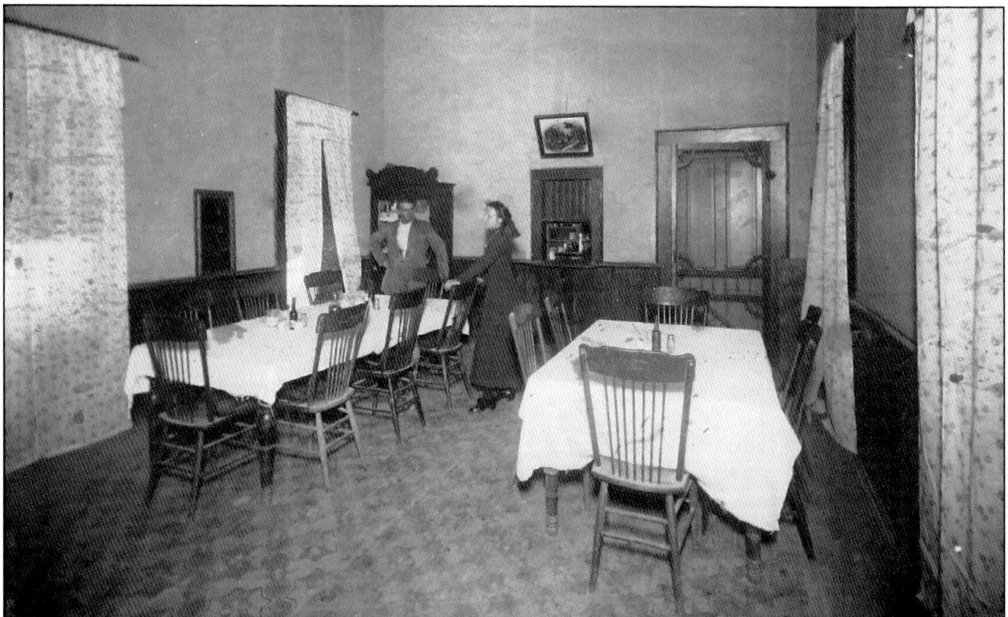

Annie and Barney Riggs had four children. Annie's daughter Eva helped her mother operate the Riggs Hotel. They became noted for their cooking, filling the Riggs dining room with patrons from near and far. In this undated photograph, Minnie Dunn, first curator of the Annie Riggs Memorial Museum, stands in the dining room with a member of the Riggs family. Annie remained loyal to all her children, including her stepson Earl.

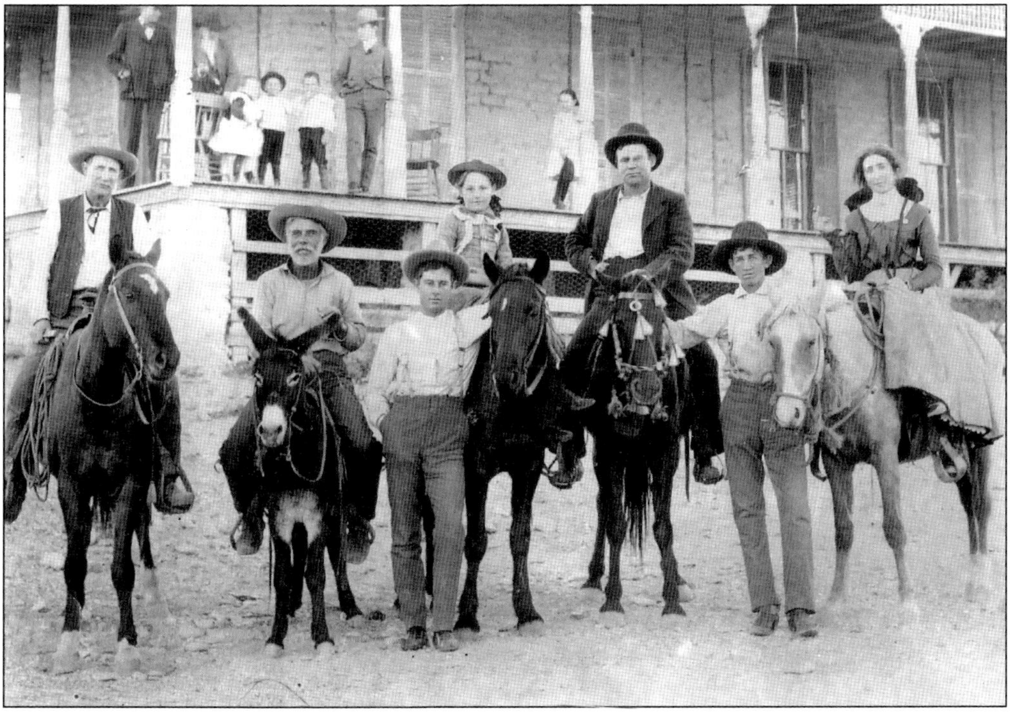

The Riggs Hotel was a popular spot in the community. Here, Earl Riggs poses with a group of riders. Pictured are, from left to right, Taylor Stephenson, Ike Hock (once part-owner of the hotel), Daisy Strickland, Theo Young, Mart Adams, Riggs, and Emma Sanders. On the porch are, from left to right, Mr. Brigham (local schoolteacher), Charles Crosby, Marjorie Livingston, Philip Rooney, Hugh Livingston, Will Haddon, and Enid Odom.

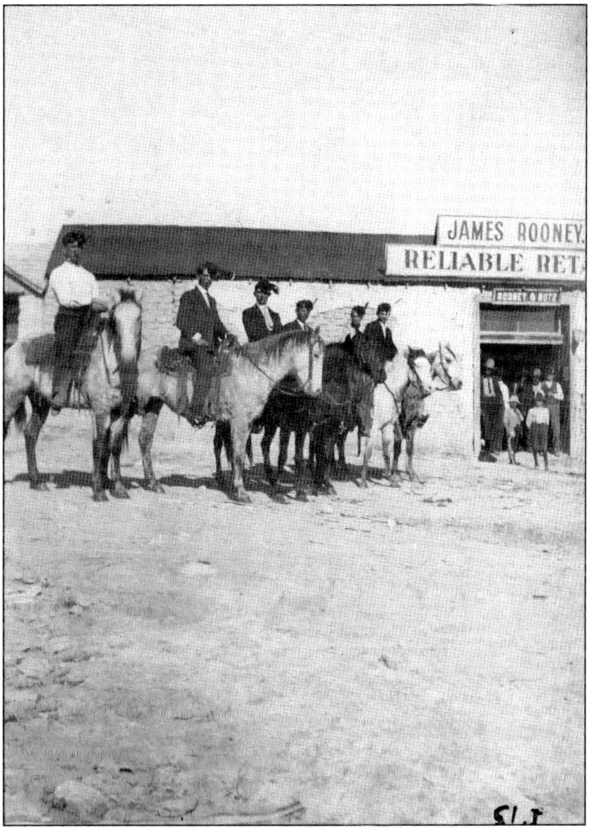

In 1904, a movement began in southern Pecos County to form a new county. Sanderson and other communities along the Southern Pacific Railroad had grown more rapidly than Fort Stockton. Southern residents resented the long ride to the courthouse and the limited amenities when they arrived. Fort Stockton, with young men clowning as Indians in front of the Rooney-Butz Mercantile, still seemed a rough and rugged frontier town.

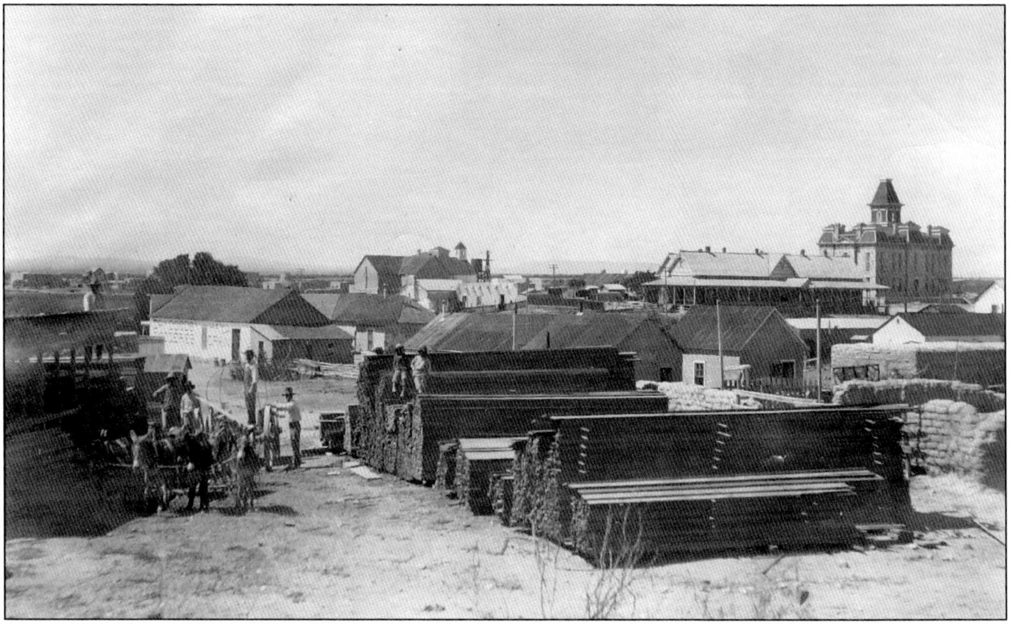

Fort Stockton was an interesting mix at the beginning of the 20th century. Here, freighters unload a wagon of lumber, hauled 85 miles from Pecos, at the lumberyard behind the Rooney-Butz store. The new Riggs Hotel, sharing the skyline with the courthouse, heralded a desire for new growth. More buildings fill in a view that was beginning to change from what was seen by Captain Wedemeyer (page 22).

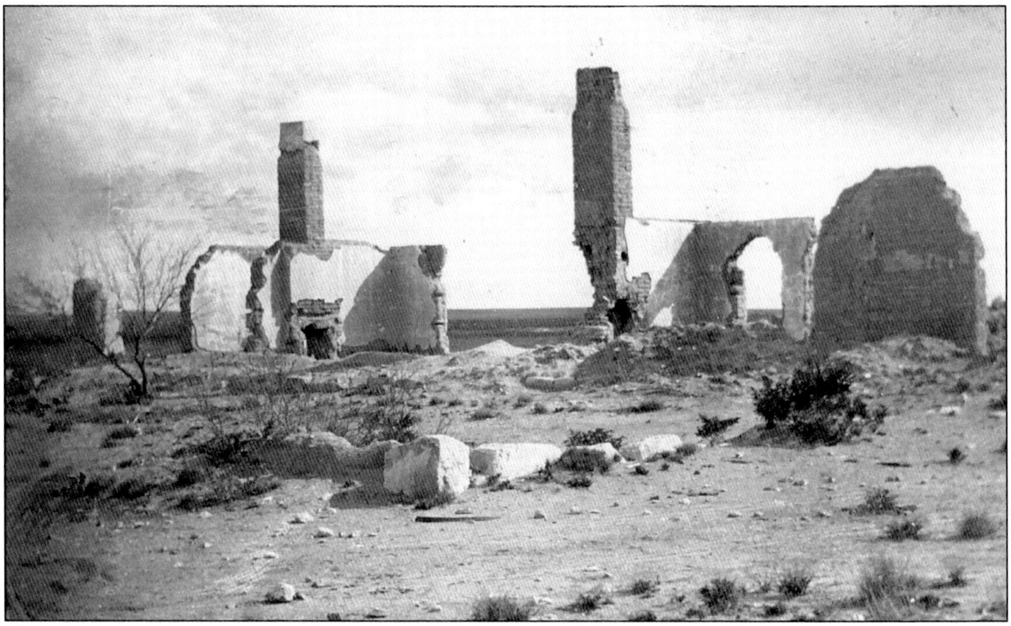

The fort hospital, built after a near mutiny among the buffalo soldiers because of the poor healthcare provided, was a crumbling ruin. Mussey and Presnall had frequently carted building materials from the fort to the Seven-d. The military years were growing distant. Still, other fort buildings survived, and the post grounds remained a center of community events over the years. (Courtesy of Mart Adams.)

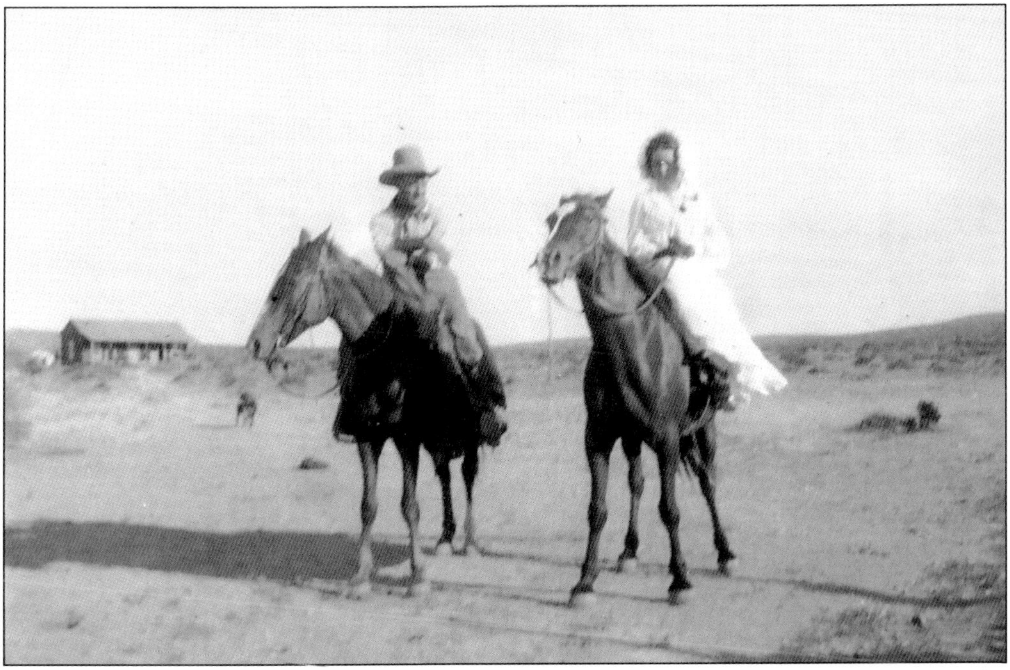

Life still retained a frontier flavor, especially away from town. Oscar Doolen Roberts and Martha Ann Rickman rode into married life on horseback in 1904. The isolated ranch house and endless terrain still resembled the open range of two decades earlier.

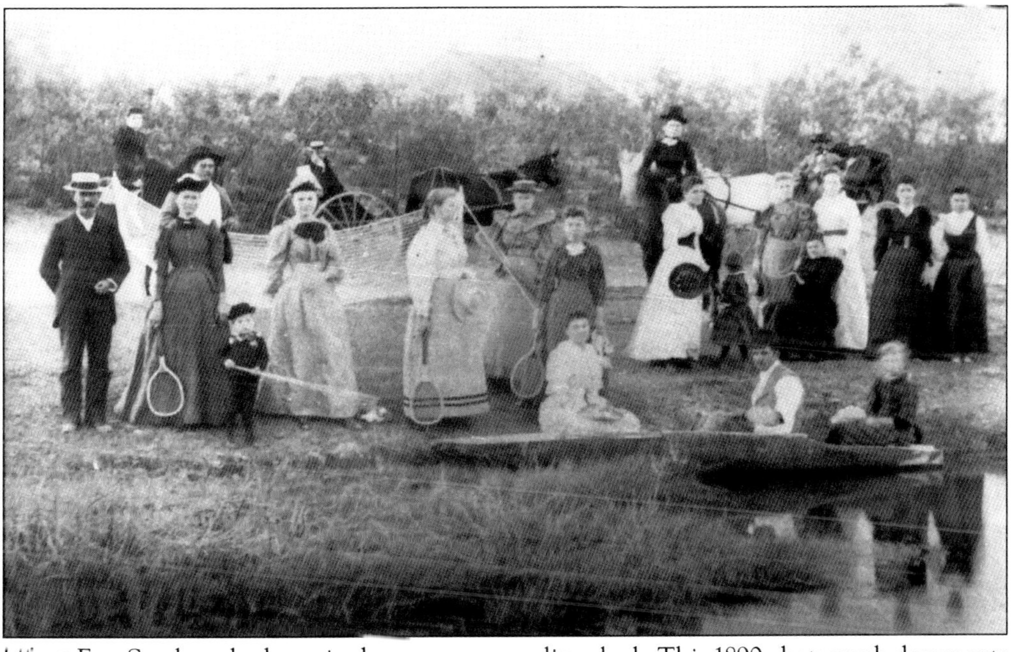

Life in Fort Stockton had acquired a more cosmopolitan look. This 1890 photograph documents a formal, rather sophisticated outing that included a tennis match. A caption on the photograph reads, "Howell Johnson, young county attorney at that time, is the fancy-dressed dude on the extreme left, mustache, straw hat, and casual pose, supposedly the best square dancer in the city." No one else earned an identification or comment.

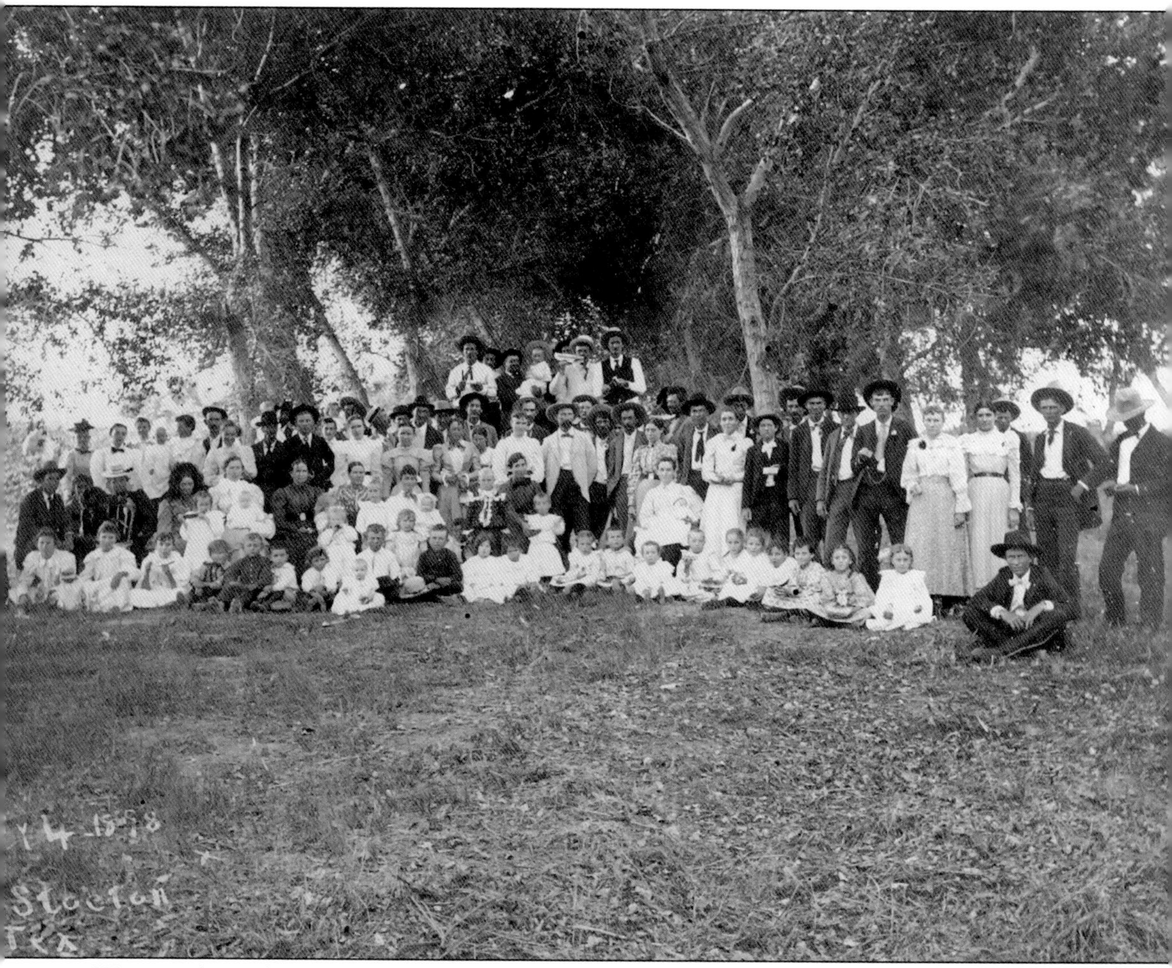

Wearing fancy dresses, ties, and straw boater skimmers, this youthful crowd of Fort Stockton citizens, pictured at a Fourth of July celebration in 1898, looked toward a future city of railroads and cars, not to one of buggies and freight wagons. In negotiating the carving away of Terrell County in 1905, Fort Stockton officials sought to retain their access to complimentary railroad passes on the Southern Pacific. So, when Pecos County attained its final dimensions on July 14, 1905, with the official establishment of Terrell County, they included a small point in the southern tip with a few miles of Southern Pacific track. Pecos County, still over 4,700 square miles in area and destined to remain the second largest county in the state, achieved its final form (see page 82).

Four

Building a Commercial Center

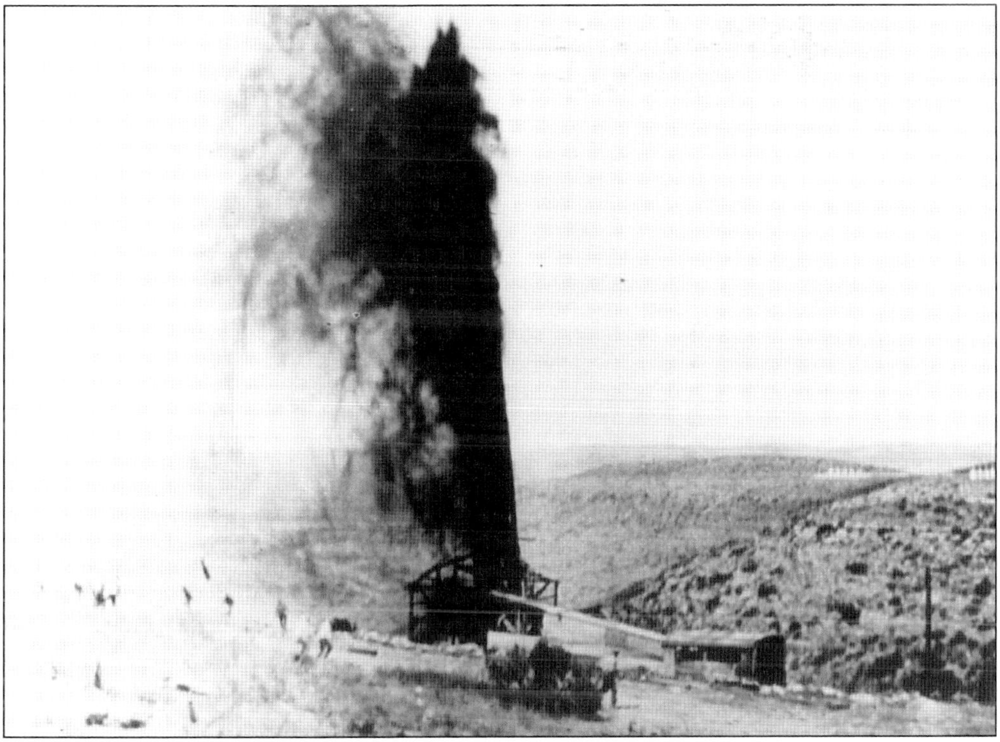

In 1905, Fort Stockton was a small, isolated rural community. By 1940, a vastly transformed city existed beside Comanche Springs. Three factors produced this change—the arrival of the railroad, the beginnings of the national highway system, and the discovery of vast oil resources. At times, the growth felt as explosive as when the Ira Yates, C-10 well (pictured) "blew in" in eastern Pecos in 1927 during the early days of the Pecos County oil boom. (Courtesy of City of Iraan Museum.)

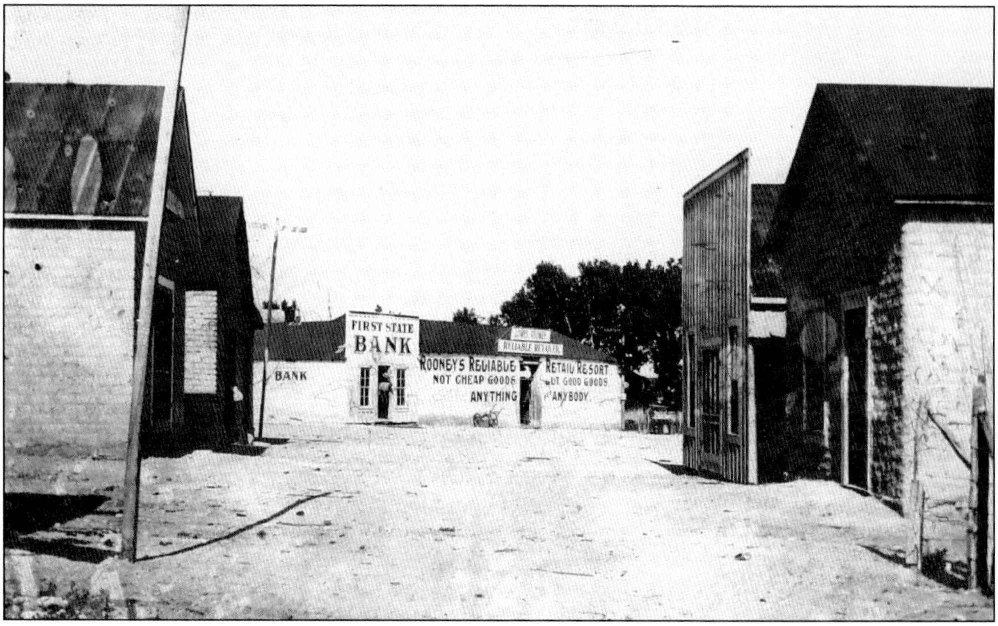

Fort Stockton did not have much of a main street. In 1904, James Rooney bought out Herman Butz's interest in their store (page 45), and Rooney's Reliable Retail Resort comprised most of the business district. Butz and Rooney remained partners in the First State Bank, (pictured in 1907, the year it opened), the city's first financial institution. Other stockholders included John Scharbauer, prominent Midland, Texas, businessman and his son Clarence.

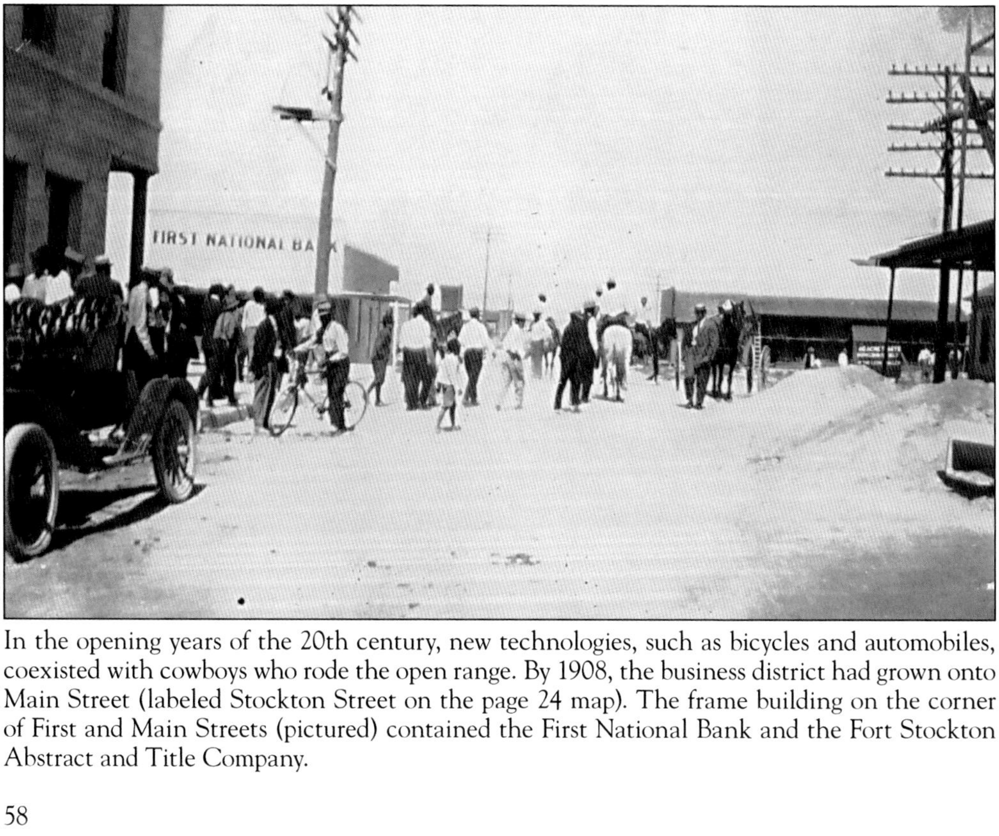

In the opening years of the 20th century, new technologies, such as bicycles and automobiles, coexisted with cowboys who rode the open range. By 1908, the business district had grown onto Main Street (labeled Stockton Street on the page 24 map). The frame building on the corner of First and Main Streets (pictured) contained the First National Bank and the Fort Stockton Abstract and Title Company.

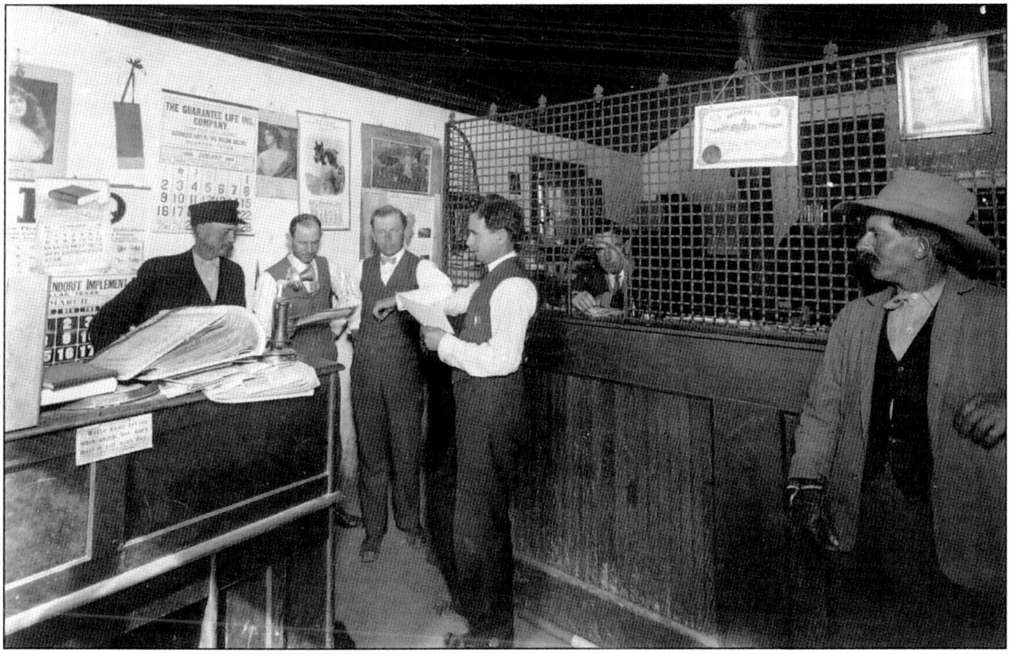

The shareholders of the First National Bank (the lobby pictured in 1910) included local pioneers James Rooney, Shipton Parke, and Herman Butz. Out-of-town investors included Herbert Kokernot, who operated the vast o6 Ranch in the Davis Mountains near Alpine. At times, more than 35,000 cattle were carrying the o6 brand on the Kokernot range, grazing approximately 400,000 acres of grassland.

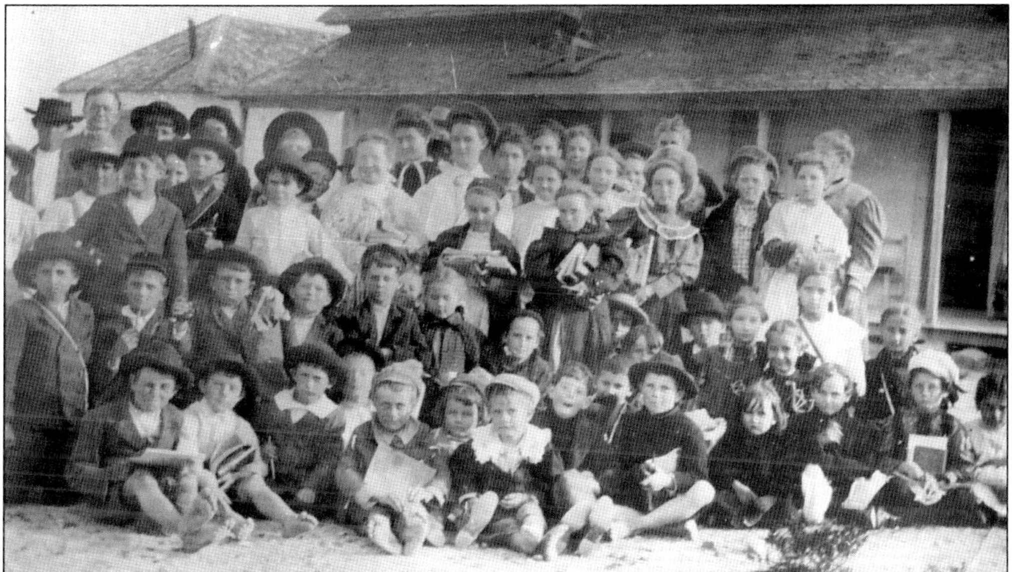

Education in Fort Stockton began with an 1867 fort school for the officers' children. When the post closed, education efforts continued. This unidentified class sits in front of the former Western Union building that became a school after the fort closed. The school had crude wooden benches, and the Mexican American and Anglo children wrote their lessons on slates for teacher Jessie Williams, sister of Judge O.W. Williams. (Courtesy of Joe Primera family.)

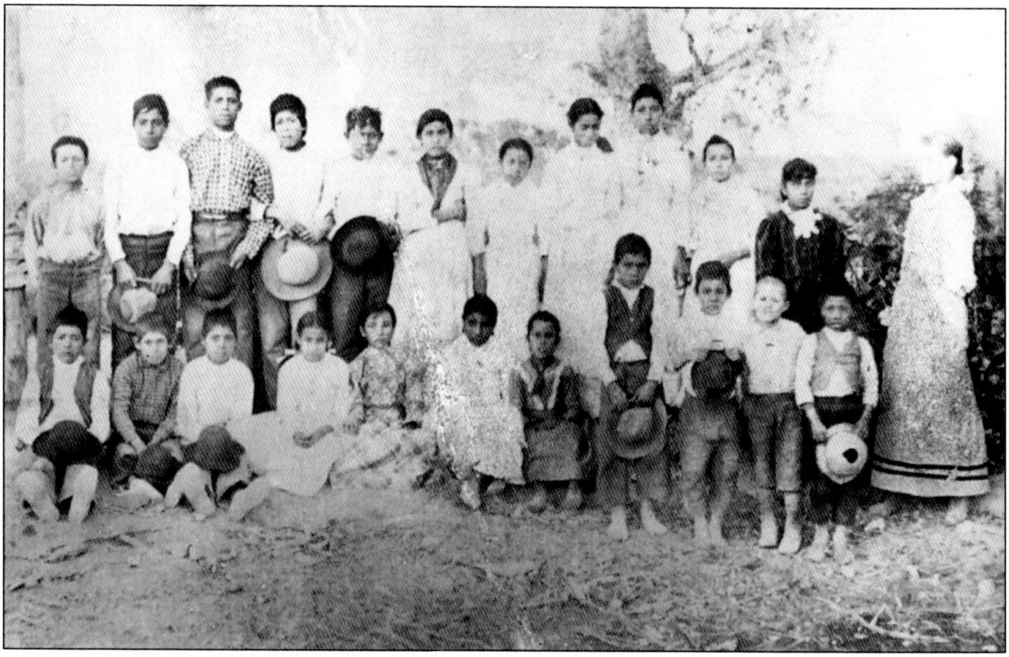

The scattered nature of the population on ranches and farms posed an educational challenge. Many ranchers' wives taught their children and those of the cowboys. The Rooney Farm, north of town, operated a school for the children in the area. Essie MacDonald (pictured on the right with her students) taught at the Rooney School. She became the wife of James Rooney.

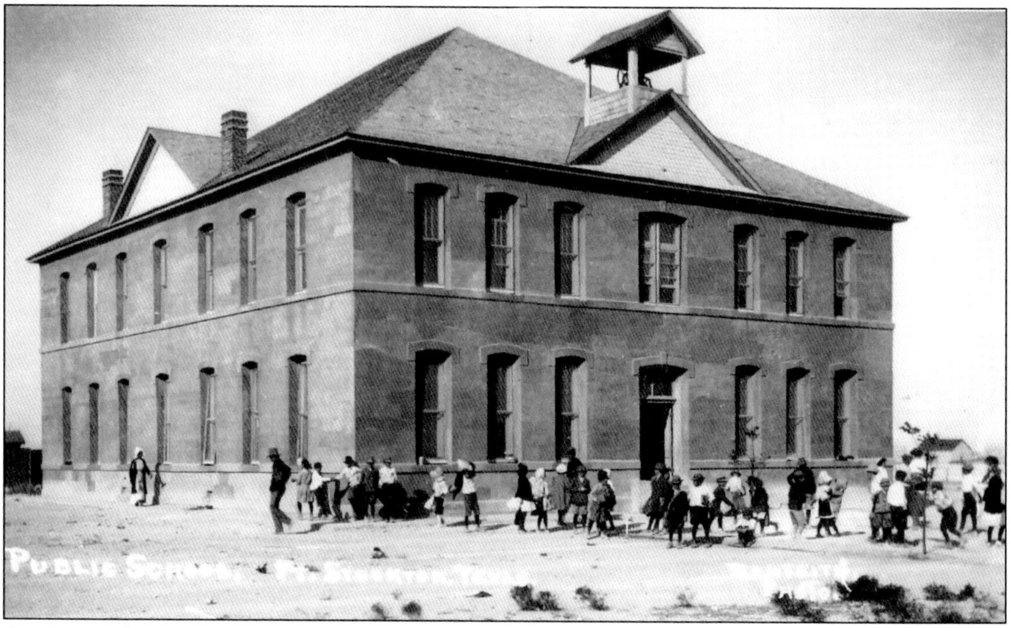

On September 7, 1908, the school year began with an enrollment of 70 students. In November of that year, a two-story grade school (pictured) was completed at a cost of $11,000. Located between First and Second Streets, the new school was for the Anglo children. Segregated education of Mexican American and Anglo children had begun. As the city grew, the divisions along Division Street became more rigidly defined. (Courtesy of Nita Stewart Haley Memorial Library.)

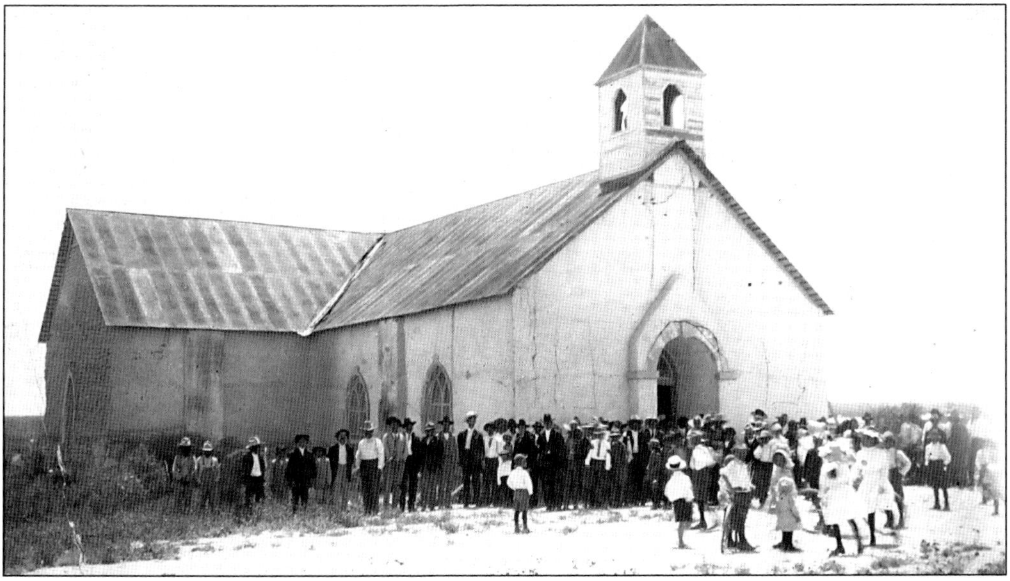

Divisions also grew along religious lines. For two decades after 1876, St. Joseph's Catholic Church (pictured) was the only religious institution in Fort Stockton. Most early pioneers were Catholic, including such prominent Anglo families as the Rooneys and the Fraziers. Yet the remote locale and the decline in the Mexican American population after the post's closing prevented the church from becoming a parish with its own priest.

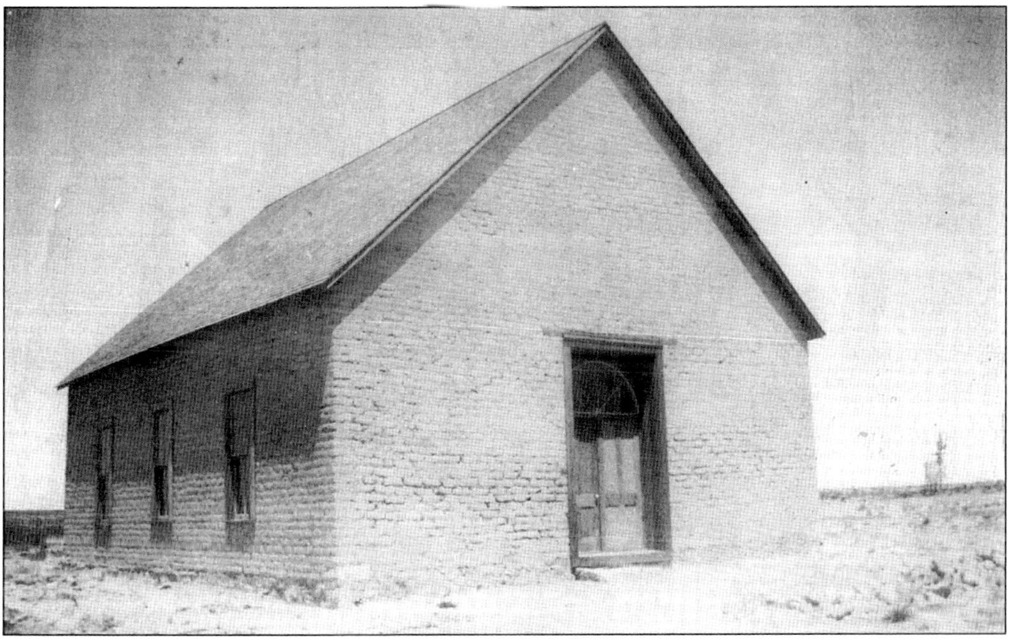

New Anglo families moving to Fort Stockton brought with them different religions. On May 29, 1887, Sallie Wheat Williams, wife of O.W. Williams, and Essie MacDonald organized Sunday school classes in the courthouse building (two for Protestants and one for Catholics). Desire for a Protestant sanctuary led to the construction of the Union Church (pictured) in 1903. Four denominations—Methodist, Presbyterian, Baptist, and Christian—met there, each having one Sunday a month.

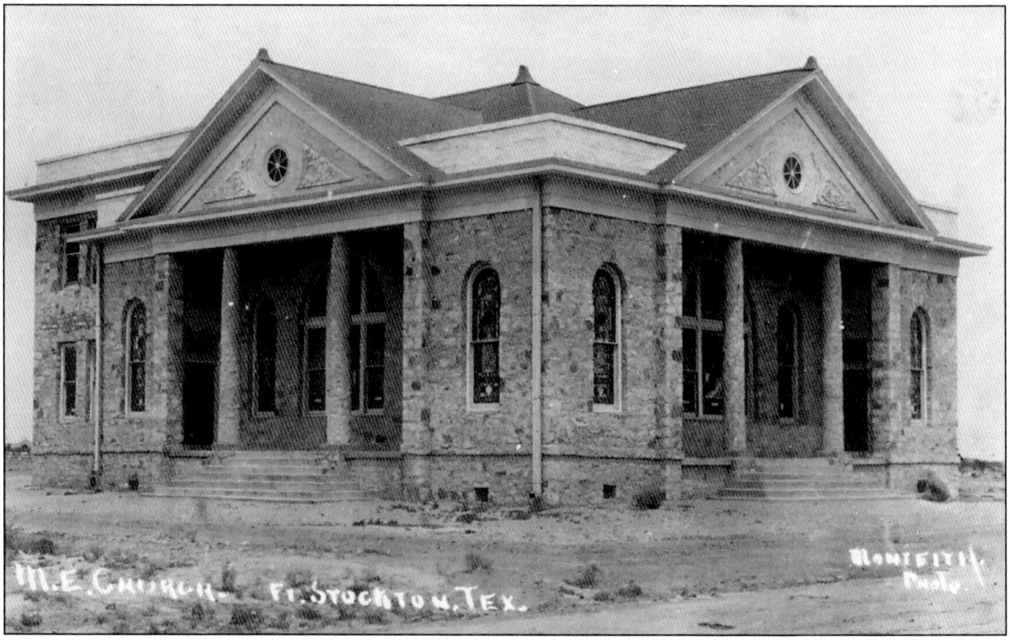

In 1899, Methodist Church South became the first organized Protestant church in Fort Stockton. The Methodists had constructed the Union Church with the stipulation that they share it with other denominations. In 1912, they completed their own building. The walls were of stone quarried from Five Mile Mesa. Sand for mortar came from local dry washes. Lime was produced by burning rocks in the old army kiln.

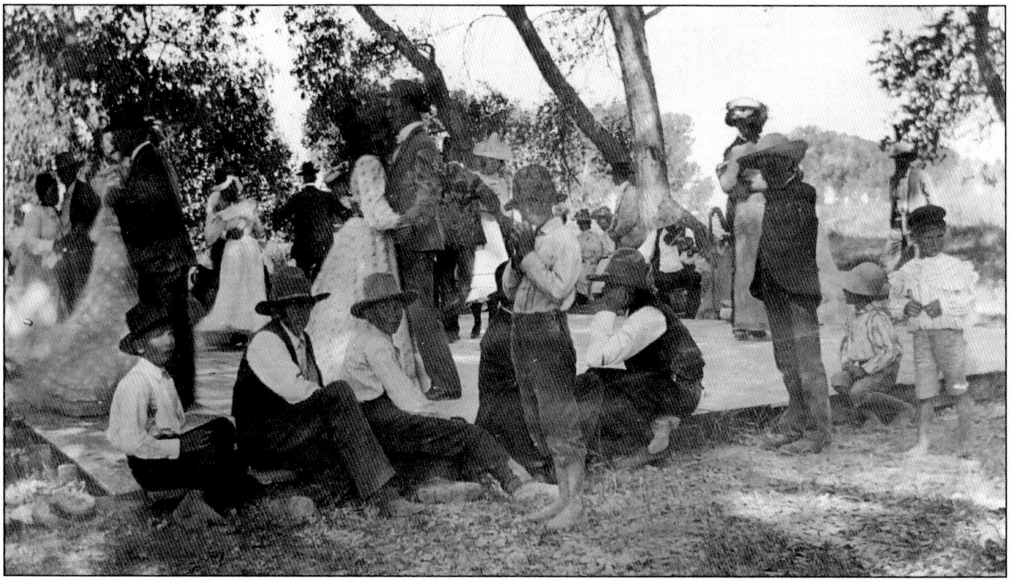

Educational, religious, and political power lines were drawn between Mexican Americans, who were largely Catholic, and Anglos, who were becoming increasingly Protestant. Yet, there was always ambiguity in these divisions. At social events, such as this July 1902 picnic, Mexican American and Anglo children watch the dancers together, while musician Chico Gomez (in the background) plays his violin. Gomez was accompanied by his brother Edubijin, who was an outstanding harp player. (Courtesy of Mart Adams.)

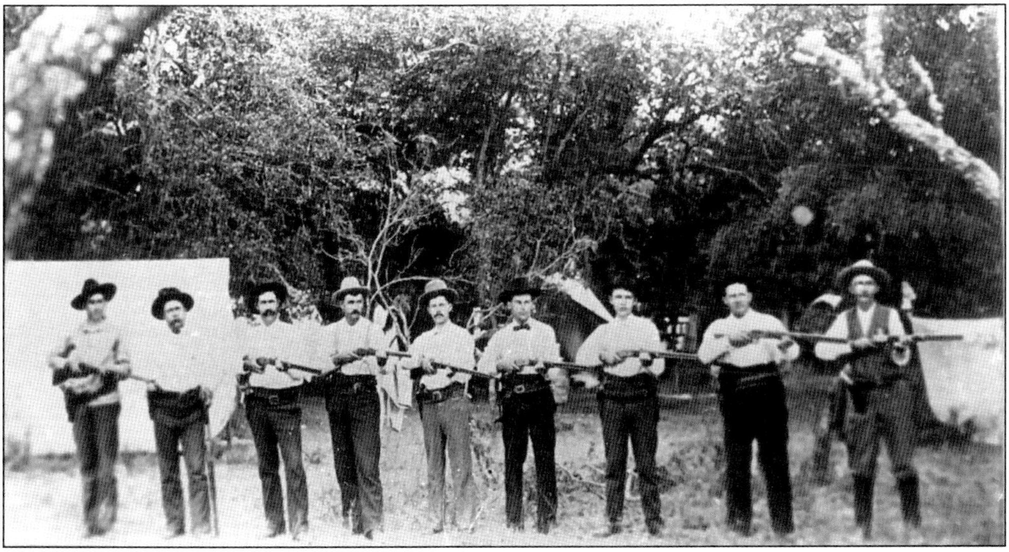

The career of Dudley S. Barker epitomizes this ambiguity. Born in Round Rock, Barker served as a Texas Ranger in 1897 and 1898. His Ranger company helped quell the 1897 San Saba range war. In San Saba, Barker met and married Lillie Campbell. This 1897 photograph of Texas Rangers on the San Saba River includes, from left to right, Ollie Perry, Jack Harwell, Ed Donnelly, Blue Bell, Bill McCouley, D.S. Barker, Van Jones, Bob McClure, and Capt. W.J. McDonald.

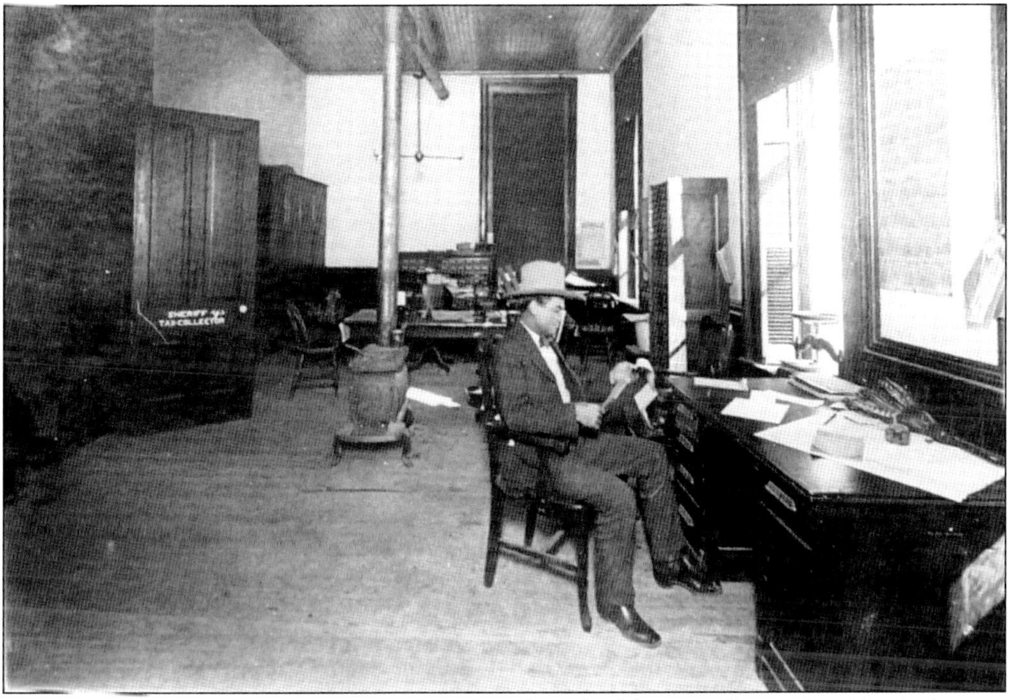

The Barkers moved to southern Pecos County and ranched for several years. In 1904, Barker was elected county sheriff and served until 1928. Pictured in his office in 1905, he became known as a fearless and efficient lawman. In a 1912 gun battle, he killed three drunken Mexican Americans over a shooting incident. Some Mexican Americans felt he treated them unfairly despite the fact that Lillie Barker was a highly respected member of St. Joseph's Catholic Church.

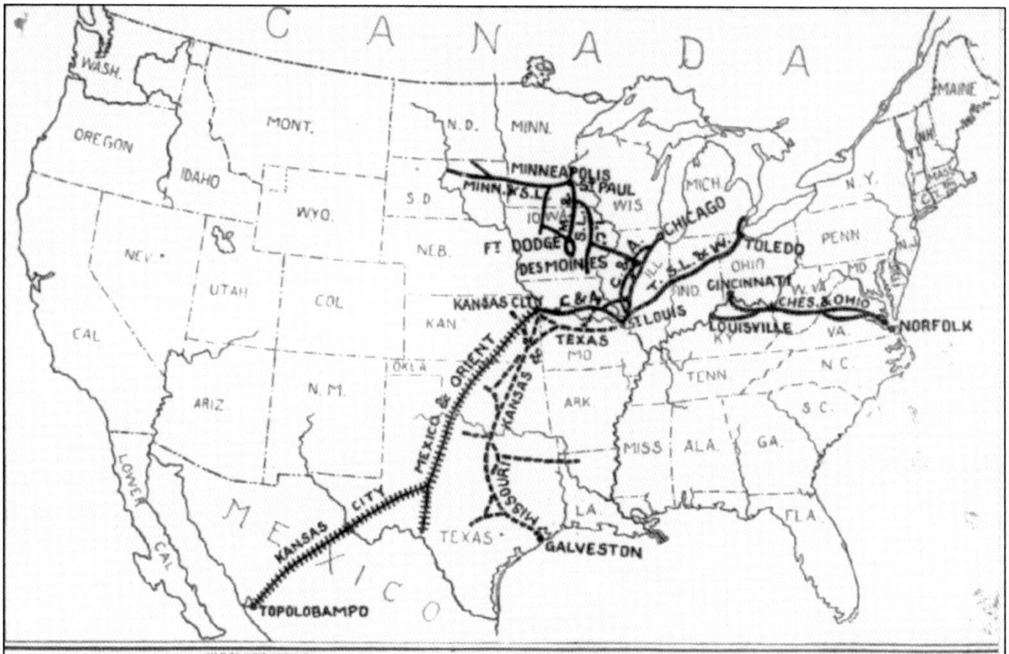

MAP OF THE HAWLEY RAILROAD LINES.

In 1912, the era of the freight wagon ended. Arthur Stillwell, enterprising railroad builder, conceived the idea of a line from Kansas City to Topolobampo, Mexico, which he claimed was the closest Pacific port to Kansas City. This map, printed in the July 1909 *American Review of Reviews*, details how Stillwell's line, the Kansas City, Mexico & Orient Railway, would connect with the Hawley Railroad system to produce a shorter Atlantic–Pacific route.

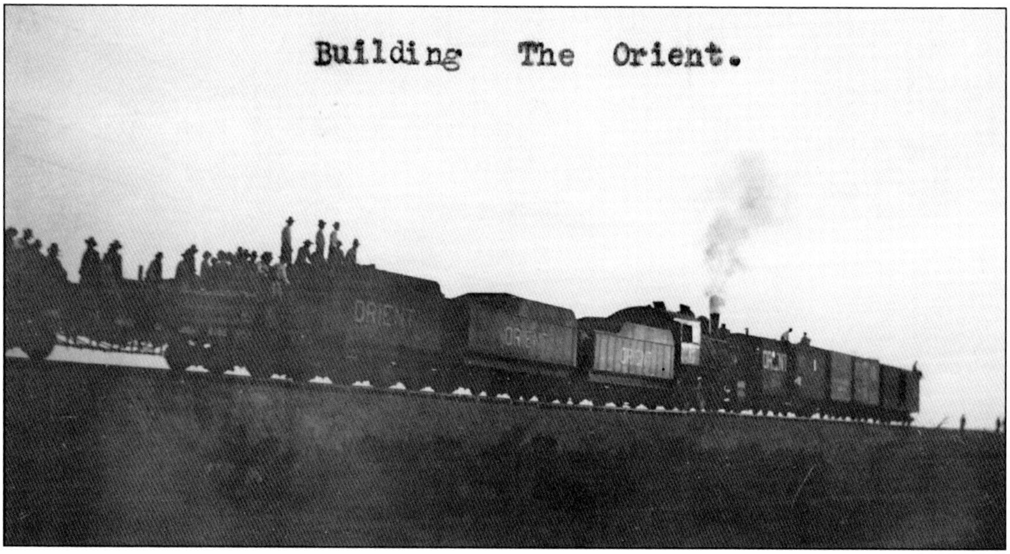

The proposed route of the Kansas City, Mexico & Orient Railway of Texas ran through San Angelo, Texas. One line ran south to Fort Stockton, Alpine, and Presidio, and a second ran to Del Rio. Stillwell had a separate agreement with the Mexican government of Pres. Porfirio Diaz for a line across the rugged Sierra Madre Mountains. In June 1909, the Orient, as it came to be known, reached San Angelo.

Fresnoes, large shovel-like implements pulled by horses and mules, built the roadbed. A Hurley track-laying machine put down the rails. Work was hindered by the inability to keep the machine loaded with material. The line (pictured under construction) was extended to Girvin in Pecos County, 32 miles from Fort Stockton, in 1911.

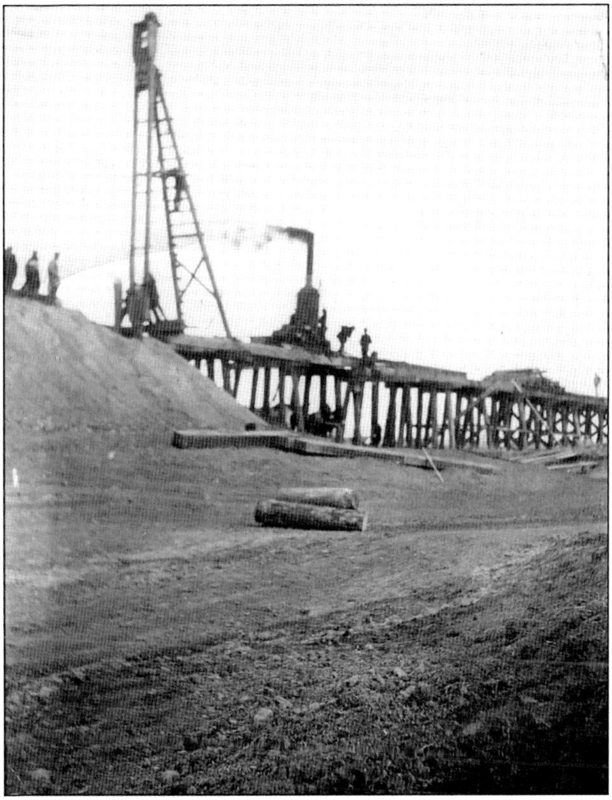

The impending arrival of the Orient launched a wave of construction in Fort Stockton. New buildings began to rise along Main Street. Stillwell, in collaboration with local interests, including the *Fort Stockton Pioneer* newspaper (established in 1908), promoted the merits of moving to West Texas. Advertisements, such as this one published in the February 11, 1911, issue of *Popular Mechanics*, provided glowing accounts of agricultural opportunity.

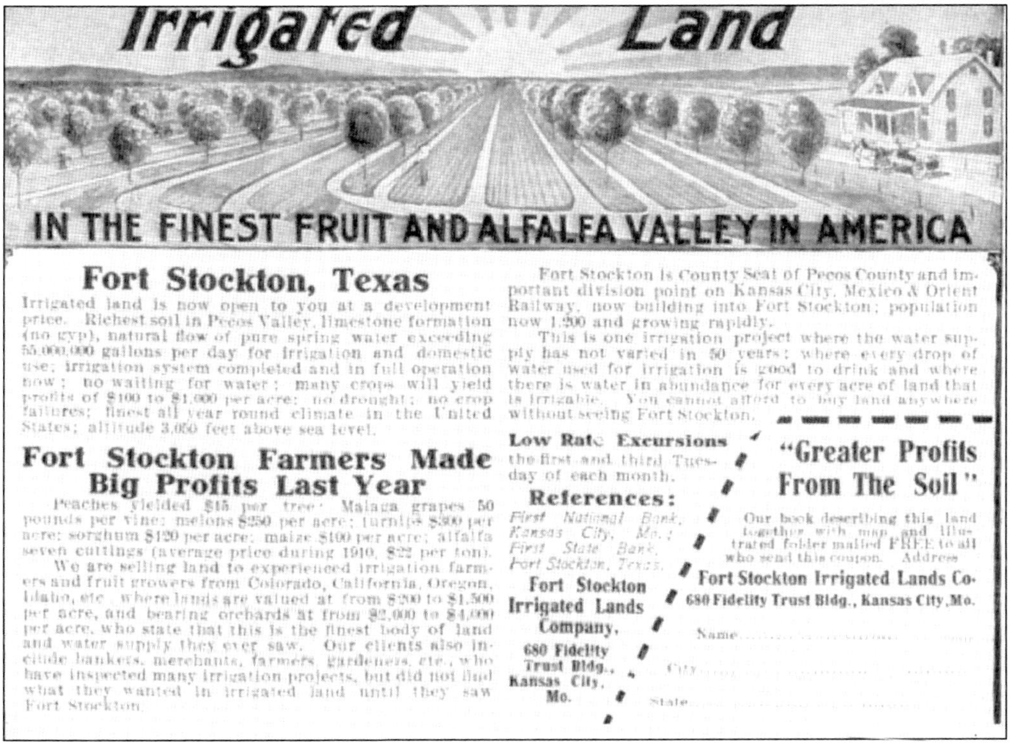

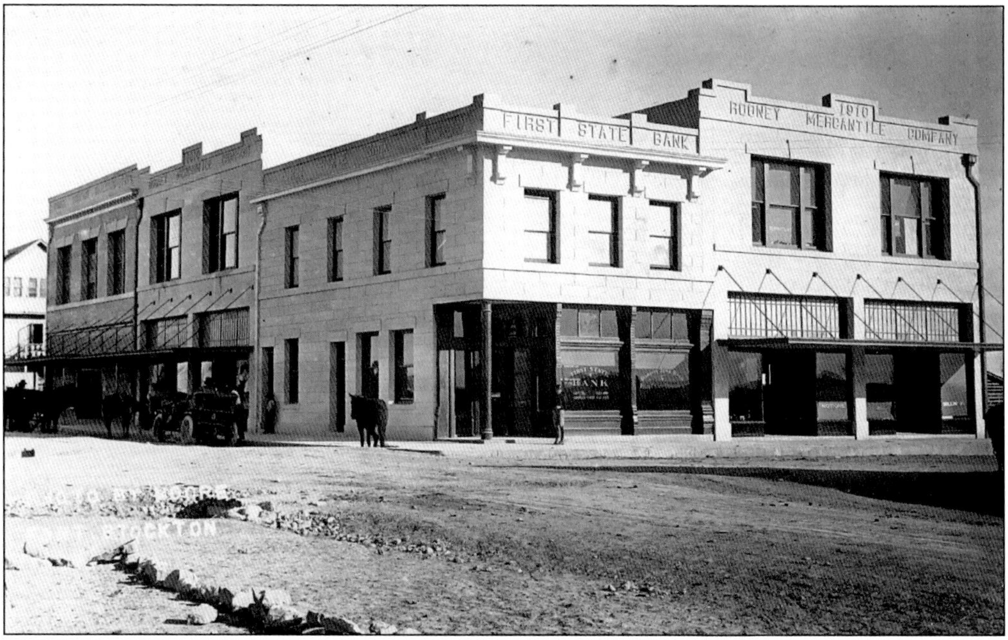

The Rooney Mercantile helped usher in a new era in Fort Stockton. Businesses moved from the creek bank to Main Street. Stone and concrete replaced adobe. Plate glass windows promoted notions, dress goods, and millinery. The store wrapped around the new First State Bank location, its windows proudly advertising its capital.

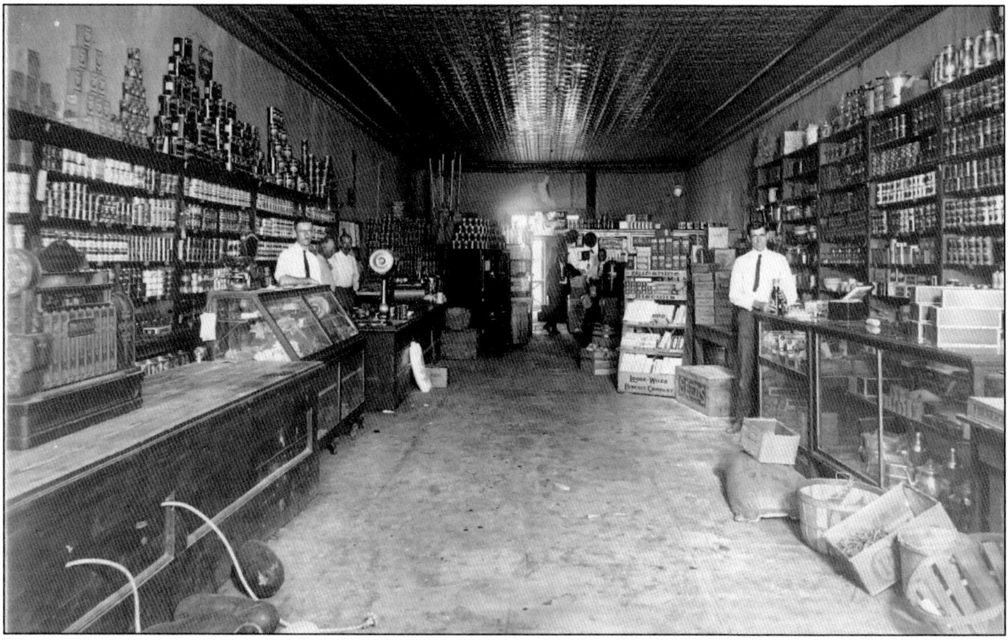

James Rooney moved his business to Main Street, establishing the Rooney Mercantile Company in 1910. The mercantile carried a large stock of goods, employed a number of clerks and other workers, and conducted an extensive retail and wholesale business. Rooney was also vice president of the First State Bank. The clerks and customers in this photograph of the store's interior are not identified.

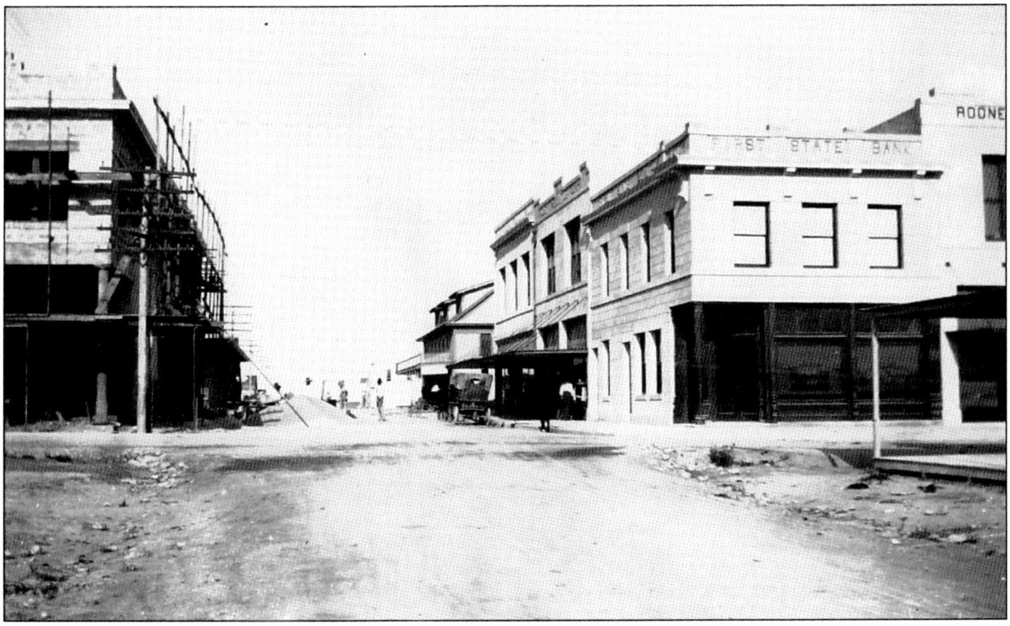

Across First Street, Rooney erected the New Rooney Hotel. In this 1910 east-facing view, the hotel is under construction on the left. It would replace the old Rooney Hotel (on the right behind the mercantile) to serve the new railroad trade. That same year, Arthur Stillwell erected a new two-story depot in San Angelo, Texas, to become the headquarters of the Kansas City, Mexico & Orient Railway of Texas Corporation. It was the only brick building in town.

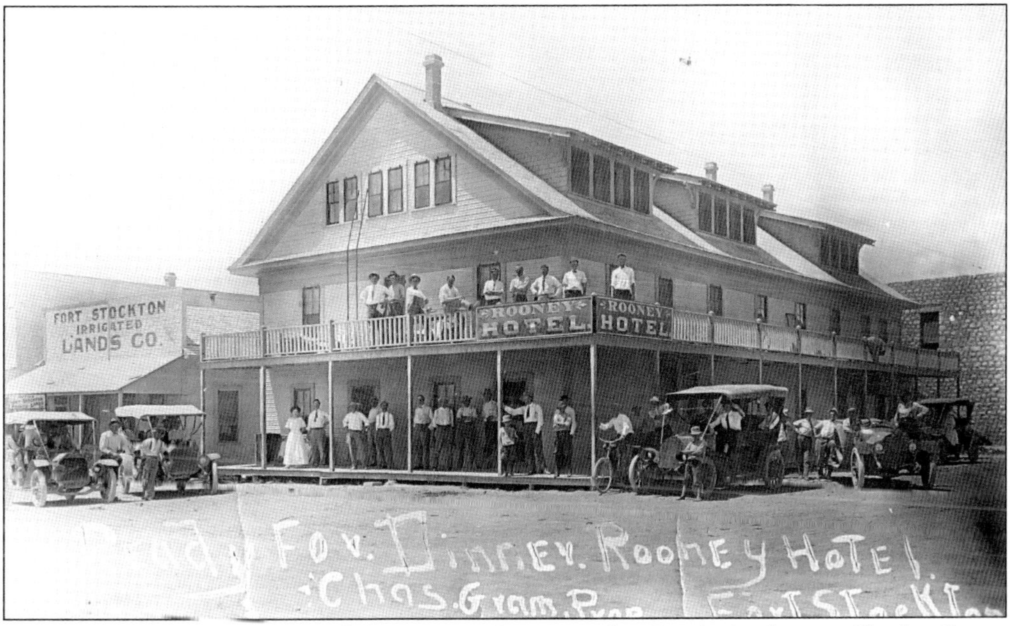

The caption on this photograph from around 1911 reads, "Ready for dinner. Charles Gram, Proprietor." The old Rooney Hotel advertised that it was "lighted throughout with acetylene gas." The hotel was moved to Big Lake, Texas, and then to Hobbs, New Mexico, where it was destroyed by a fire. In 1912, Mr. and Mrs. H.H. Tracy of Cleveland, Ohio, replaced Gram as the proprietors.

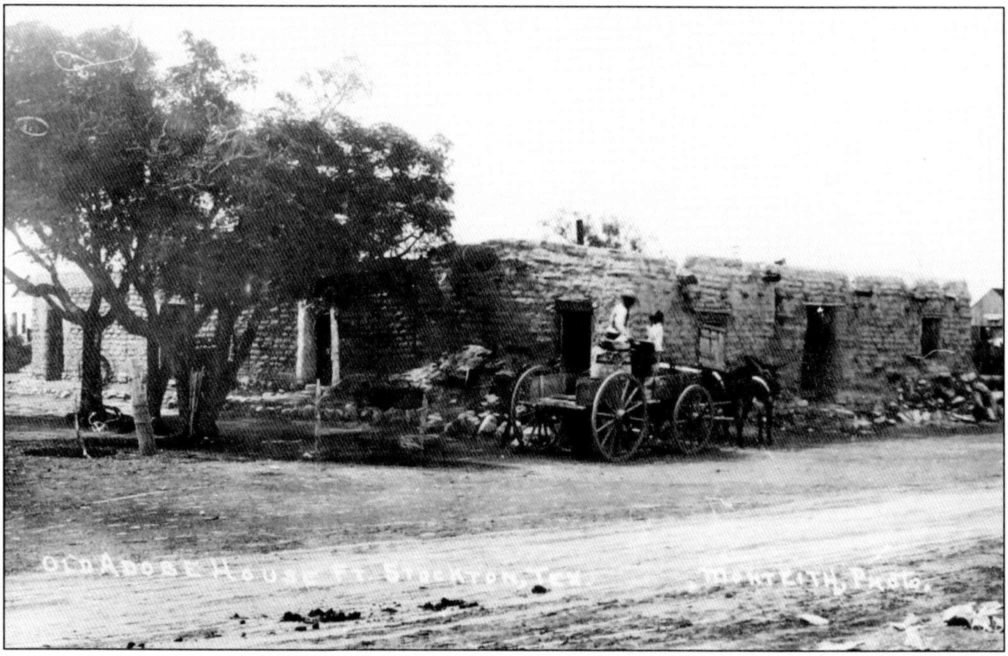

Along with gas lighting, more infrastructure was added. For decades, water was hauled from Comanche Creek and delivered in barrels, as seen in this photograph. In 1910, James Rooney and Herman Butz drilled a well north of town and erected a 10,000 gallon elevated tank. W.F. Zarbach and Charles A. Schraff began providing electricity in 1911. It cost 18¢ per kilowatt-hour for homes and 15¢ per kilowatt-hour for businesses.

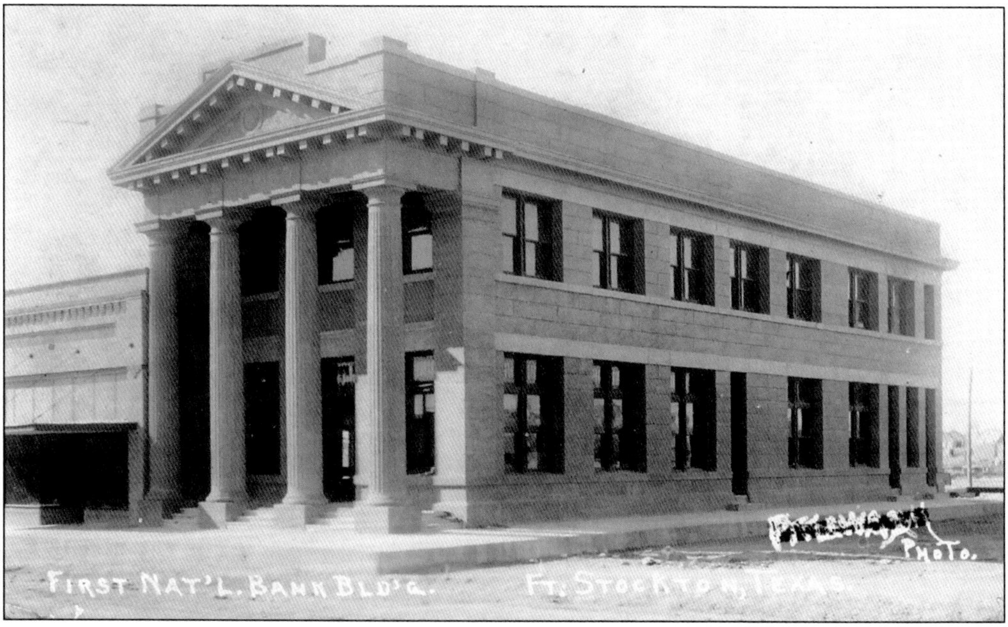

In 1912, the First National Bank moved from its small wooden building and erected a two-story stone building with a granite finish in the Greek Revival style. The new structure stood on the corner of Second and Main Streets. The building cost $16,000, but the investment paid off. Between November 1910 and February 1913, the bank's deposits grew from $13,000 to over $65,000.

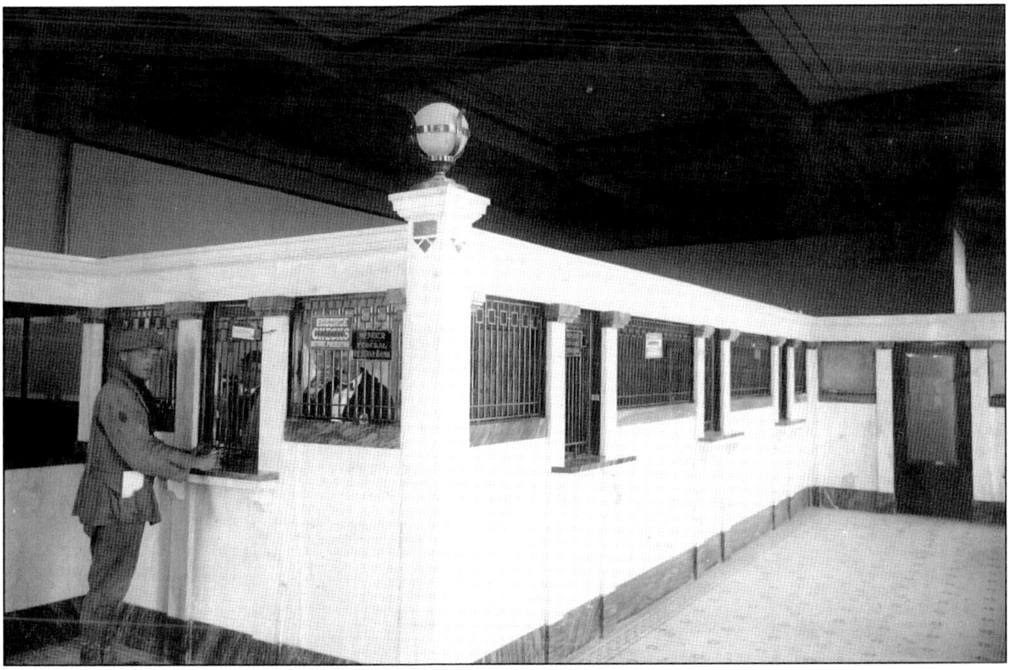

The interior of the new First National Bank had a more elegant appearance than its predecessor (page 59). The tile floors, the granite trim, the elegant ceiling, the cashier in coat and bowtie, and the four cashier windows were all there to convey a sense of solid finance to both locals and passengers arriving on the Orient. The name of this road-worn customer has been lost.

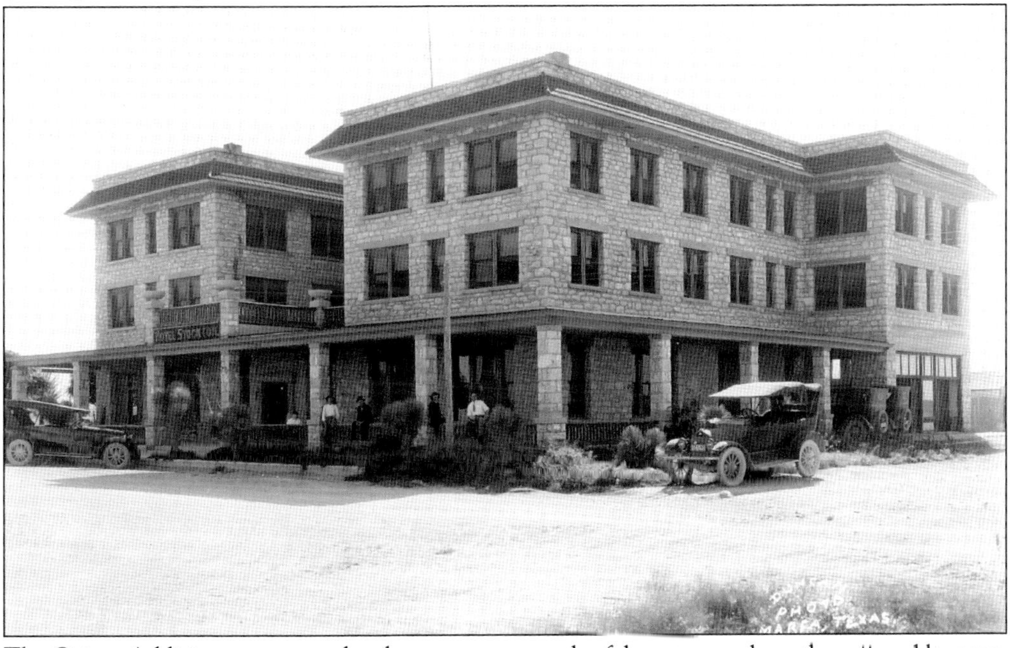

The Orient Addition was a new development area north of downtown where the railroad line was planned. The Hotel Stockton was built there in 1911 at a cost of $50,000. When completed, the hotel had 70 rooms, steam heating, electric lighting, and a sewer system. A 1912 advertisement in the *Fort Stockton Pioneer* read, "Good beds, clean linen, baths—$2.00 and up."

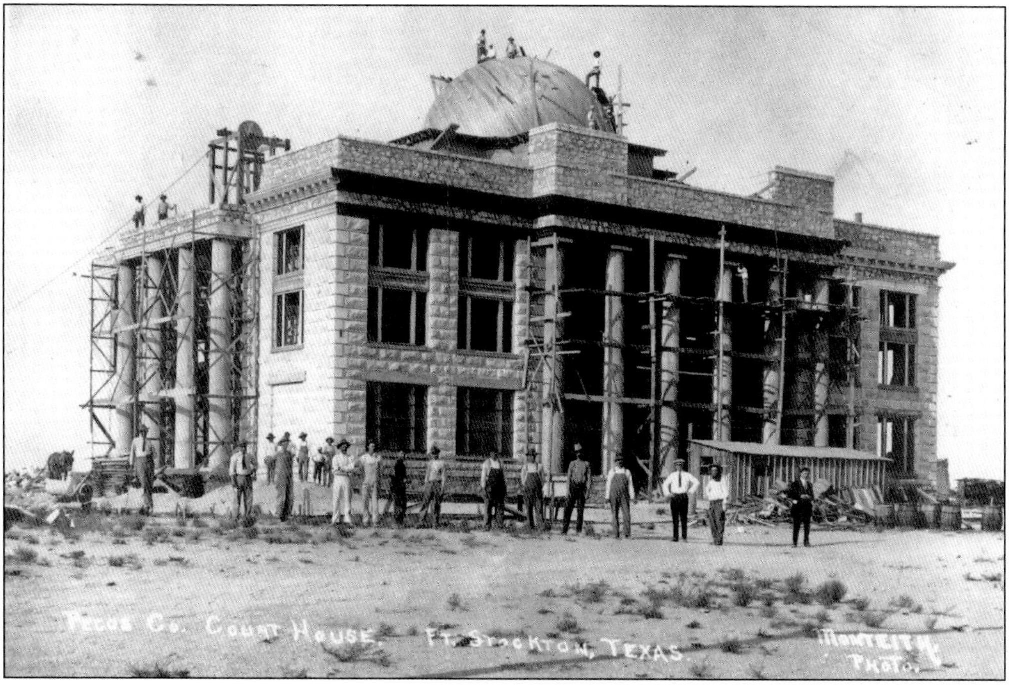

A growing, modern county needed a new courthouse. In 1912, the commissioners' court advertised for bids for alterations and additions to the courthouse and jail. Falls City Construction Company of Louisville, Kentucky, won the remodeling bid at $73,000. The courthouse, pictured under construction, retained some of the old foundations and stones. (Courtesy of Nita Stewart Haley Memorial Library.)

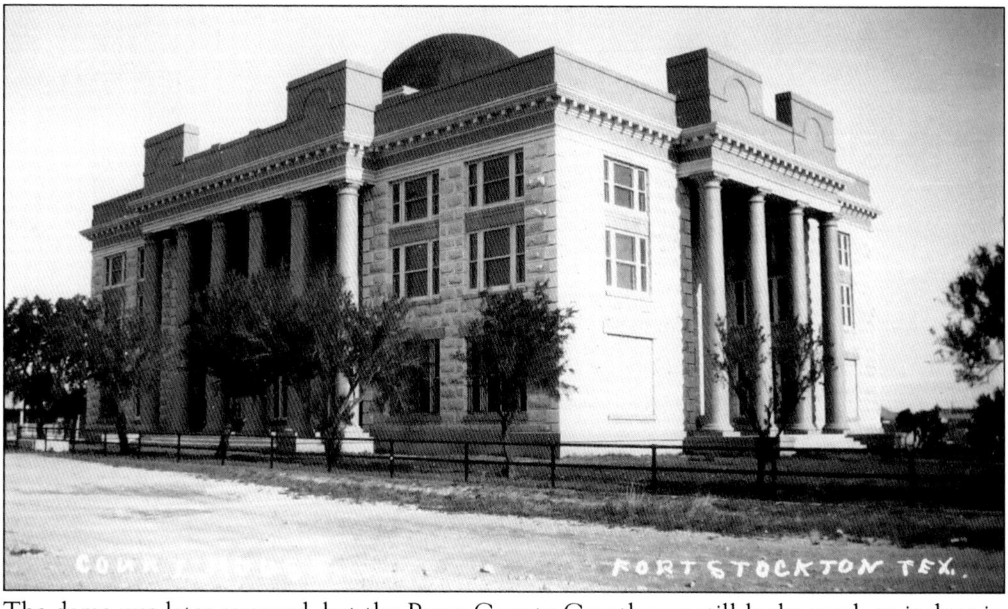

The dome was later removed, but the Pecos County Courthouse still looks much as it does in this old postcard. Pecos County had about 6,000 residents when the courthouse was completed in 1913, of which 1,750 lived in Fort Stockton. Over 28,000 acres were under cultivation. With 100,000 head, Pecos had more cattle than any other Texas county.

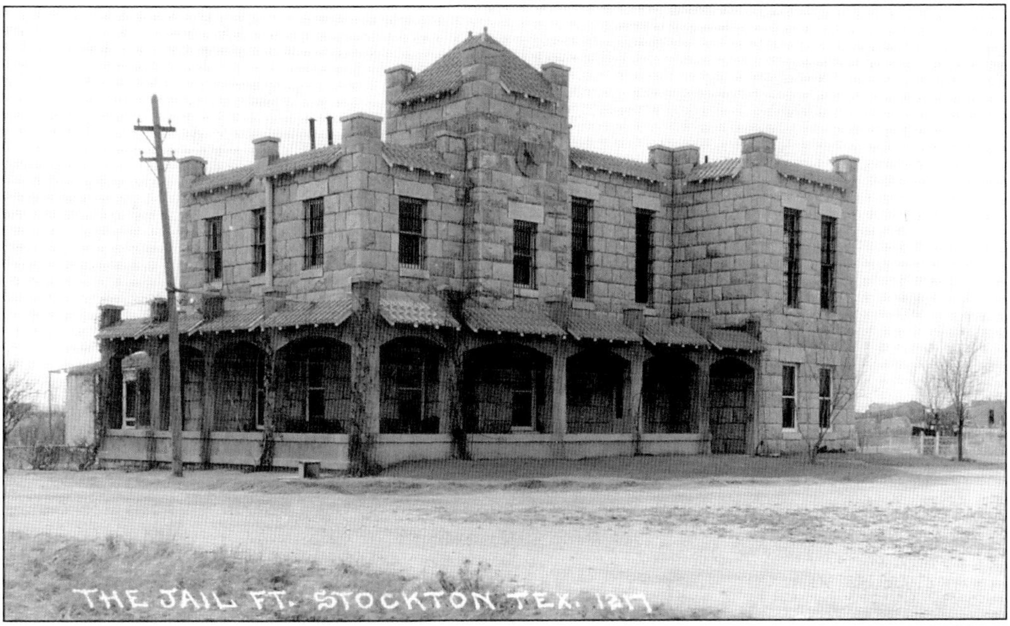

The 1883 jail (page 25) was enlarged with a wide porch around two sides. Prisoners were held on the second floor, and the sheriff, deputy sheriffs, or jailers lived on the ground floor. Life there could be interesting. Betty Christall recalls how her mother quieted a jail full of drunken braceros by spraying them with a water hose. In December 2000, when Sheriff Bruce Wilson retired, he became the last sheriff to live in the jail.

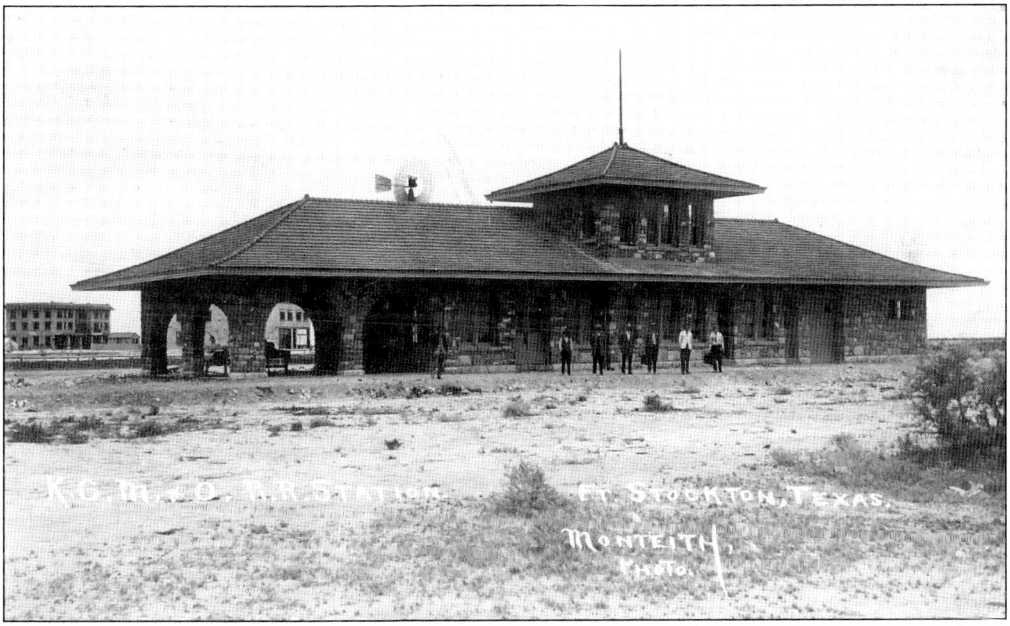

The depot was the capstone of the new construction. Begun in August 1910, it was completed in October 1911. Almost half of the $16,000 cost of the two-story stone building went to labor. The depot included a general waiting room, a smoking room, toilets, a women's waiting room, and a colored waiting room. With the newly-completed Hotel Stockton in the background, city leaders (pictured) wait for the track to arrive.

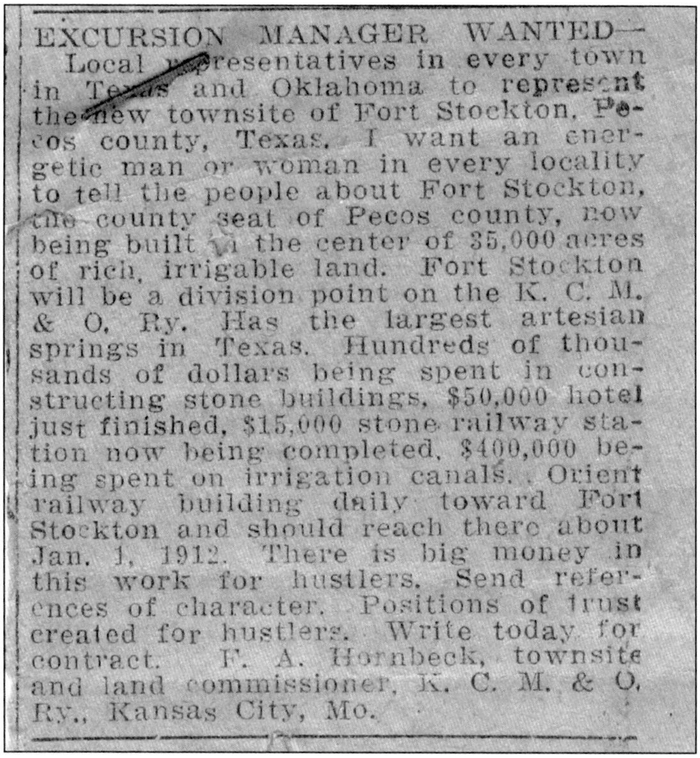

EXCURSION MANAGER WANTED—Local representatives in every town in Texas and Oklahoma to represent the new townsite of Fort Stockton, Pecos county, Texas. I want an energetic man or woman in every locality to tell the people about Fort Stockton, the county seat of Pecos county, now being built in the center of 35,000 acres of rich, irrigable land. Fort Stockton will be a division point on the K. C. M. & O. Ry. Has the largest artesian springs in Texas. Hundreds of thousands of dollars being spent in constructing stone buildings, $50,000 hotel just finished, $15,000 stone railway station now being completed, $400,000 being spent on irrigation canals. Orient railway building daily toward Fort Stockton and should reach there about Jan. 1, 1912. There is big money in this work for hustlers. Send references of character. Positions of trust created for hustlers. Write today for contract. F. A. Hornbeck, townsite and land commissioner, K. C. M. & O. Ry., Kansas City, Mo.

In April 1908, a group of local businessmen established the *Fort Stockton Pioneer.* Managing editor Jesse McKee hired 10-year-old Fred Achterburg as printer's devil (apprentice). In 1910, Elias Barry moved from Columbus, Texas, to become editor and publisher. The young paper promoted the Orient Railway. This advertisement for an excursion manager proudly proclaimed, "There is big money in this work for hustlers."

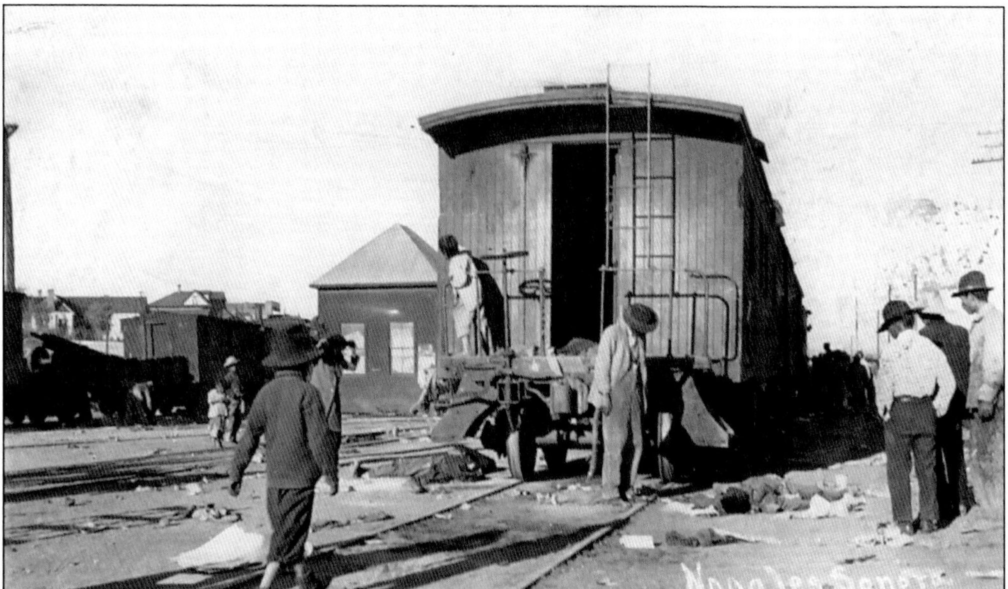

Complications developed for the railroad. The anarchy in northern Mexico caused by the Mexican revolution destroyed much of the completed work. Pancho Villa, once a contractor for the project, demolished miles of the track he helped build. Scenes such as this, taken after a battle in Nogales, Sonora, Mexico, also befell the Orient lines. The incomplete railroad failed to generate enough revenue, and the company fell into receivership in March 1912.

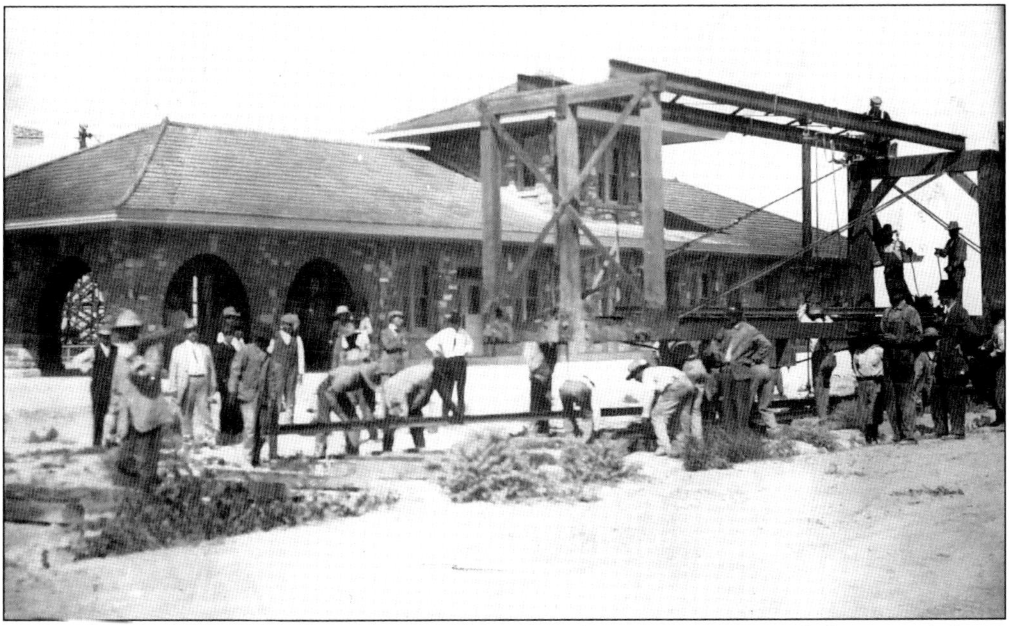

Mayor James Rooney presided over a mass meeting held on May 10, 1912, to help raise a $15,000 bonus to extend the line to the city. The Fort Stockton Irrigated Lands Company raised another $15,000. The receivers resumed work in July. In October, rails were laid to the depot (pictured).

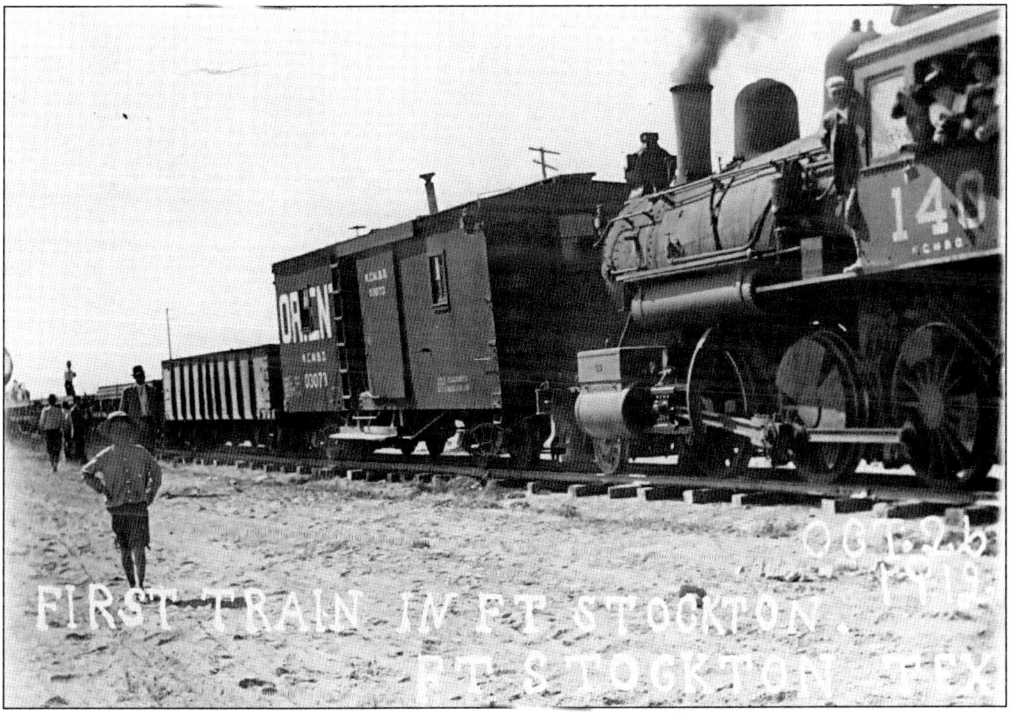

The caption on this photograph reads "First train into Fort Stockton, Texas, October 26, 1912." The engine is full of excited locals. In the background, men unload the first cargo from the freight cars. The Orient line continued on to Alpine, where it connected with the Galveston, Harrisburg & San Antonio Railway (the Southern Pacific) in 1913.

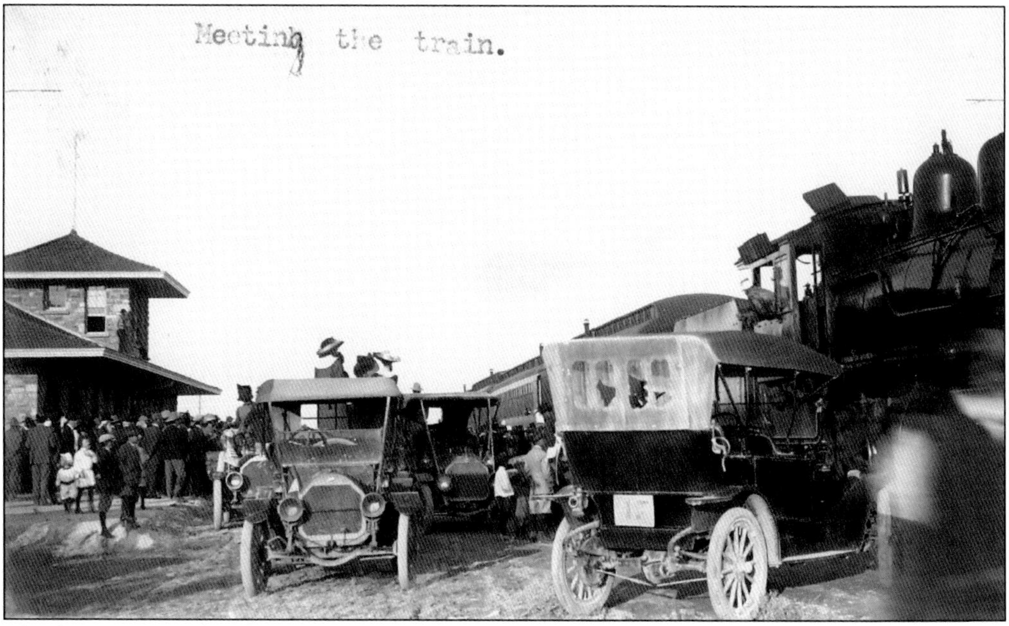

The first Orient railroad excursion train arrived in Fort Stockton on Tuesday, November 19, 1912, at 4:45 in the afternoon. In this photograph of the event, the depot area is filled with a large crowd. A group of women sacrifice a bit of decorum and stand up in one of the cars for a better view. The license plate on Herman Butz's car on the right is "17."

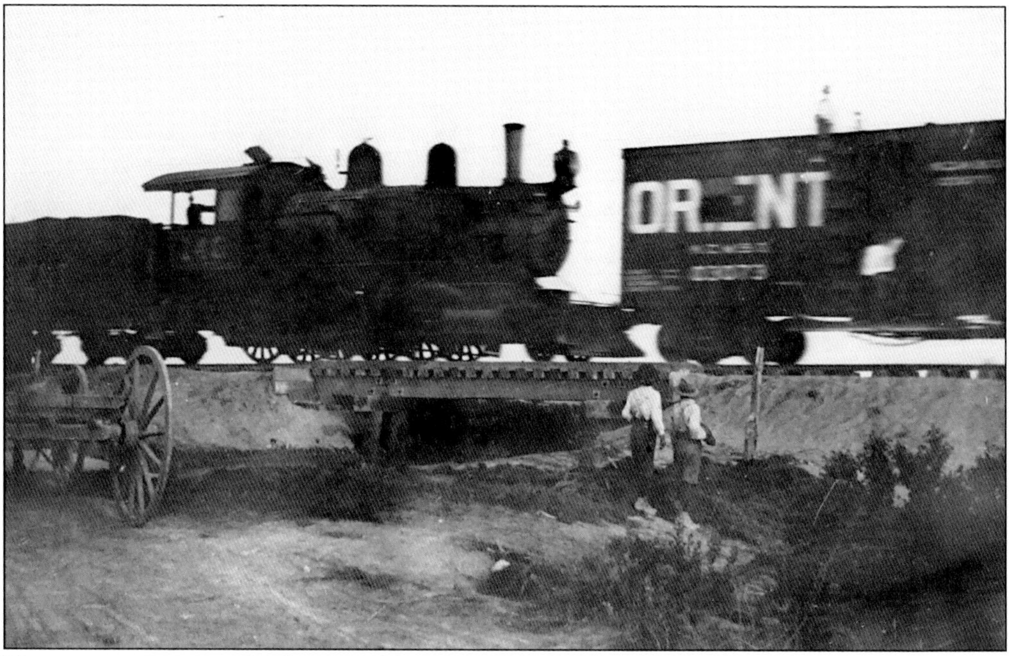

The train, roaring by the fascinated boys in this 1912 photograph, embodied technology that produced a faster moving, more interconnected nation and transformed Fort Stockton from adobe to stone seemingly overnight. Residents of the 21st century have great difficulty comprehending the dramatic significance of an event such as the arrival of the railroad in a frontier town. It forever changed the lives of young boys like these.

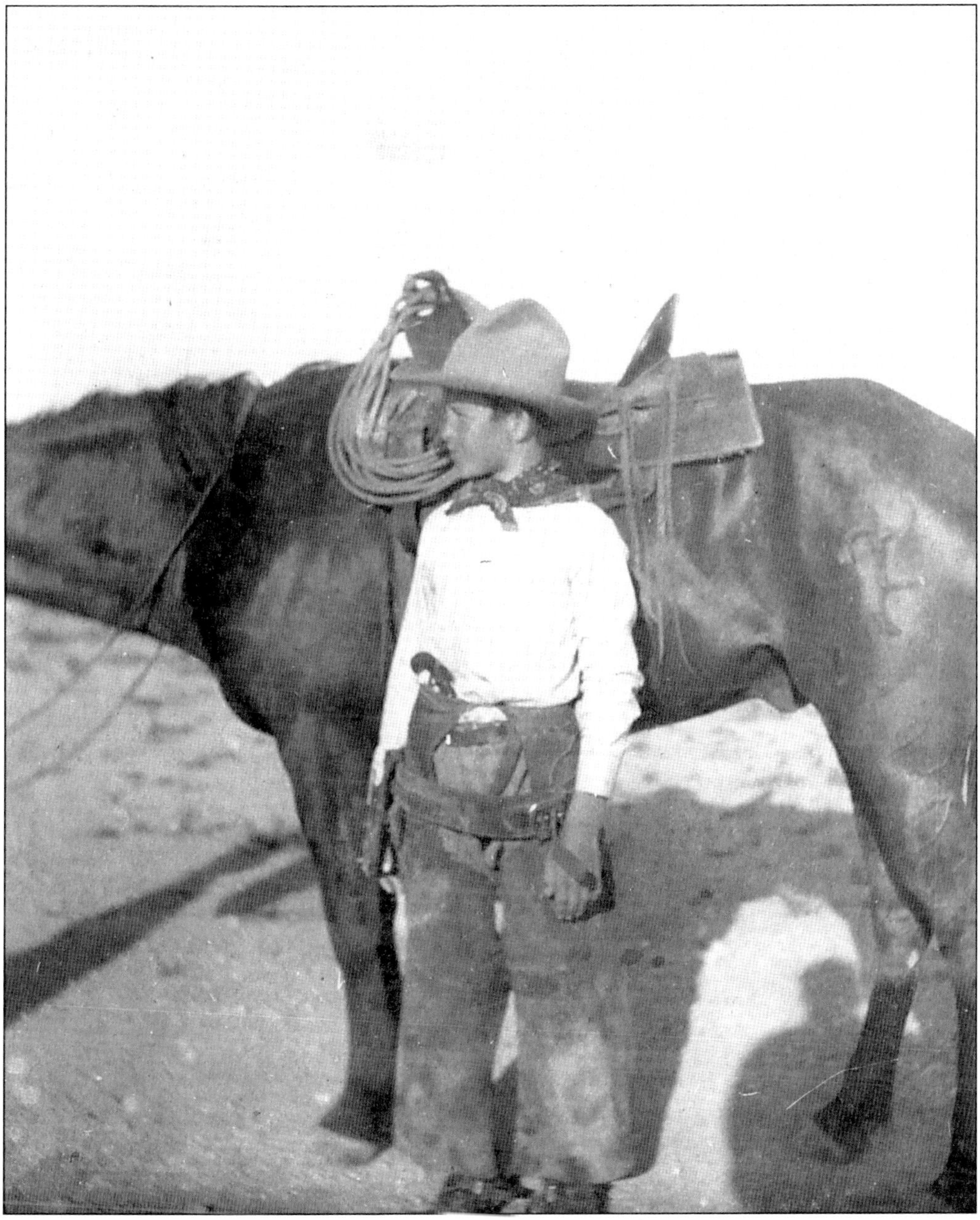

Douglas Adams was among the Fort Stockton boys who knew the world before the trains arrived. He was born in 1901 in one of the old officers' quarters of the fort. Doug was the son of Mart Adams, a local businessman and saloon keeper (see page 53). As a boy, he attended church at the adobe Union Church with the Presbyterian congregation. At the age of 10, he witnessed the arrival of the trains. In 1915, his father died, and Doug had to find work on local ranches, where transportation reverted to horses and wagons. He worked beside cowboys who recalled the days of the open range. In this photograph from that time, a young cowboy believed to be Doug stands beside his horse with a pistol in his belt. Doug Adams later returned to Fort Stockton and married Lorene James from Quanah, Texas, who, as a young girl, watched her father ride beside the Comanche chief Quanah Parker during the local parades. (Courtesy of Mart Adams.)

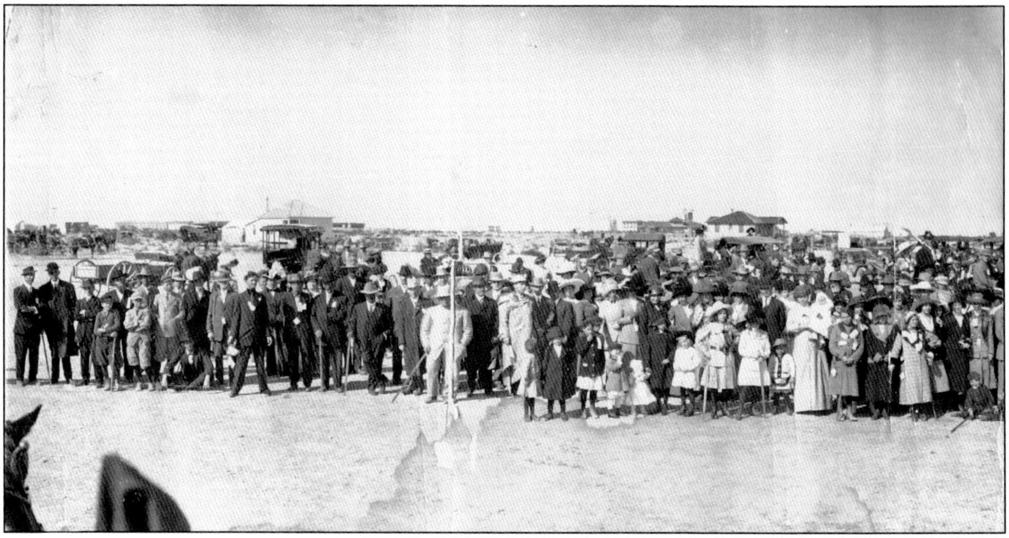

San Angelo, Texas, sent a delegation of businessmen to Fort Stockton on the excursion train. The 16-member band they brought was welcomed by Fort Stockton's Booster Band. The new rail line would provide greater economic connections between the two cities. After the greetings and speeches, the group trooped over to the old fort parade ground for this panoramic shot. In this first segment from the left, the depot and Hotel Stockton are visible in the background. Wagons and automobiles form a jumbled line behind the crowd.

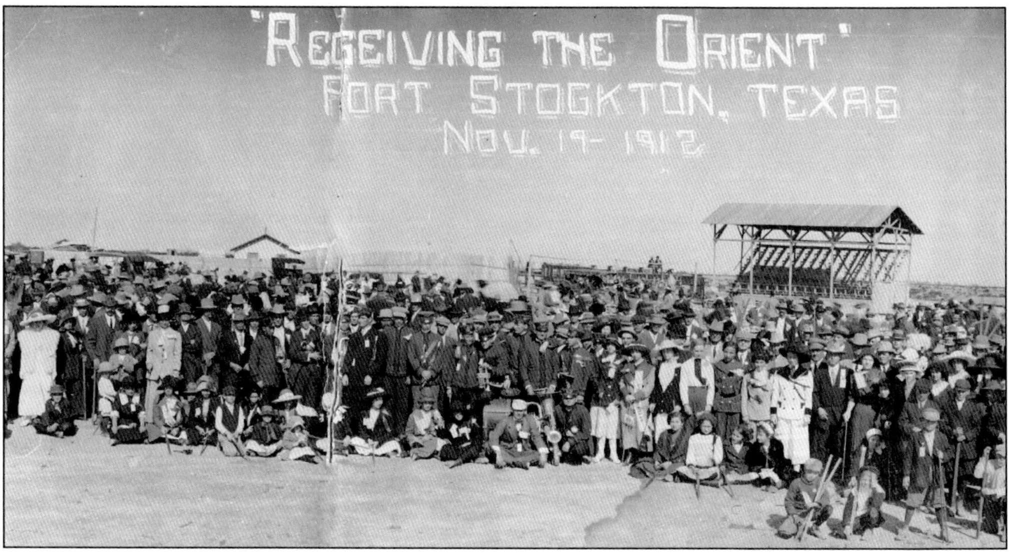

The center section of the panorama bears the caption "Receiving the Orient, Fort Stockton, Texas, November 19, 1912." The two bands occupy the center. The baseball field stands are in the background. A number of people hold yardsticks, probably a promotional item. Children line the front. In the mass of people, certain hats, clothes, and poses stand out from the rest.

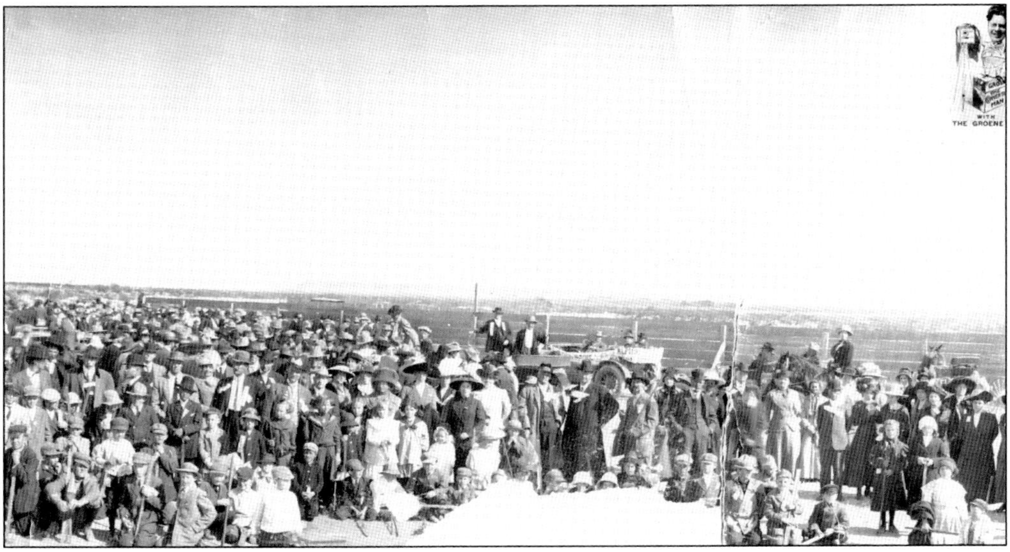

The right segment of the photograph includes several groups in automobiles. The two near the center are part of a delegation from Alpine, Texas. One matron sits astride a horse. Seven-Mile Mesa is visible on the horizon. A San Angelo football team in beanies forms a small cluster in the background to the left. No definitive conclusion can be drawn, but the Mexican American community appears to be absent.

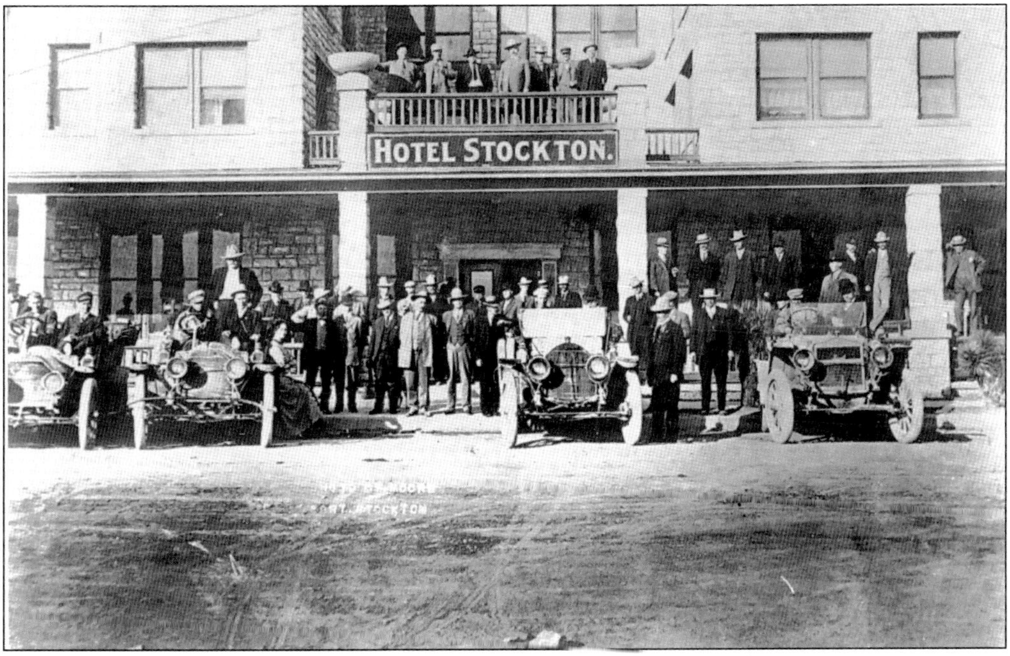

Besides the San Angelo delegation on the train, visitors drove in from Alpine, Marfa, and Pecos. The *Fort Stockton Pioneer* reported a "brilliant assembly at Hotel Stockton" that evening. Here, a group lines up along with their automobiles in front of the new hotel. Interestingly, the group includes only one woman, seated on the automobile just to the left of center.

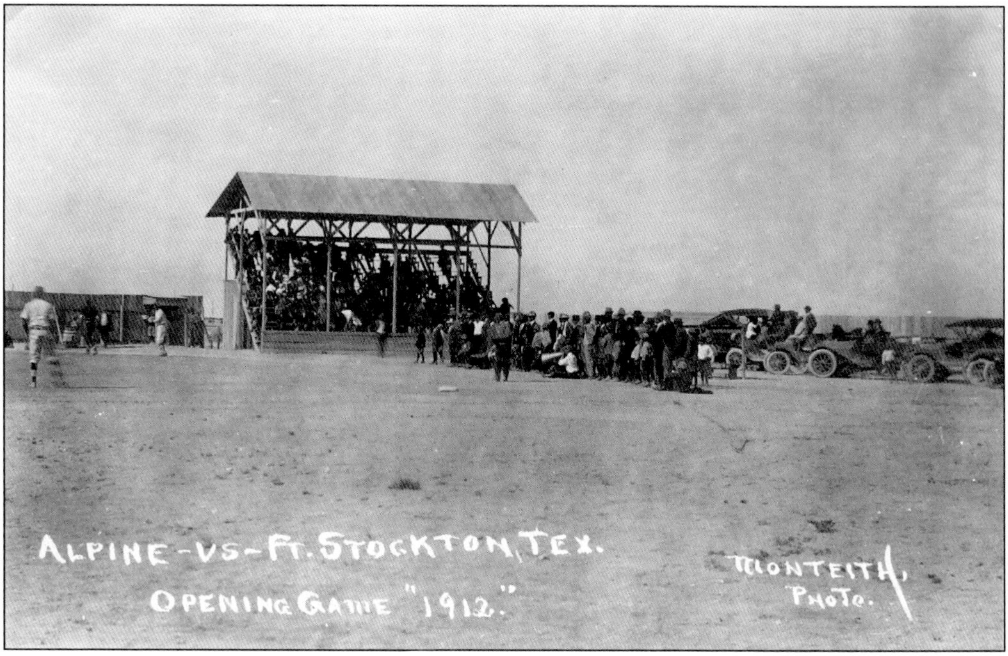

A Fort Stockton baseball team existed for several years around the turn of the century. They played area teams from as far away as Midland (whom they defeated in 1911). This photograph records a moment in the opening game of 1912. The stands are screened, but spectators apparently had no fear of standing unprotected near home plate.

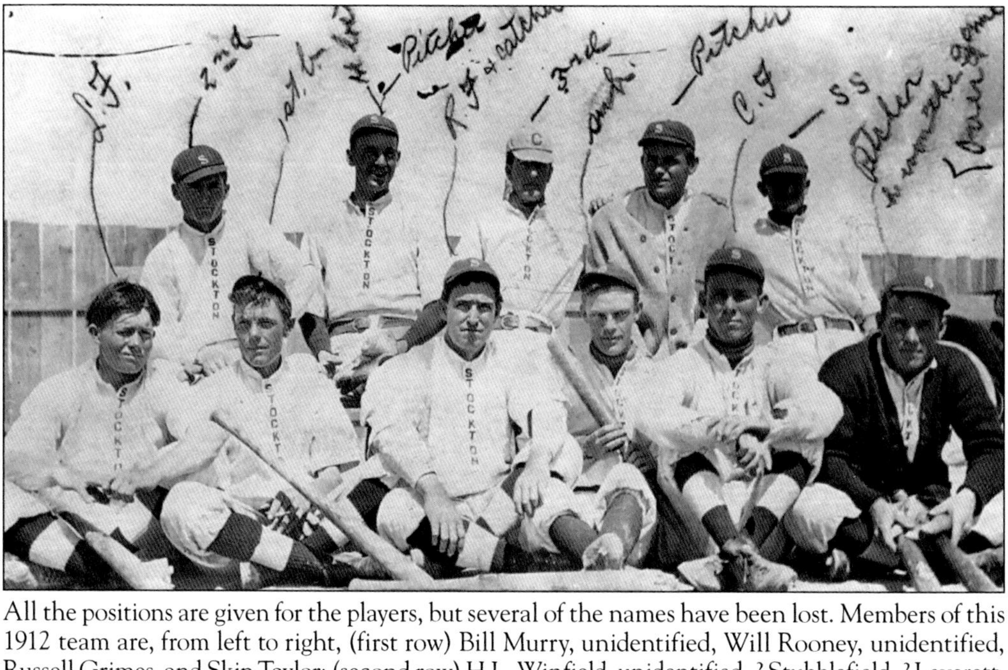

All the positions are given for the players, but several of the names have been lost. Members of this 1912 team are, from left to right, (first row) Bill Murry, unidentified, Will Rooney, unidentified, Russell Grimes, and Skip Taylor; (second row) H.L. Winfield, unidentified, ? Stubblefield, ? Leverett, and an unidentified shortstop. Other towns played besides Midland and Alpine included Pecos, Marfa, and Big Spring.

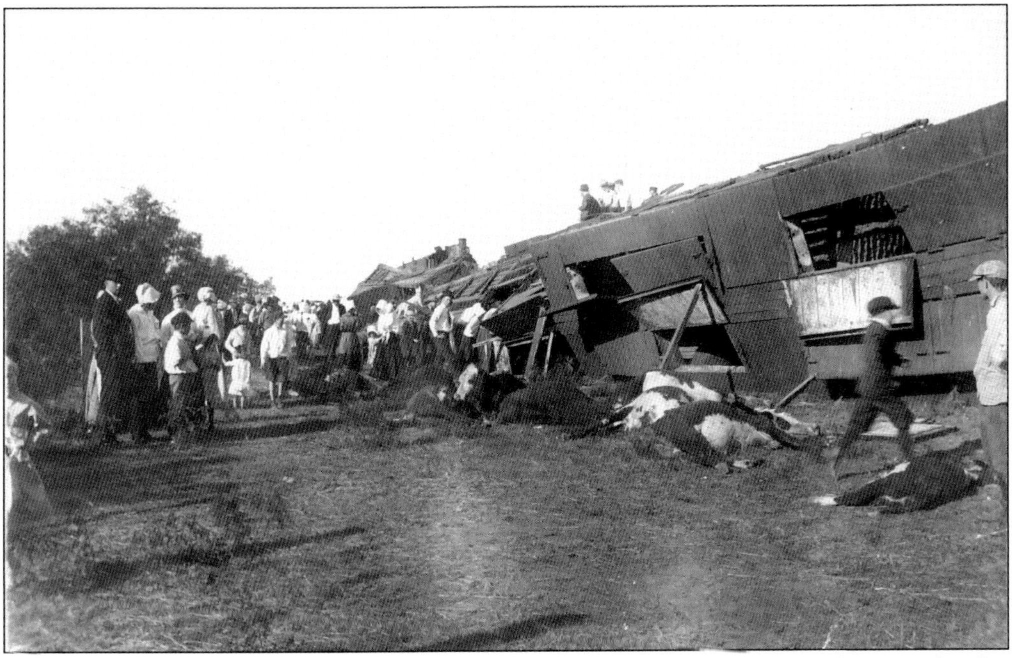

The Orient owners regained their line in 1914, eventually extending it to the Mexican border, but Stillwell's dream of Pacific trade never materialized. The railroad proved highly unprofitable. Wrecks like this one, often deadly to human and animal passengers, were common in the early years. The discovery of oil at Texon ushered in new petroleum business that encouraged the Atchison, Topeka & Santa Fe Railway Company to purchase the Orient in 1928.

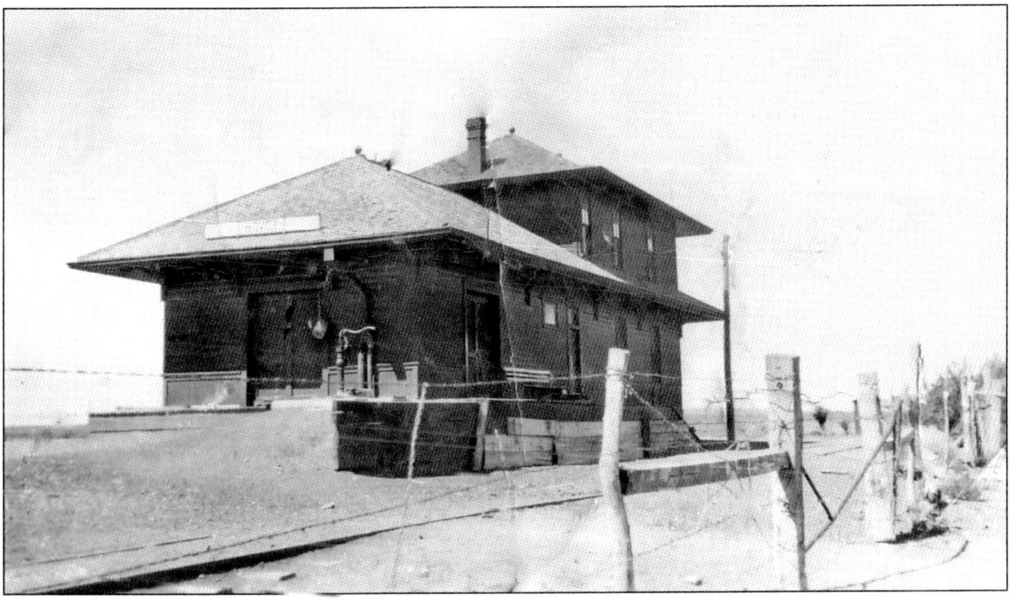

As the Orient line extended south, a side track was created about every 10 miles to allow trains to pass. Sidings also facilitated the loading of stock and the storage of freight cars. The Hovey station (depot pictured), located 35 miles south of Fort Stockton, was established in 1913. A small community of railroad workers, farmers, and ranchers grew up around the station and post office there. (Courtesy of Nita Stewart Haley Memorial Library.)

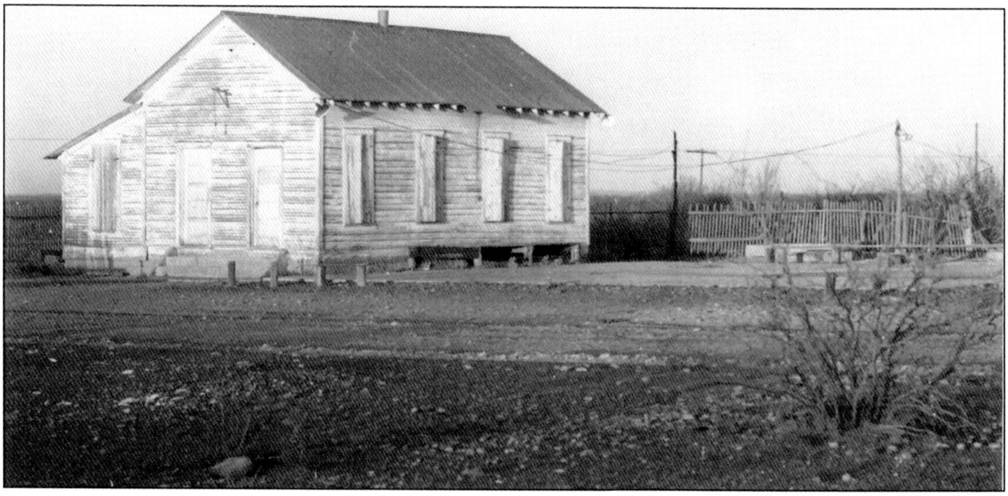

Area families wanted a school for their children. In a building on the Beatty Ranch, five miles northeast of Hovey, Mary Lou Fulcher became the first teacher, earning $50 per month. When that building burned, Pecos County contracted with W.C. Schaffer to construct a new school. With one large classroom and two small rooms serving as a teacher residence, the school, pictured in the 1950s, was built near the railroad at Hovey.

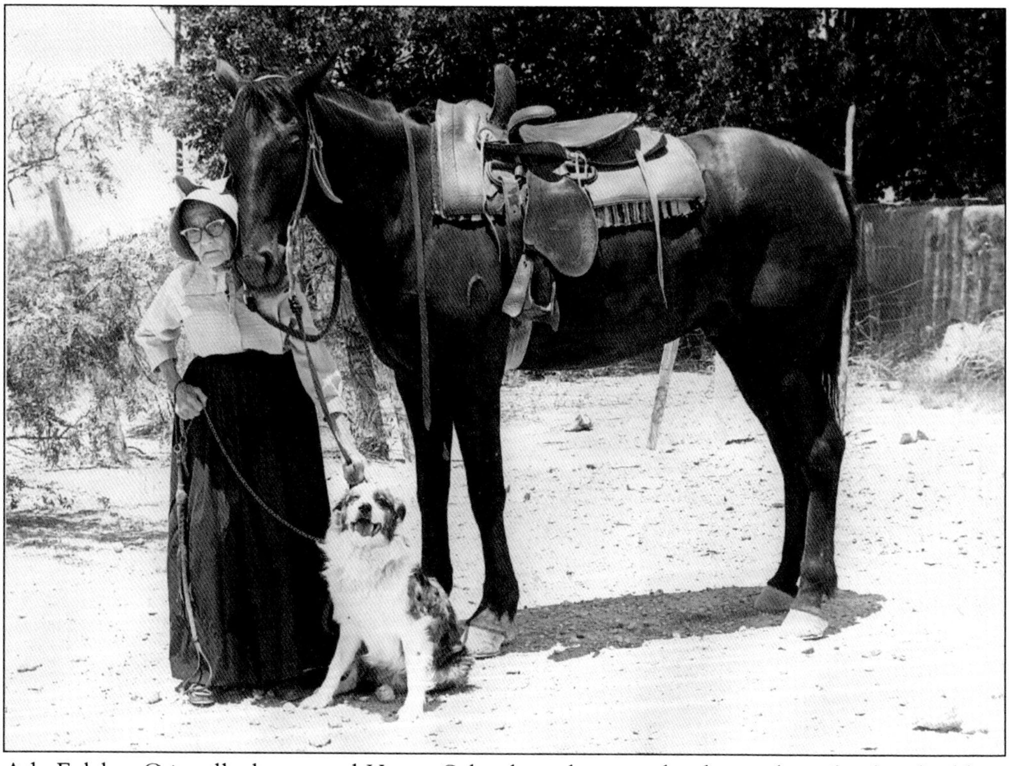

Ada Fulcher Criswell, the second Hovey School teacher, taught there when the first building burned. The fire in the woodstove was built up to provide heat, and this started the blaze. With no fire protection, the structure burnt to the ground. Ada and the students saved the desks and books. This photograph of Ada at 80, with her horse and dog, captures the tough spirit of this pioneer teacher.

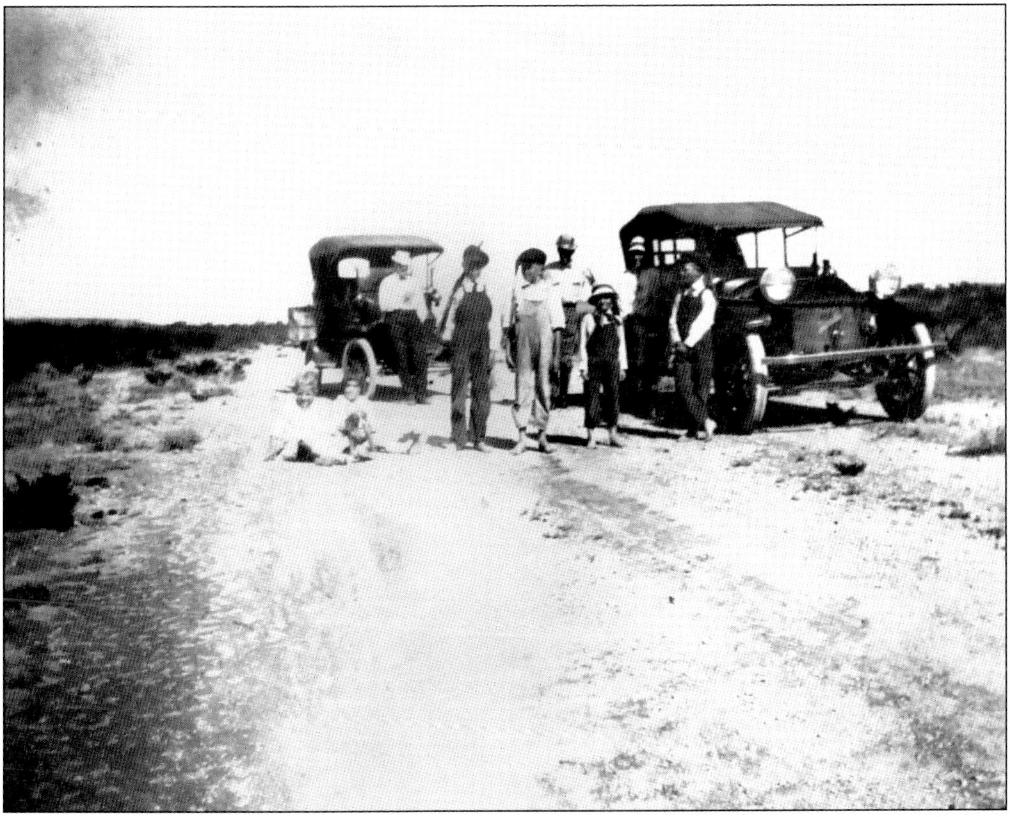

Highways around Fort Stockton remained primitive. The caption on this photograph reads, "On road to Kerrville, 1916, the Haddens, Mrs. Lockett, Cecil Lang, and Frommes." As automobile use grew, demand for better roads also increased. The principal goal of the Good Roads movement, started by bicyclists, was to decrease rural isolation. In 1911 and 1912, the Texas Legislature voted $5 million in bonds for rural road improvement.

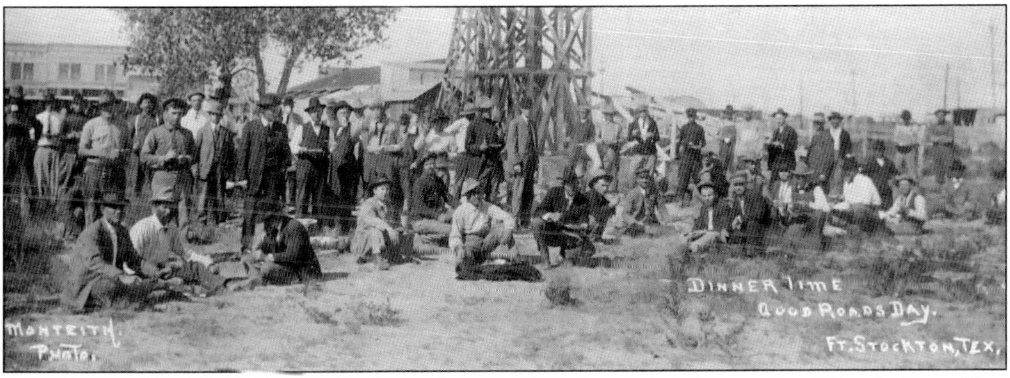

Texas governor O.B. Colquitt proclaimed November 5 and 6, 1913, as Good Roads Days. Fort Stockton organized a Good Roads Association, with W.A. Hadden as president. On November 5, businesses closed and everyone turned out with tools to work on the streets. Lunch (pictured) was served before the group departed to clear rocks and fill bad chuck holes along 30 miles of the Alpine Road.

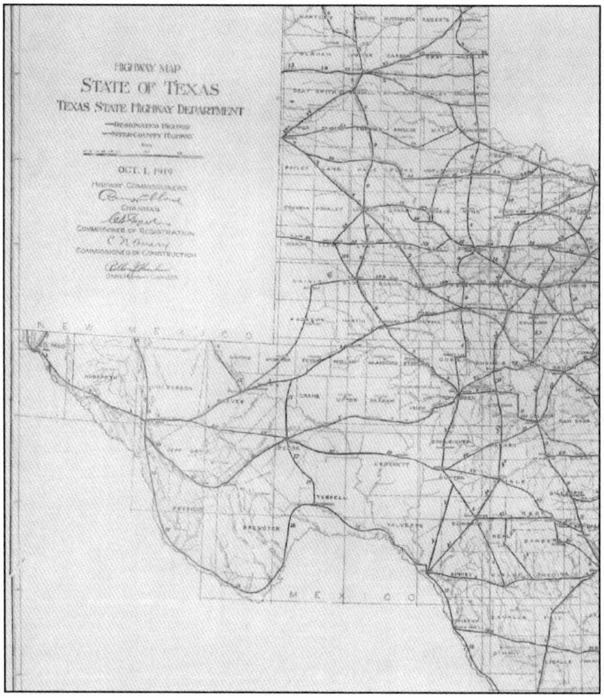

The establishment of the Texas Highway Department in 1917 shifted highway responsibility from the counties to the state. This 1919 highway department map defines an early plan for state highways. The map also establishes the importance of Fort Stockton as a convergence point for several roads, many of which followed old Comanche routes or those used by stage lines and the military. (Courtesy of Nita Stewart Haley Memorial Library.)

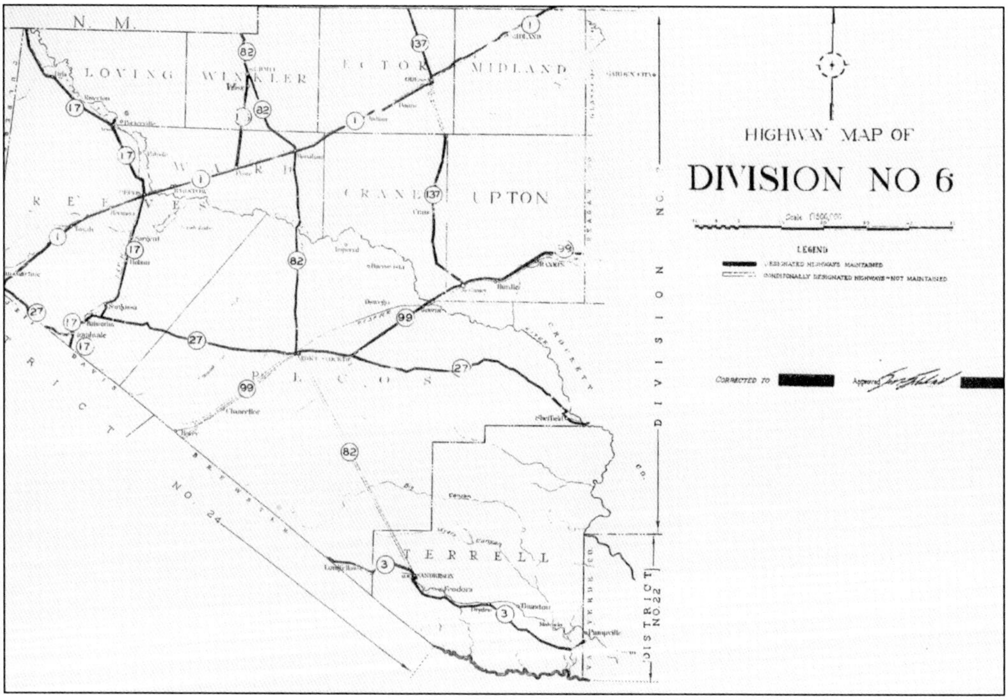

This highway division map from the 1920s provides a clearer picture of the reality of Pecos County roads. Most remained improved dirt at best. The roads south carry the designation "conditionally designated highways—not maintained." Despite their rough surfaces, highways were growing in national importance. They played an increasing role in Fort Stockton's future. (Courtesy of Nita Stewart Haley Memorial Library.)

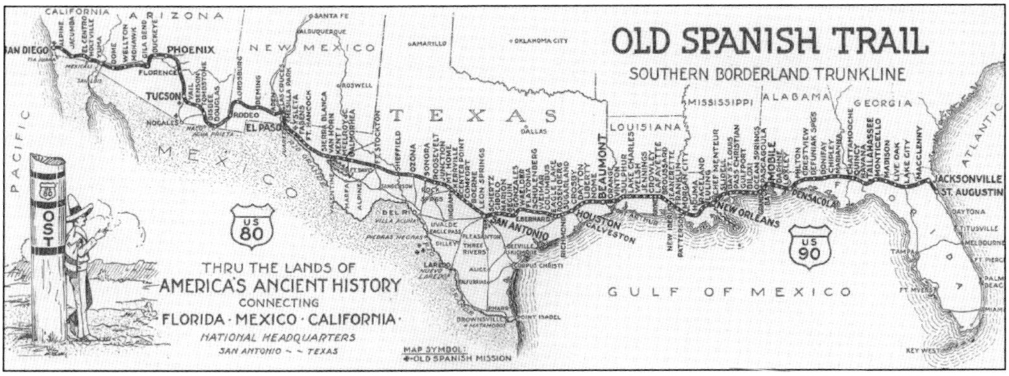

The Old Spanish Trail movement organized to promote a paved automobile highway (pictured) across the southern United States. It would connect six centers of historical interest—St. Augustine, New Orleans, San Antonio, El Paso, Tucson, and San Diego. In 1919, San Antonio became the headquarters of the movement, with Harral Ayres as managing director. In 1926, Ayers secured United States highway status for the Old Spanish Trail, including a central Texas segment that brought the highway through Fort Stockton. (Courtesy Old Spanish Trail Centennial.)

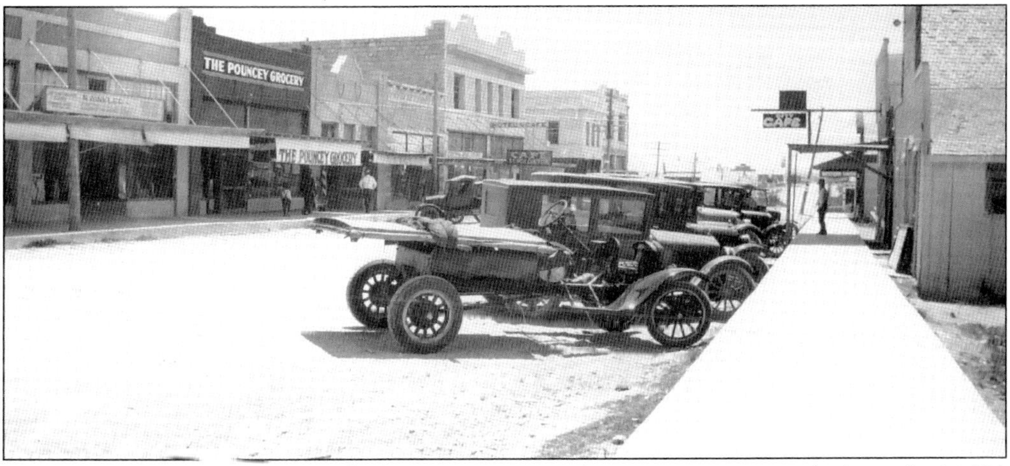

The 1923 Old Spanish Trail guide described Fort Stockton as "a prosperous little city" of 1,300 people. Businesses listed included Pace Auto Company, the Old Spanish Trail Headquarters, Rooney Mercantile ("the Big Store"), Jacob's Café ("All tourists stop here"), and R.O. Gonzales General Merchandise. Another important store was Winkler's Department Store (at left), which was started by German immigrant Nathan Winkler in 1912.

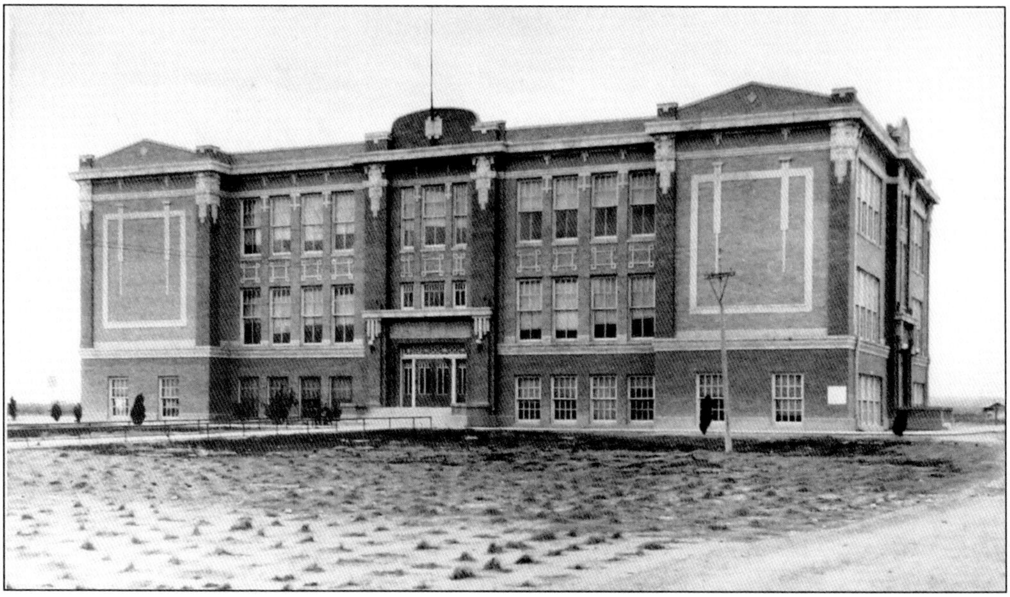

The prosperous little city requested the creation of the Fort Stockton Independent School District in 1917. That same year, the new high school, costing $60,000, opened. It was three stories tall and had its own windmill-powered water system. The basement contained the physics and chemistry labs, the domestic science department, and the manual training department. The superintendent's office, the library, and seven classrooms occupied the first floor. The top floor held more classrooms and the auditorium.

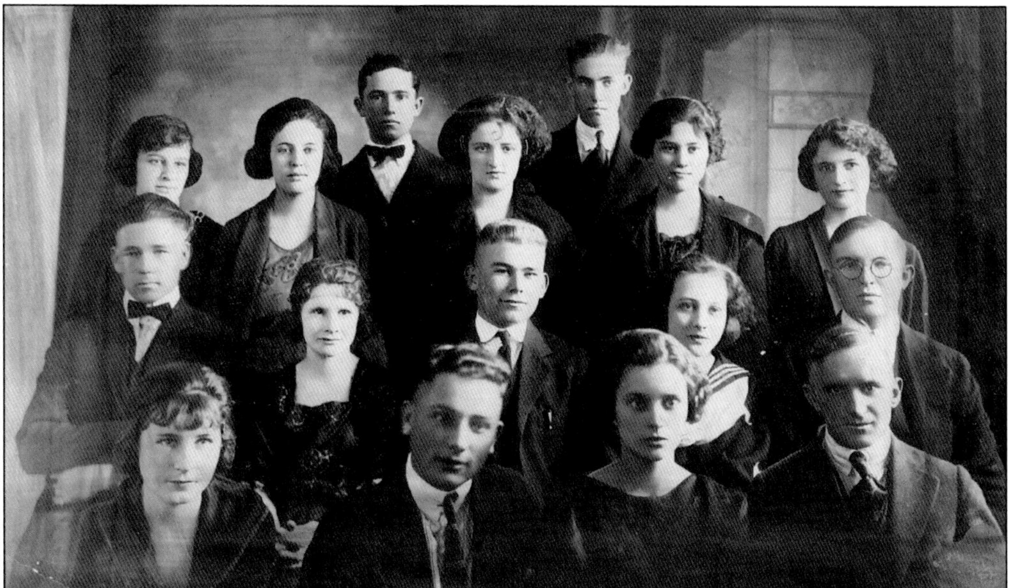

The first graduating class was in 1922. Class members were, from left to right (first row) Freida Downs, Irvin Akin, Mary Timon (treasurer), and Earl Livingston; (second row) Frank Stephenson, Lilla Mae Leatherwood, Karl Butz (class president), Louise Barrett (secretary), and Shipton Parke; (third row) Hazel Wheeler, Maurine McDonald, Minnie Swinney, Edna Reinertsen, and Christine Rigsbee (vice president); (fourth row) Waldo Powers (historian) and Earl Taylor.

The grade school (page 60) was sold to the Jesuits for a novitiate in 1916. Pecos County repurchased the school in 1926 and consolidated the three Mexican-American schools. The new school had 248 students and six teachers. A domestic science department was started that year, and a Mexican parent teacher association, with 70 members, was organized. This is one of the pages of a yearbook devoted to the Mexican school.

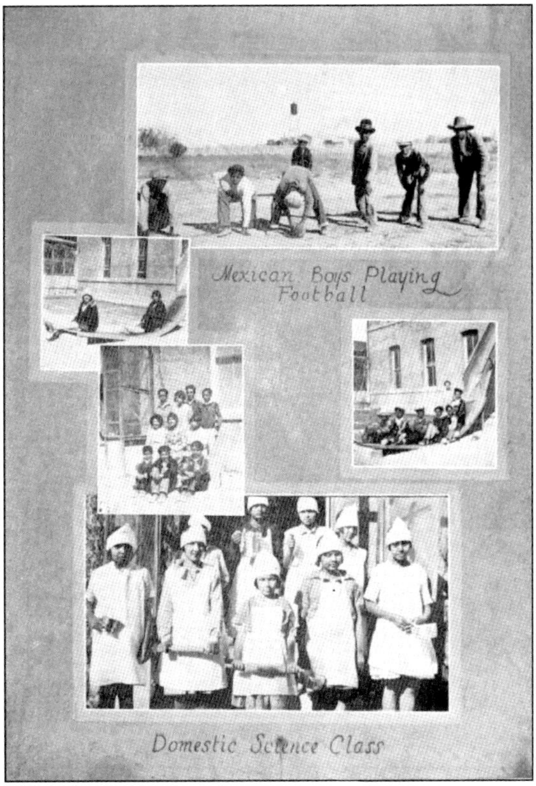

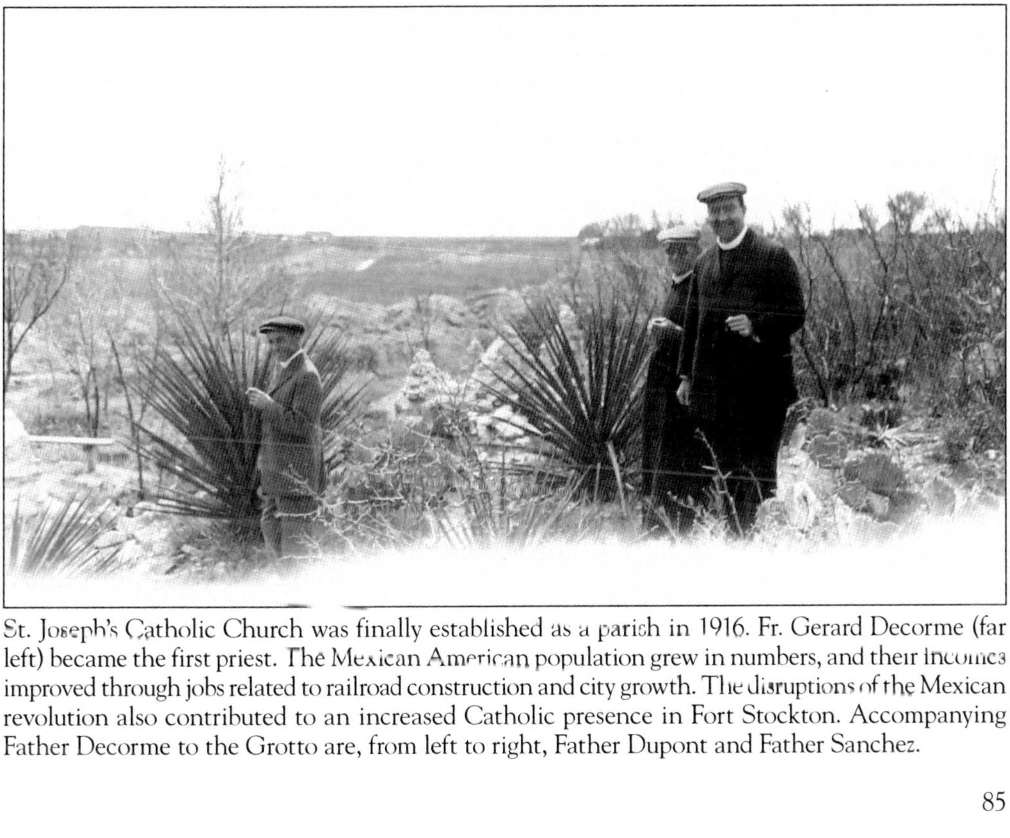

St. Joseph's Catholic Church was finally established as a parish in 1916. Fr. Gerard Decorme (far left) became the first priest. The Mexican American population grew in numbers, and their incomes improved through jobs related to railroad construction and city growth. The disruptions of the Mexican revolution also contributed to an increased Catholic presence in Fort Stockton. Accompanying Father Decorme to the Grotto are, from left to right, Father Dupont and Father Sanchez.

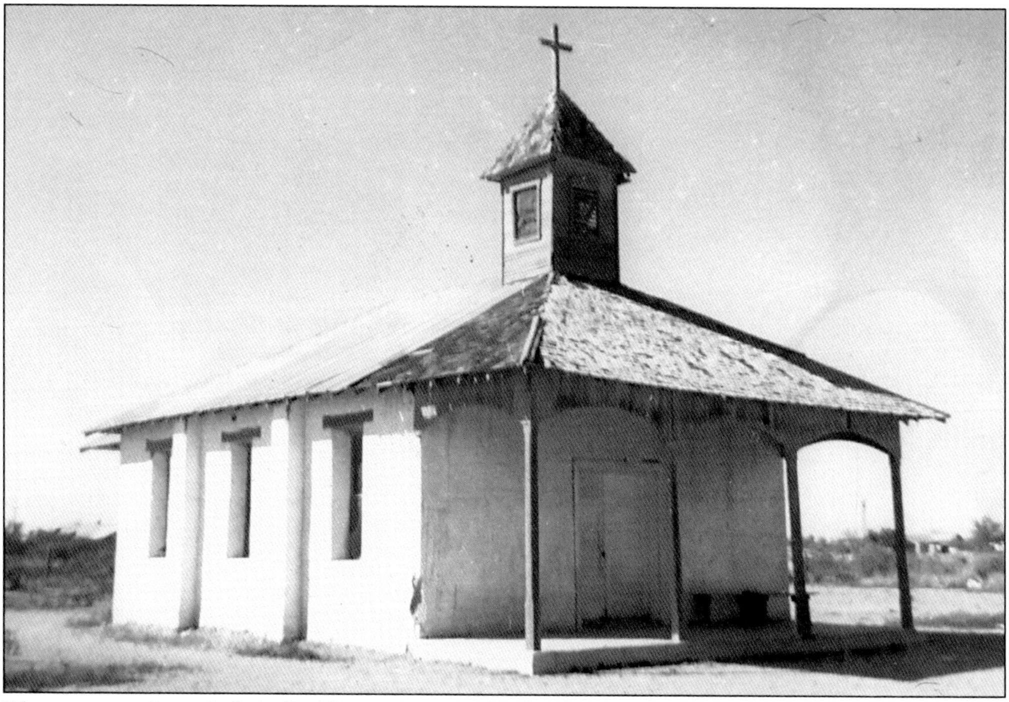

The new parish included all of Pecos County. Father Decorme provided religious services at six chapels. These churches ranged from Little Mexico, three miles north (pictured), to Sheffield, 75 miles to the east (visited only four times a year). Several Protestant churches were organized in these years as well, including Presbyterian (1903), Baptist (1906), Disciples of Christ (1907), and Church of Christ (1915).

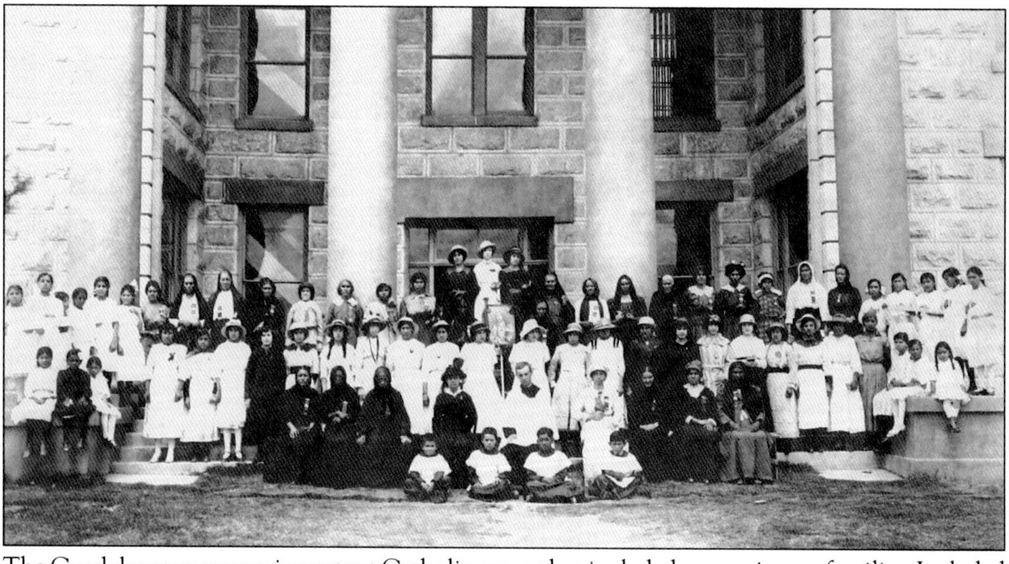

The Guadalupanos was an important Catholic group that included many pioneer families. Included in this group photograph on the courthouse steps around 1916 are Antonia Sosa, wife of Pedro, a brick mason from Mexico; Matilda Pena, who owned the oldest house; Virginia Barron, who came to the area in 1870; Jeronima Gonzalez; and Padre Gerardo Decorme (second row, center). (Courtesy of M.R. Gonzalez Jr.)

From the earliest days, Mexican American families were a central part of the workforce, especially in farming, sheepherding, and ranching. Lazaro Acosta came to Fort Stockton in 1910 to work on the El Sonora Ranch, located south of town. Lazaro stands with his wife, Miguela, and their family. Their children are, from left to right, Albert Acosta, Beatrice Acosta, Calistra, and Juanita. The El Sonora later became part of La Escalera Ranch. (Courtesy of Pablo Valenzuela.)

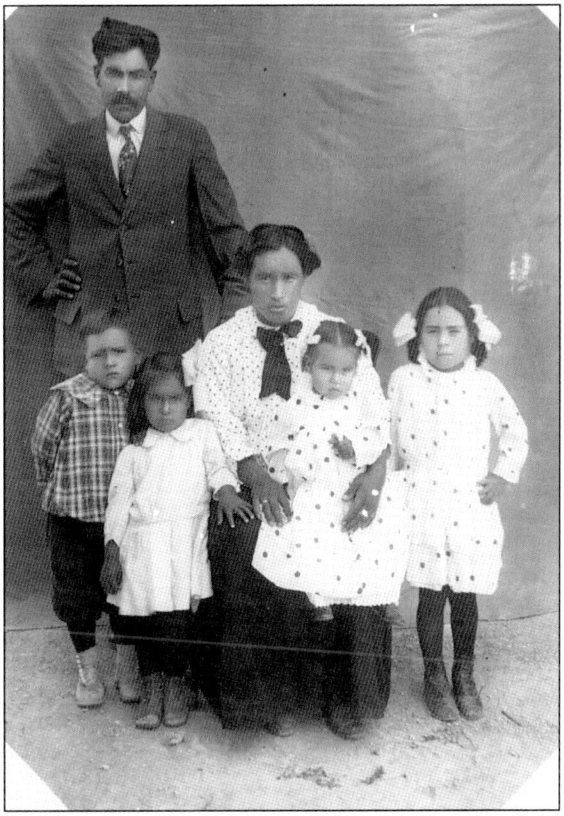

In town, Mexican Americans found employment in local businesses. Rooney Mercantile employees included, from left to right, Lupe Terrazas (who drove the delivery truck), Pilar Duran, Velma James, Doug Adams, E.O. Gonzales, Cleve Nunn, and R.H. Hughes. Fr. Alvin Wilde, local historian, said of the Mexican Americans, "They were the manpower of all enterprises, well looked upon and regarded for the necessity of their work." (Courtesy of Joe Primera family.)

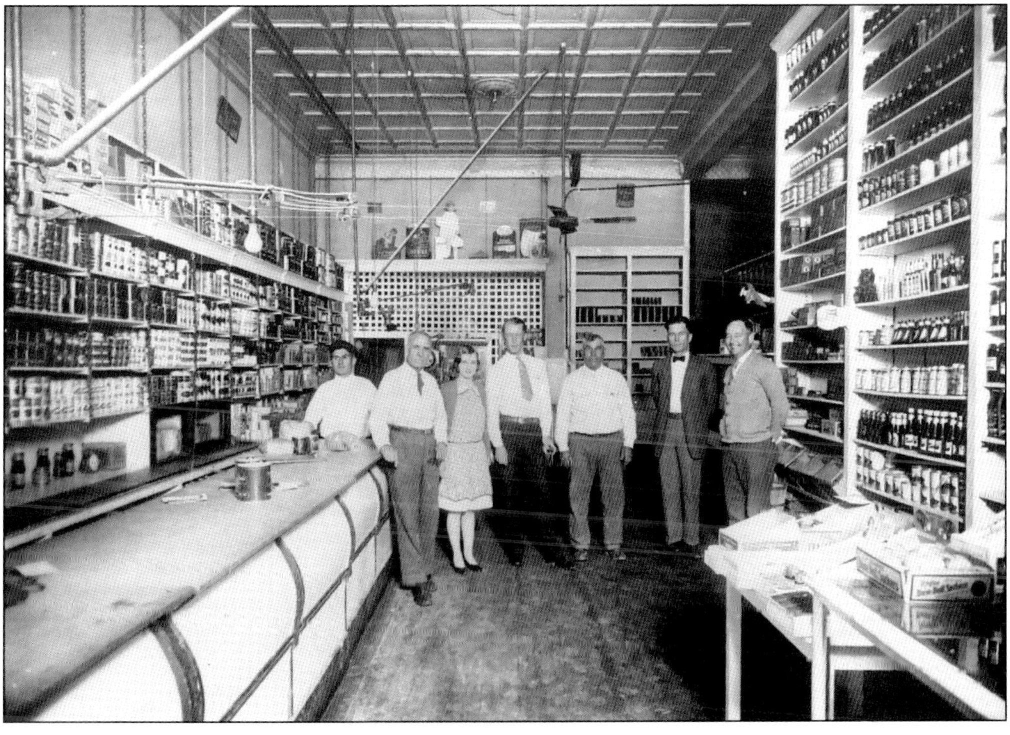

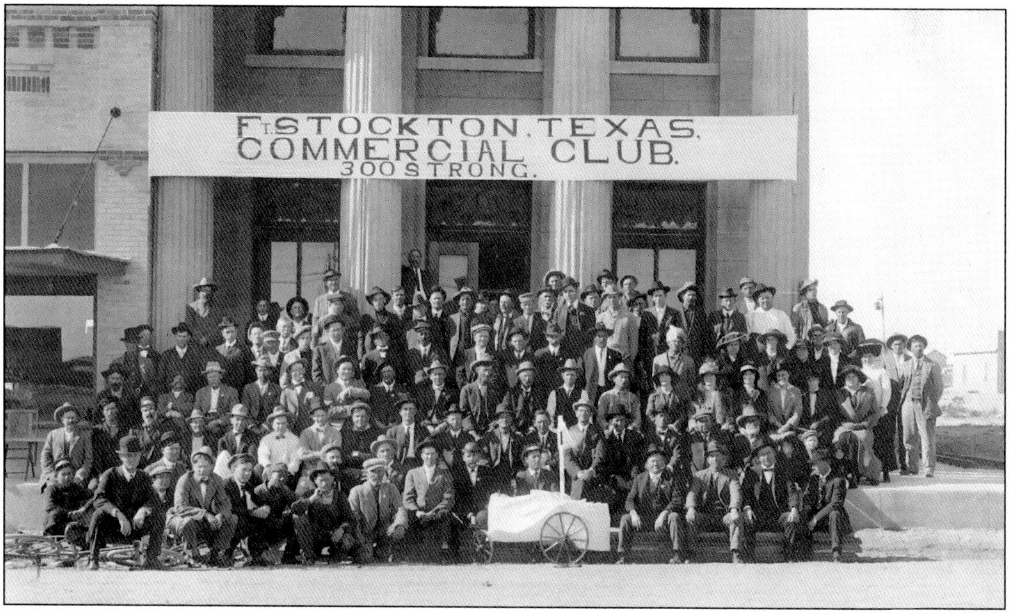

In May 1913, another important group formed—the Fort Stockton Commercial Club, a chamber of commerce–style organization. Mayor James Rooney exhorted those present to get together and "put Fort Stockton on the map in boxcar letters." The club, with James Rooney as temporary chairman, was made up of 85 members. Club members pose on the steps of the First National Bank. The headquarters was in the Stockton building, at 500 First Street.

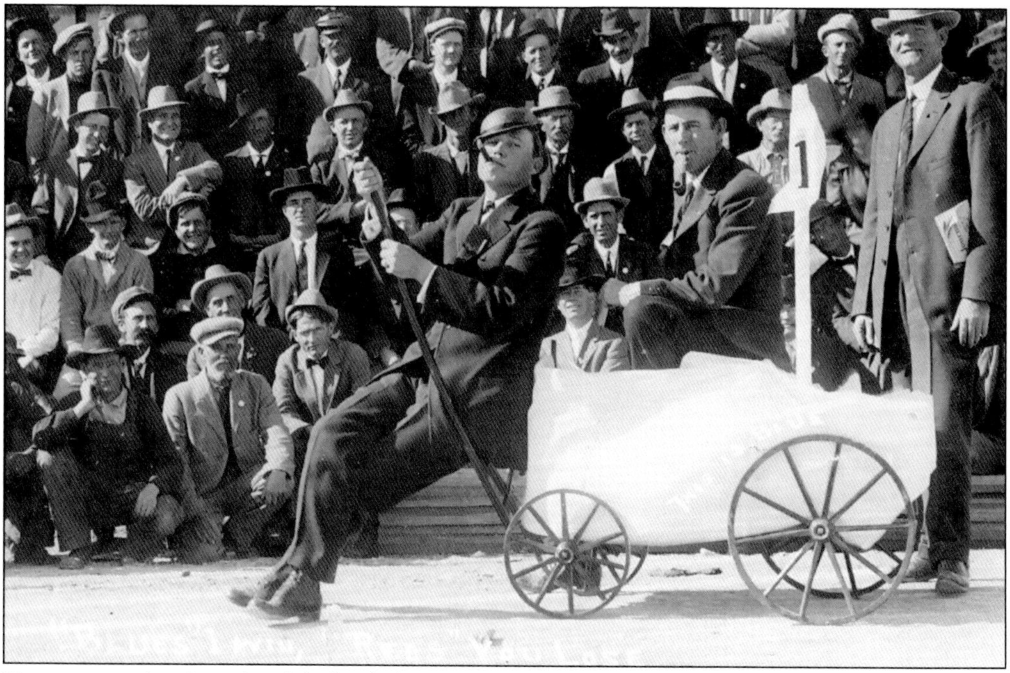

To grow membership, the club divided into two teams, Blues and Reds, to recruit new members. At the club banquet in December 1913, the winning Blue team was treated. In this photograph, Red team leader W.R. Chancellor (left) clowns with Blue team leader Marshal Lea as over 300 club members observe their antics.

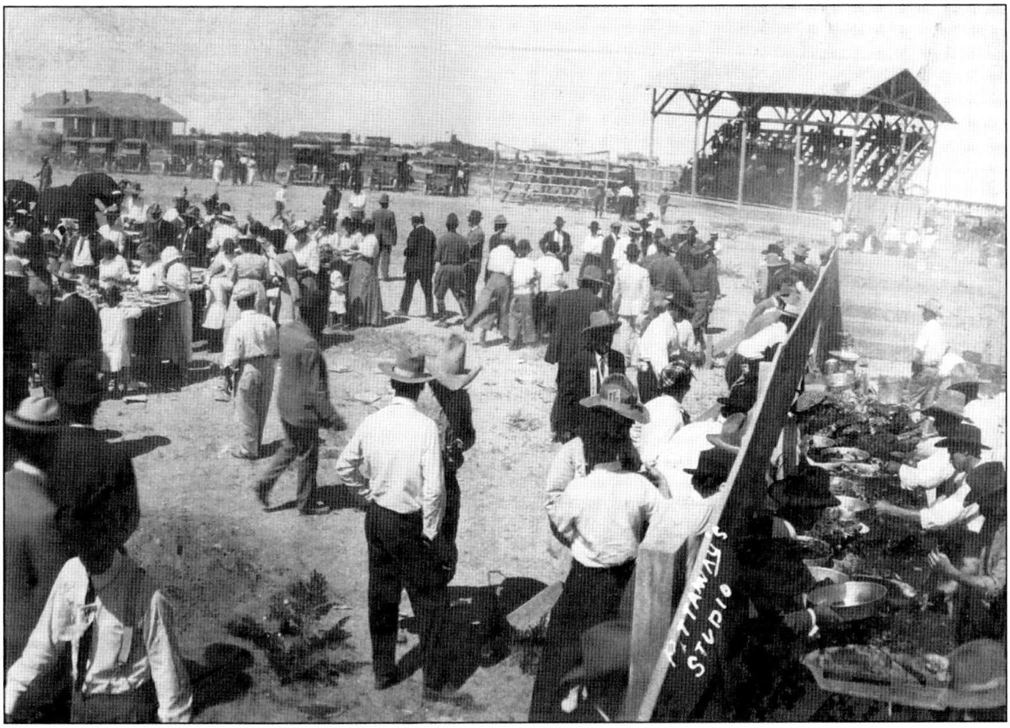

In 1914, the Commercial Club sponsored the first Fort Stockton Fair, which took place September 24 through 26. Local ranchers, including Clarence Scharbauer, donated cattle for the event. On the 25th, some 3,000 people attended a free barbeque on the old fort ground. To the right in this image, waiters fill dishes to serve the crowds, while guests dine standing at long tables. The *Fort Stockton Pioneer* reported, "The meats were very fine, cooked to a turn, and all the fixings were there."

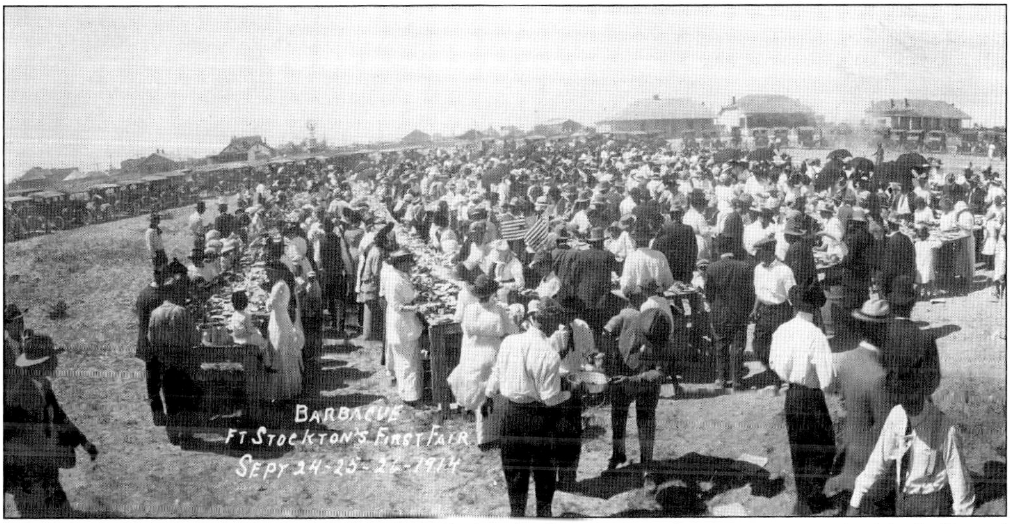

These guests dining at the September 25th free barbeque were later entertained with drills and maneuvers on the parade grounds by Troop F of the 15th US Cavalry. Three officers' quarters remain standing in the background to the right. The *Fort Stockton Pioneer* reported, "Once more the glorious Stars and Stripes will float over that hallowed spot."

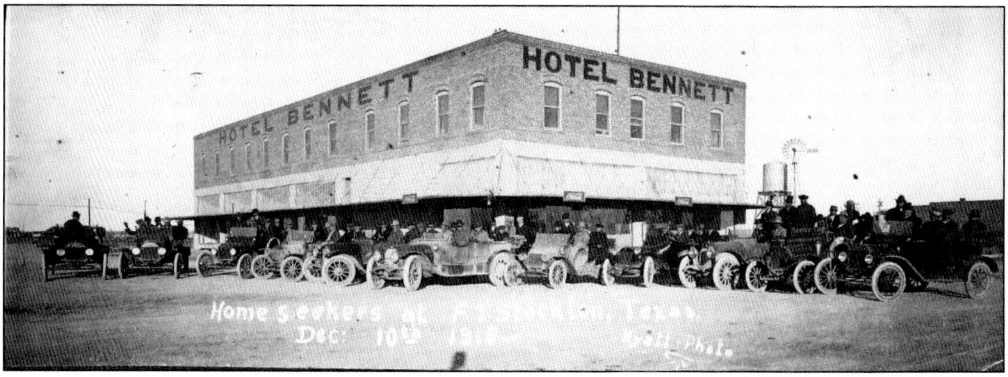

Commercial clubs and advertising brought new people to Pecos County. As many as 50 prospective buyers at a time were shown land in the Imperial Valley. This motorcade stopped long enough for a photograph in front of another new hotel, the Bennett. New or expanding agricultural projects took place along the Pecos River and west in the Leon Valley. Ranching extended into remote western sections of the county.

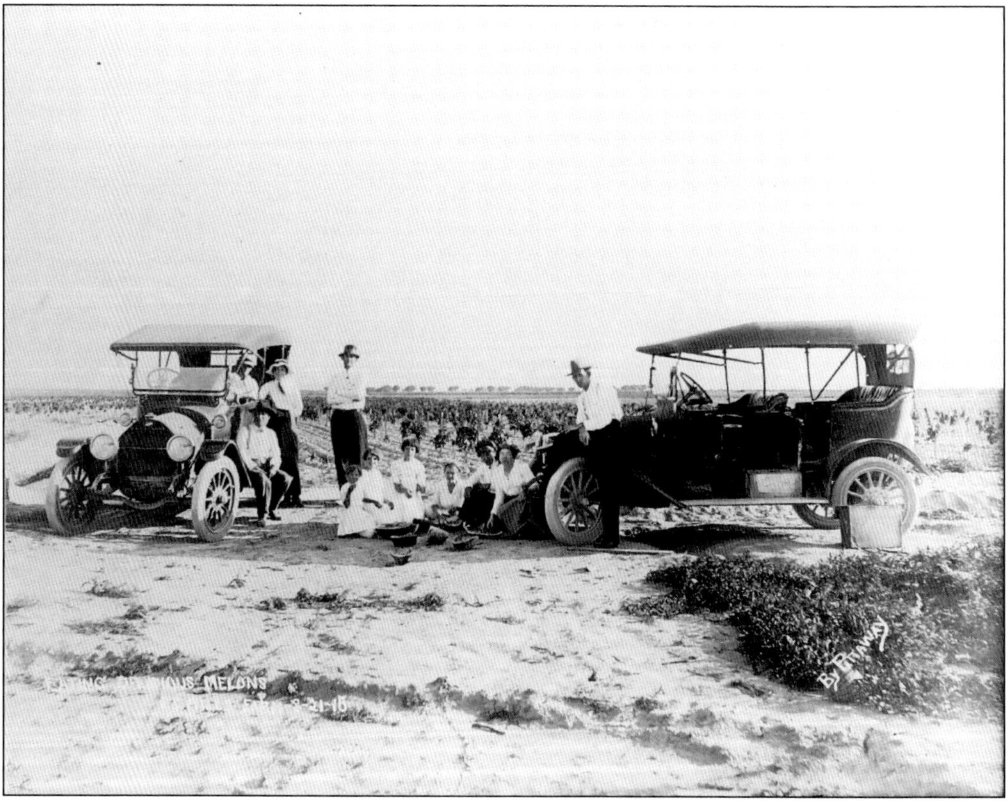

In 1910, Gerald Beeman and J.Y. Webb purchased the land containing Leon Springs, eight miles west of Fort Stockton, and organized the Leon Springs Irrigation Company. Gerald persuaded his son Del to relocate from Seattle, Washington, to construct a dam and irrigation system. The primary crops were cotton and alfalfa, but other things were grown as well. This caption reads, "Eating Delicious Melons, F.S. Mills, 8-21-15."

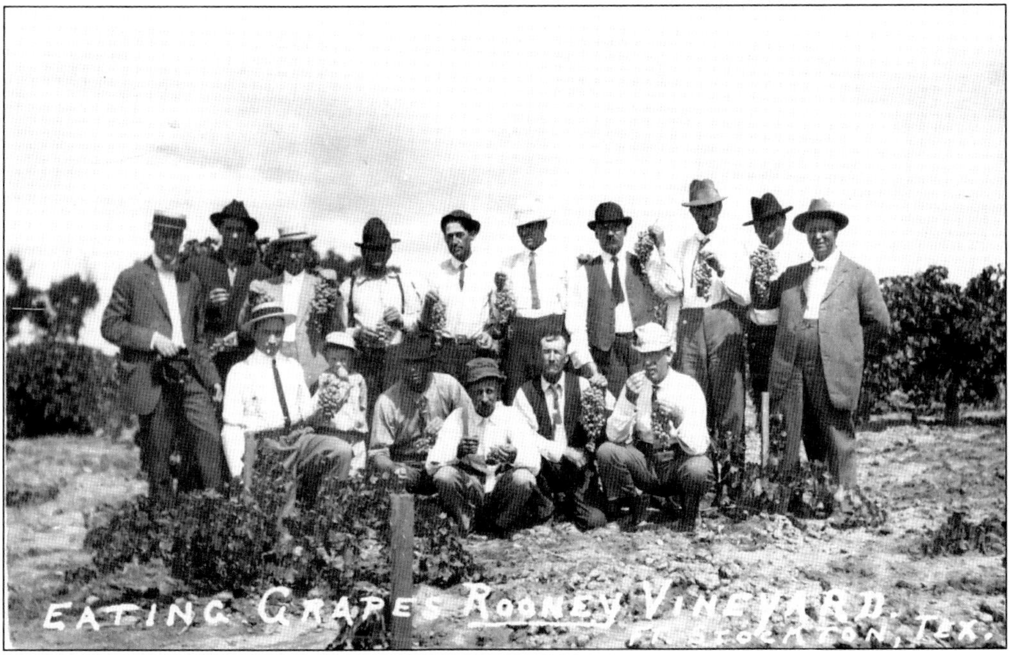

Grapes proved to be another successful crop in the area. Both Beeman and Rooney Farms had productive vineyards. An unidentified group enjoys grapes directly from the vine at the Rooney Vineyard. In 1913, the *Pioneer* commented as follows: "This section is destined to be the greatest grape section in the world. After ripening, they will not rot on the vine, but will remain sweet and good for weeks."

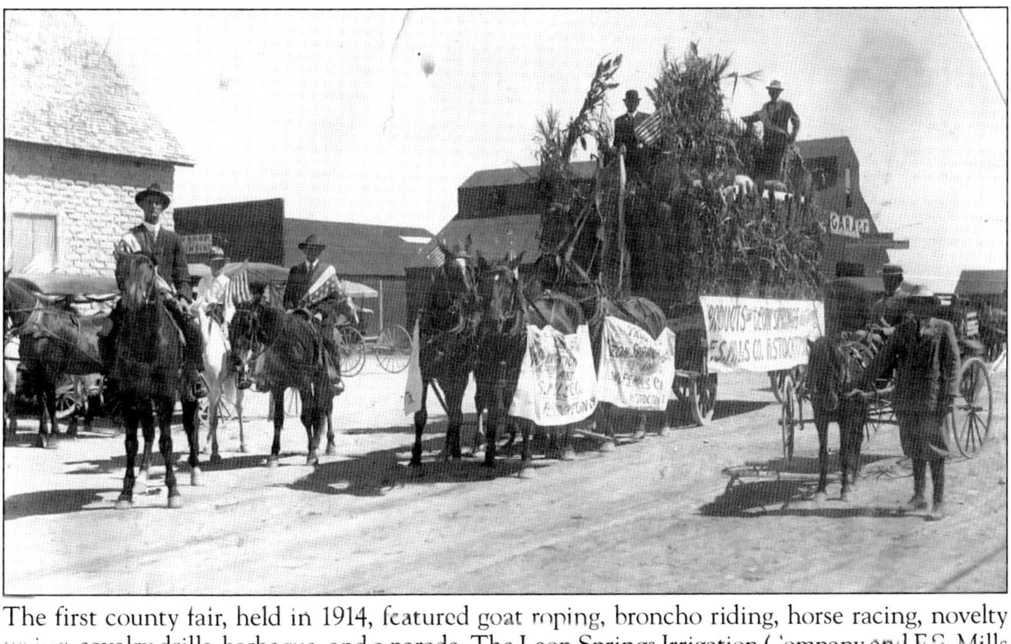

The first county fair, held in 1914, featured goat roping, broncho riding, horse racing, novelty racing, cavalry drills, barbeque, and a parade. The Leon Springs Irrigation Company and F.S. Mills created a popular display of horses and wagons draped in flags and agricultural products. Other Leon Valley crops included Egyptian wheat, onions, peanuts, soudan grass, cane, cantaloupes, chili peppers, okra, lima beans, and squash.

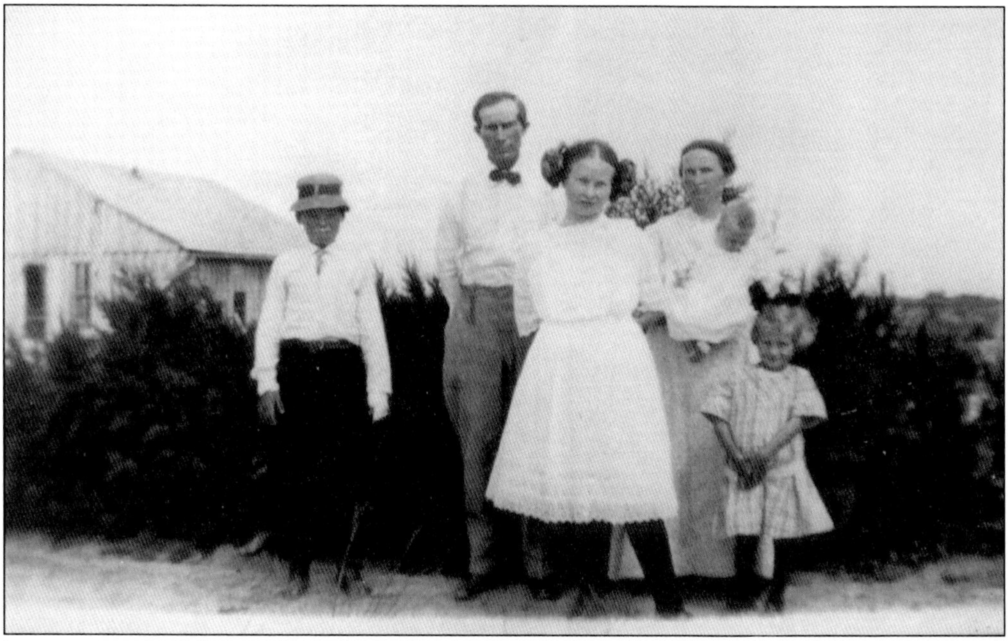

Irrigation projects began along the Pecos River as early as 1877 but were abandoned as failures. In 1909, D. Zimmerman began constructing a large reservoir in the Imperial Valley. Agents advertised Fruitdale as a land of opportunity with fertile bottomlands and plenty of fresh water. Arthur Loar brought his family there in 1913. In this photograph, Arthur's wife, Mary, holds son James. Daughters Ruth (left) and Isabelle stand with an unidentified neighbor boy.

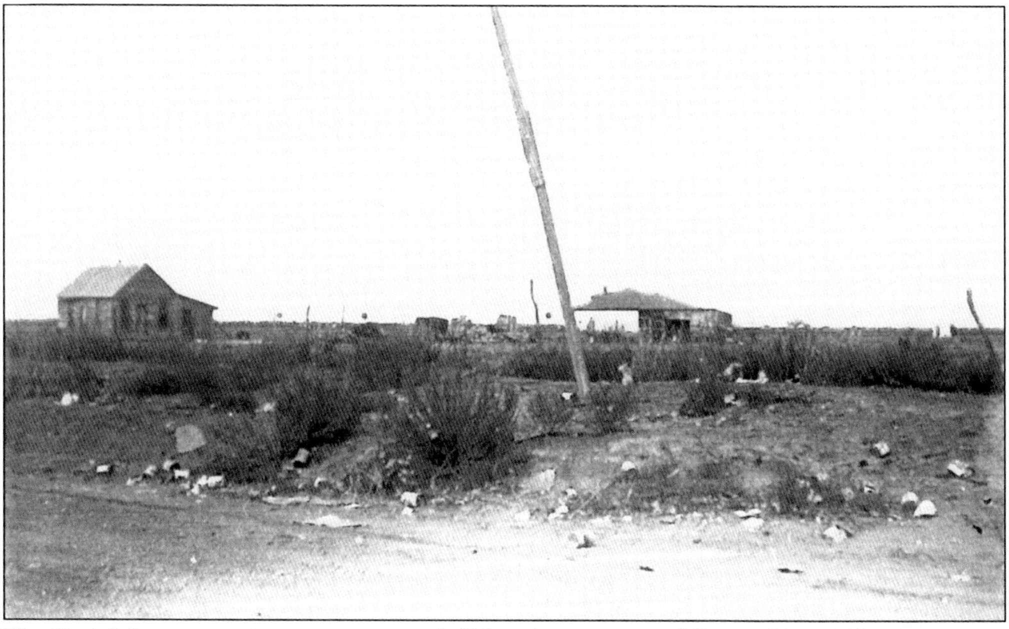

The Fruitdale community grew to around 600 and was renamed Buena Vista. The Loars soon found there was little fresh water. When there was enough water in the river, only cotton or alfalfa could be grown with the salt-laden water. The Loars left in 1918. A few others lasted until the 1930s. The caption on this photograph reads, "Buena Vista, who knows what?"

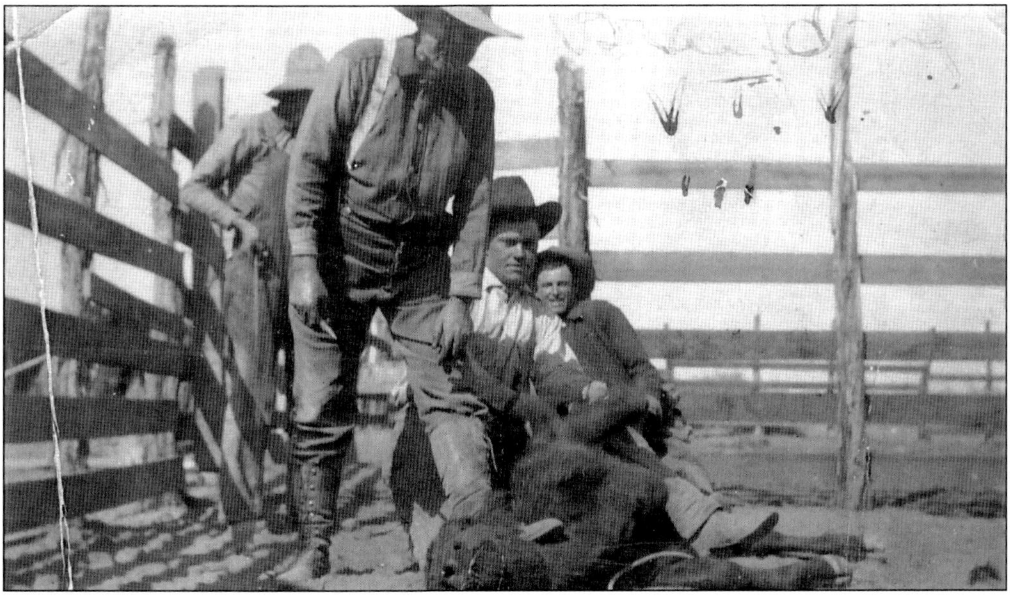

By the 1920s, the open range was fenced and cattle breeding grew in importance. S.L. Stone (standing, in suspenders) took up ranching when a hurricane destroyed his Sealy, Texas, rice farm. He brought registered Hereford to his west Pecos County ranch. Helping him with branding in 1913 are an unidentified cowboy (standing), Bill Addison (in black hat), Hal Burnett, and another unidentified cowboy. (Courtesy of Stone family.)

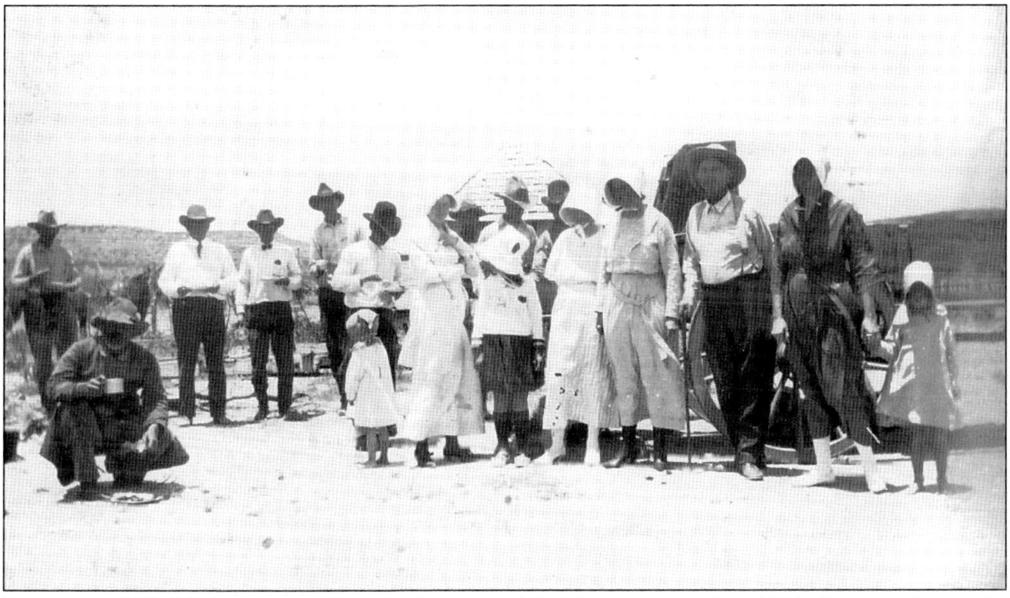

Ranches still held chuck wagon meals (see page 33). The group in this 1920 photograph on the Clarence Scharbauer Pecos County Ranch includes (on the left, in white shirts) John Scharbauer, Clarence Scharbauer, and John Billings (foreman). The woman in the center is Mrs. J.H. Burke, with her daughter Christine on her right. On the far right are Cora Billings and her daughter. All others are unidentified.

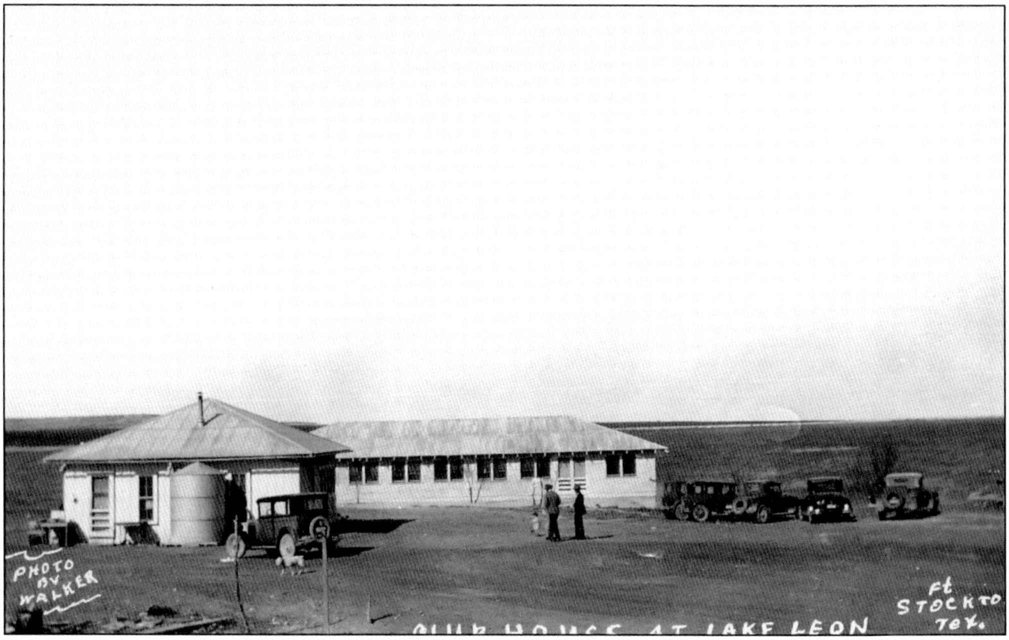

Leon Lake, stocked with fish, became a favorite recreation site in the 1920s. Del Beeman provided land for the Leon Lake Club House (pictured). The clubhouse floor was hardwood. Most of the dances in Fort Stockton in the late 1920s and early 1930s were held at Leon Lake.

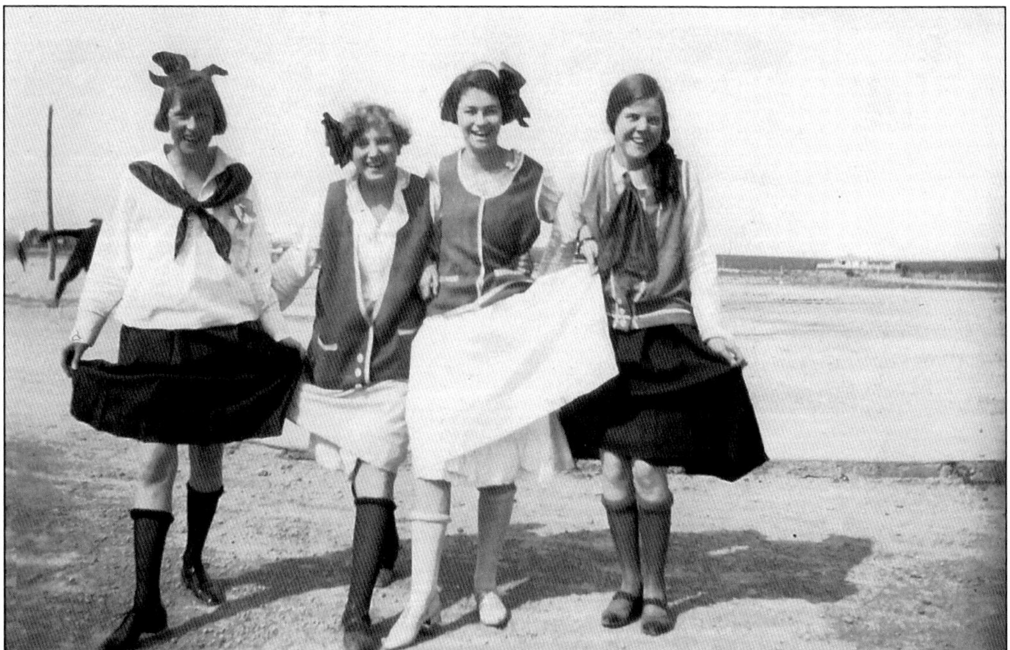

Life was good in 1920s Fort Stockton. The Pecos and Rio Grande telephone line brought connections to the outside world. The Airdome offered "better shows at sensible prices," and the new Palace Theater was built north of Winkler's store. The younger generation had time for fun. Clowning for the camera in this c. 1924 photograph are, from left to right, Dorothy Rooney, Maidie Butz, Ruth Rollins, and Doris Lea.

James Rooney died in 1927. He had been an economic force in Fort Stockton for over two decades. His many enterprises, including a city water system, a mercantile, banks, and hotels, as well as his service as first mayor of the city, led many to refer to Fort Stockton as "Rooney Town."

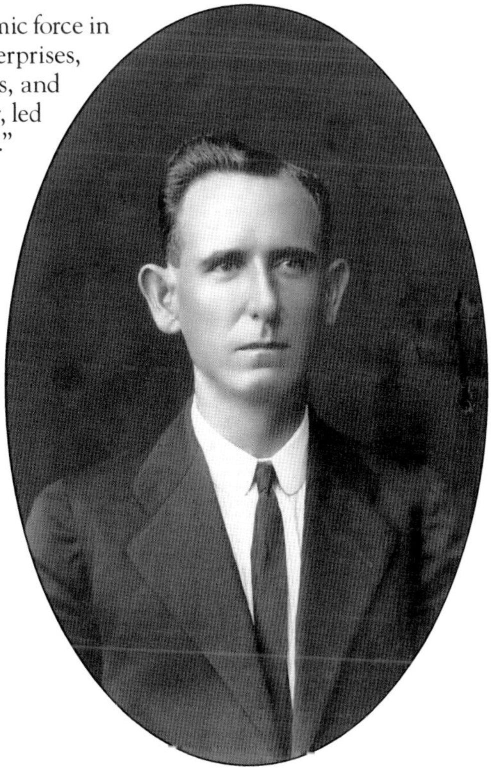

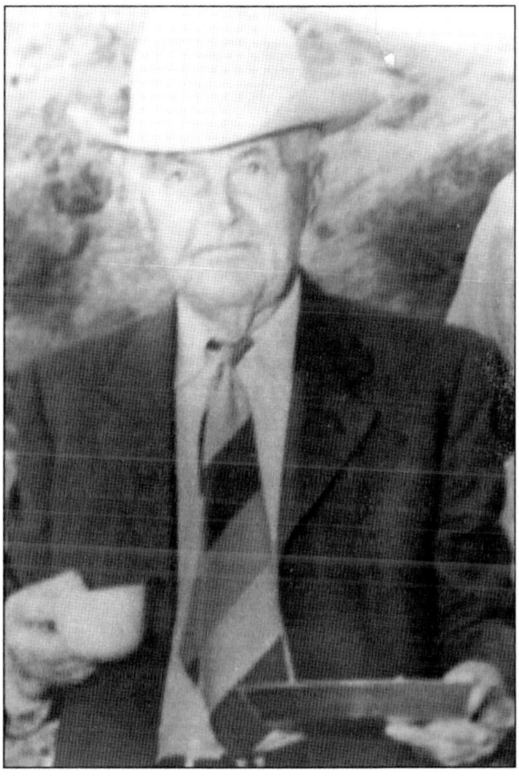

In 1926, Dudley Barker, after 20 years in office, lost the county sheriff office to William Patrick Rooney. Barker—six feet tall and wearing his black hat and pistol—had run the county his way, chasing bootleggers for hundreds of miles and arresting or shooting lawbreakers. He even dealt with carnival bears. Legend holds that he killed 20 men. For the rest of his life, he listed his occupation as "Sheriff, retired."

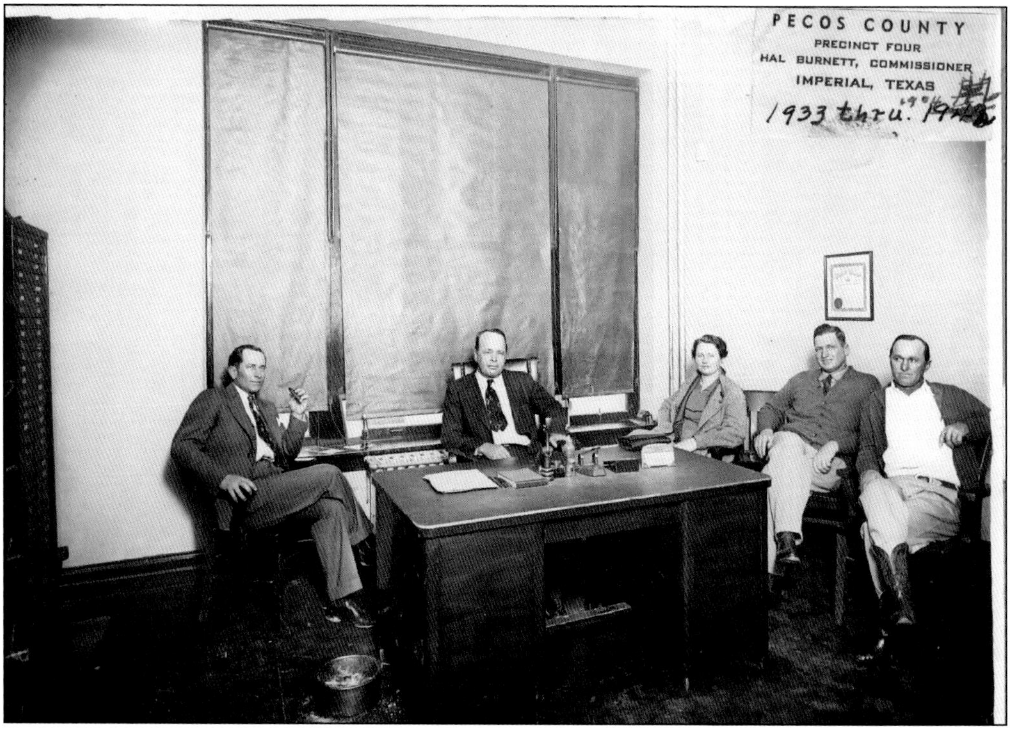

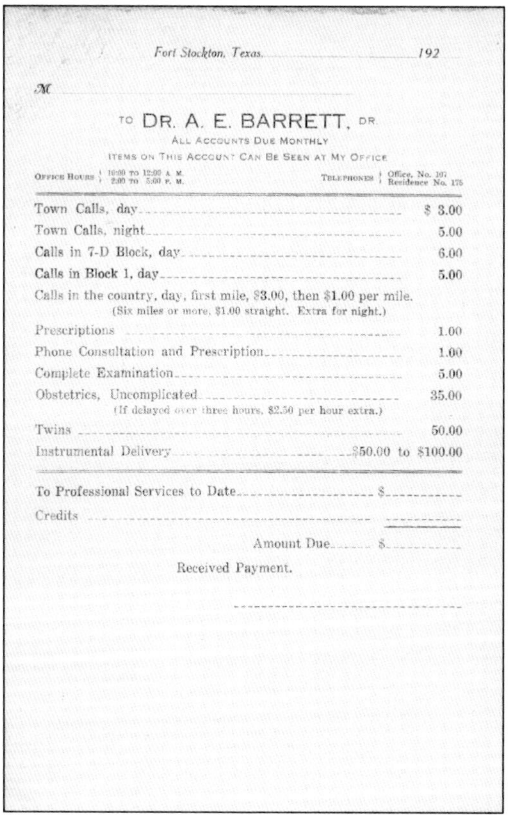

Fort Stockton, Texas.............192

M

TO DR. A. E. BARRETT, DR.

ALL ACCOUNTS DUE MONTHLY

ITEMS ON THIS ACCOUNT CAN BE SEEN AT MY OFFICE

OFFICE HOURS { 10:00 TO 12:00 A. M. / 2:00 TO 5:00 P. M. TELEPHONES { Office, No. 107 / Residence No. 175

Town Calls, day	$ 3.00
Town Calls, night	5.00
Calls in 7-D Block, day	6.00
Calls in Block 1, day	5.00
Calls in the country, day, first mile, $3.00, then $1.00 per mile. (Six miles or more, $1.00 straight. Extra for night.)	
Prescriptions	1.00
Phone Consultation and Prescription	1.00
Complete Examination	5.00
Obstetrics, Uncomplicated (If delayed over three hours, $2.50 per hour extra.)	35.00
Twins	50.00
Instrumental Delivery	$50.00 to $100.00

To Professional Services to Date............ $..........

Credits

Amount Due........ $..........

Received Payment.

A new group now held political power. Some were the descendants of pioneers, and some were newcomers. Members of the 1935 Pecos County Commissioners Court included, from left to right, Clayton Williams Sr., commissioner and son of O.W. Williams; Judge Ed Casebier, who arrived in 1912; Lyman Webb, commissioner; Hal Burnett, commissioner, who moved to Imperial in 1923; and F.B. "Buck" Pyle, commissioner.

The city also needed doctors. Dr. Alfred Barrett moved west for his asthma condition. He came to Fort Stockton when the 1918 flu epidemic turned the schoolhouse into a makeshift hospital, and he served the city for over 50 years. Barrett used this form to record patient calls. In 1919, Dr. D.J. Sibley set up his dental practice in the Stockton Hotel. For 15 years, he was the only dentist in the county.

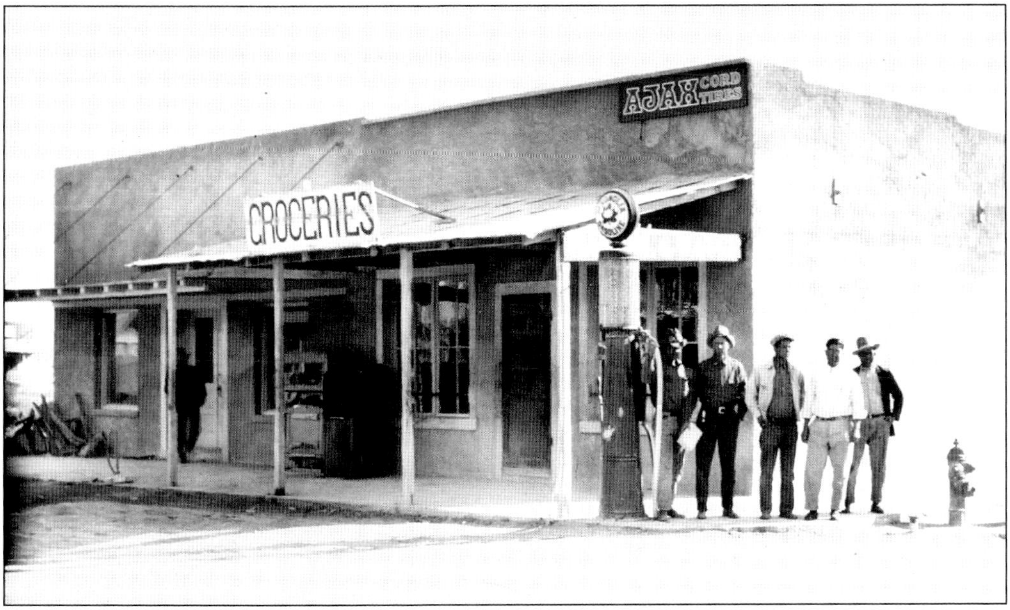

Manuel Ramirez "M.R." Gonzalez operated a grocery store on the corner of Nelson and Division Streets. There were no establishments on Main Street owned or run by Mexican Americans before 1955. However, Mexican American businesses did exist to the west, on Nelson and Callaghan Streets. When tough times came in the 1930s, M.R. closed the store and saved his stock for better times. (Courtesy of M.R. Gonzalez Jr.)

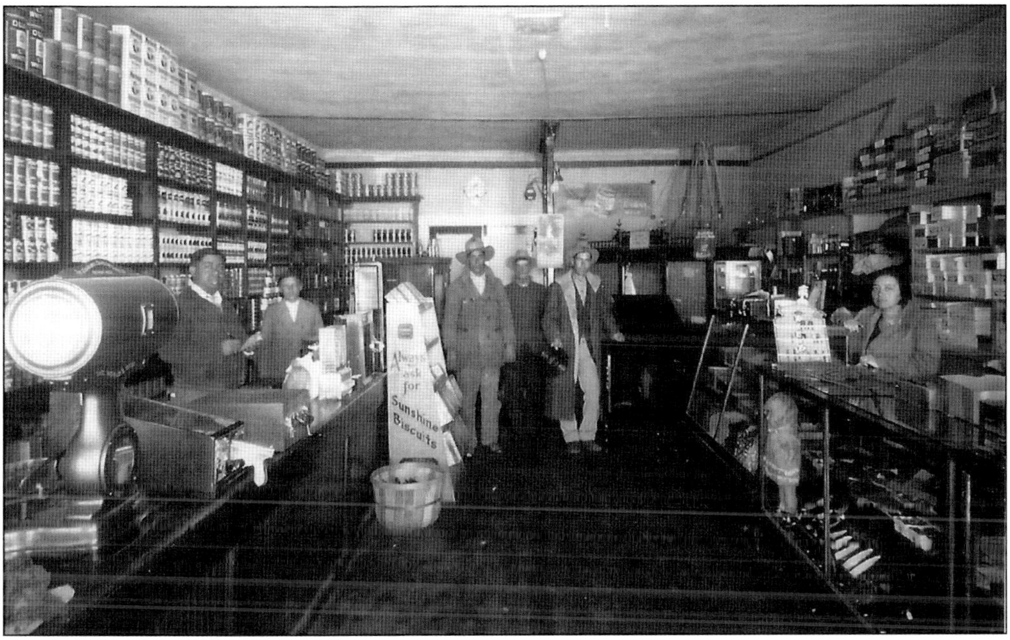

In 1927, Carmen Gutierrez, granddaughter of a Spaniard, rode the train with her mother and a cousin from Chihuahua, Mexico, on her way to a new life in Chicago. At the stop in Fort Stockton, the cousin left them stranded. When M.R. Gonzalez delivered groceries to the home in which she was staying, he was smitten. They married, and Carmen (right) helped M.R. (far left) in the store. (Courtesy of M.R. Gonzalez Jr.)

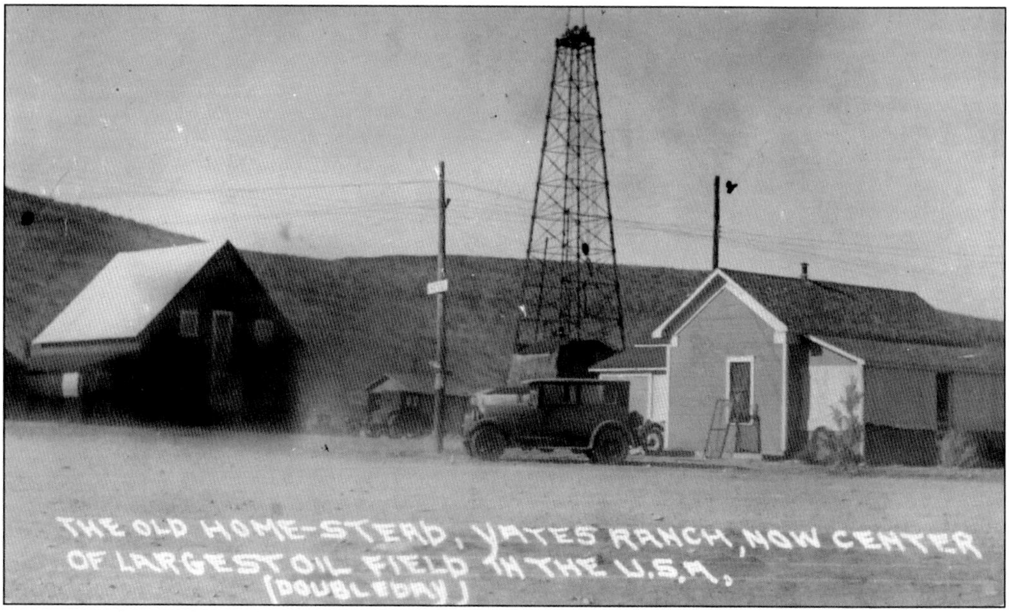

In 1926, oil transformed Fort Stockton. In 1915, Ira Yates traded his grocery store in Rankin, Texas, for the Tom Hickox ranch in eastern Pecos County. Yates leased his land to Mid-Kansas Oil and Gas, despite the common belief the county lacked major oil reserves. On Yates's 67th birthday, the No. 1 Yates erupted, smearing the hillside with black oil. His Red Barn, Texas, ranch (pictured) became a boomtown. (Courtesy of City of Iraan Museum.)

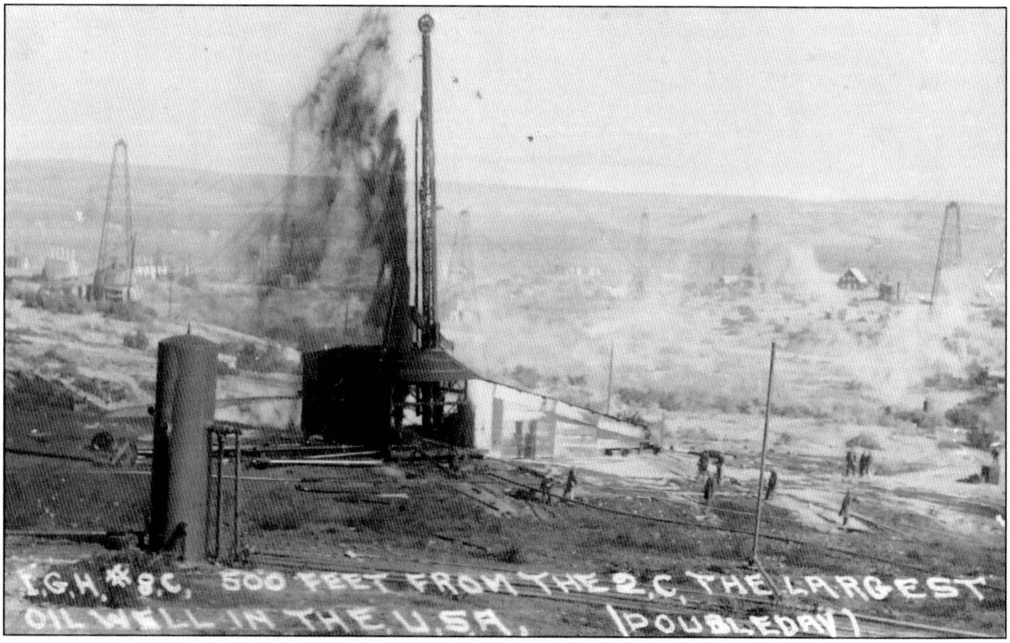

The Yates quickly grew into a huge field. The Yates A-30 tested at 200,000 barrels per day. As the field grew, so did new boom towns. A red light district flourished in nearby Gruby. Red Barn was more respectable, though a careless smoker burned down the new hotel. Oil camps sprang up near the fields, and wives and children joined the men, living in rows of tents. Things grew more respectable. (Courtesy of City of Iraan Museum.)

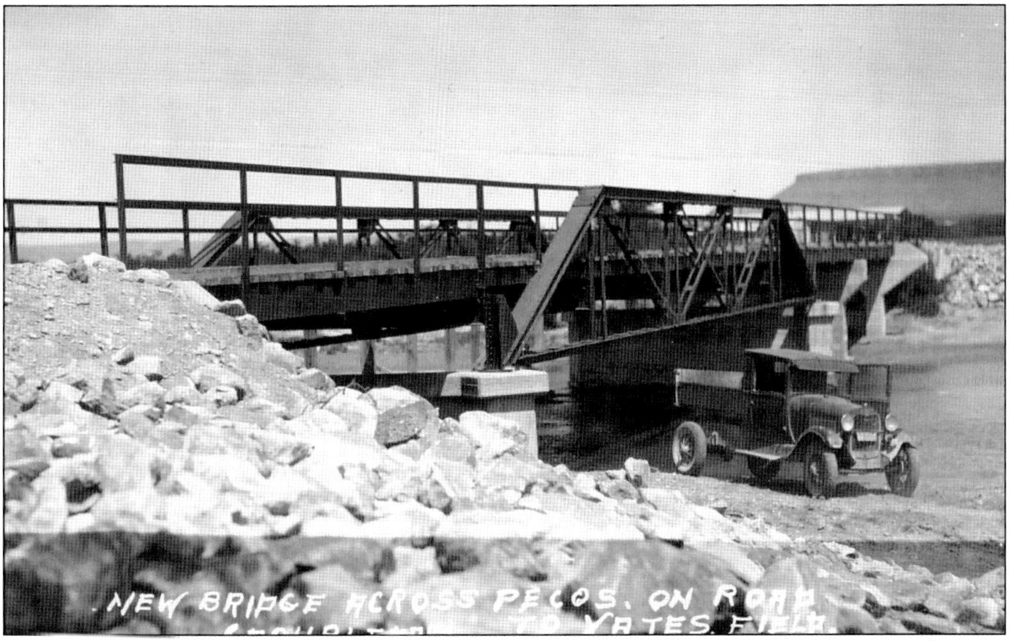

The first major problem confronting the oil companies was getting the crude oil to market. An eight-inch pipeline was laid to the Orient Railway in McCamey, Texas, to carry 10,000 barrels a day. In 1927, two Pecos County crews built roads into Yates Field and the new town of Iraan (a combination of Ira and his wife Ann's names). This bridge was one of those built across the Pecos River to the oil fields. (Courtesy of City of Iraan Museum.)

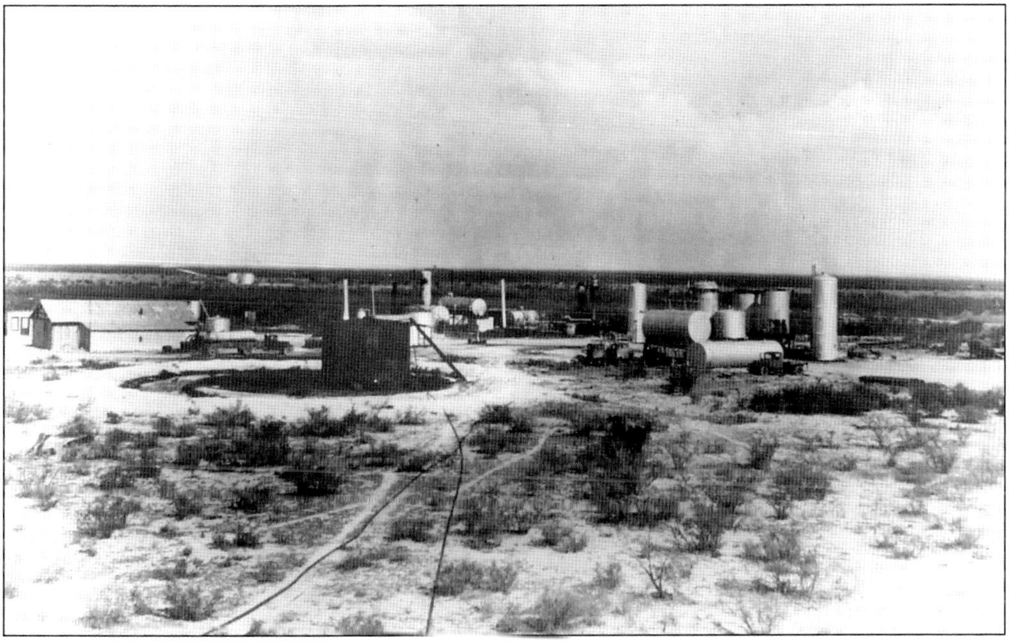

The Yates Field discovery inspired companies to drill exploratory wells across the county, and other fields soon developed. Fort Stockton promoters were quick to add the oil industry to the economic attractions of the area (page 2). Pipelines, tank farms, and gas refineries, such as the Aero Gas Refinery (pictured in 1930), soon joined sheep, cattle, and fields as part of the landscape.

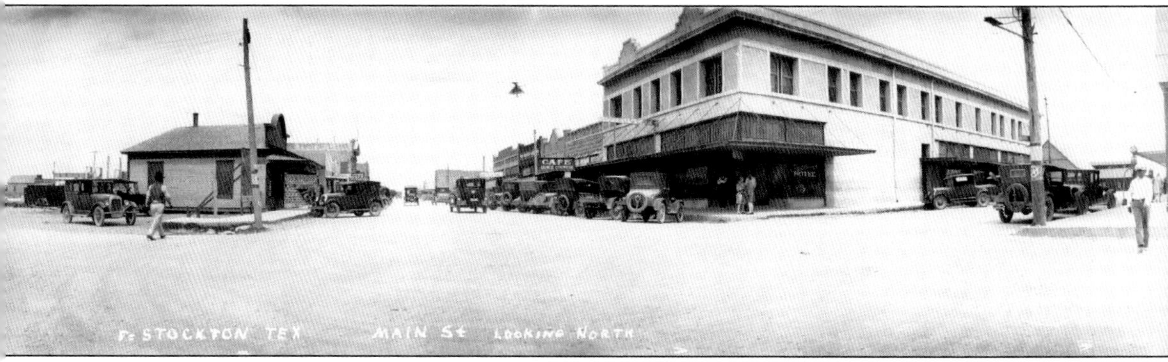

By the time this 1930s photograph was taken, Fort Stockton had grown into a very different city from the rural frontier town it had been. The diversity achieved in these years provided the core from which the city has operated ever since. From the early 1920s, Fort Stockton has been the largest community on the San Antonio to El Paso highway between Kerrville and El Paso, a total distance of 500 miles. The Great Depression, World War II, and the vast changes of the late 20th century would all leave their marks, but the Fort Stockton built in these early years endured.

Five

Celebrating Comanche Springs

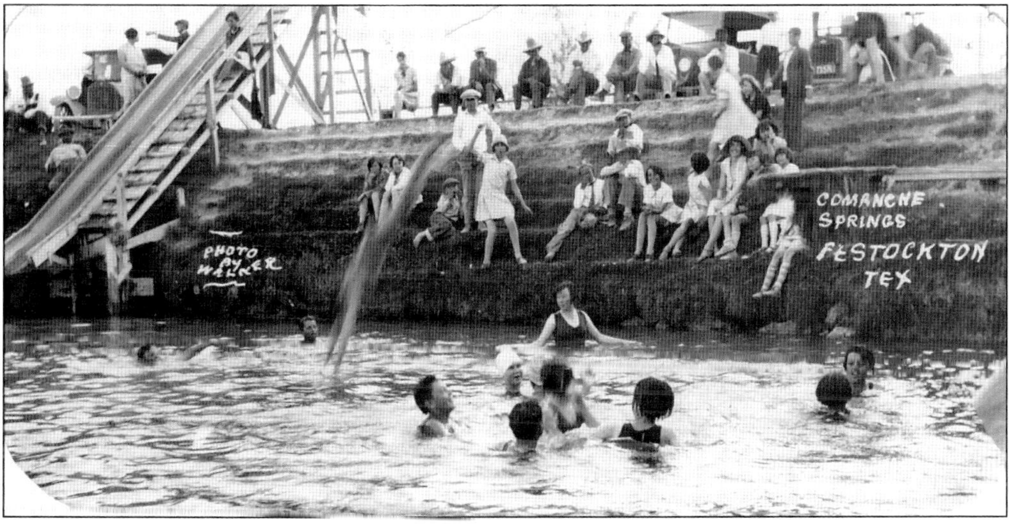

Comanche Springs had always provided the water critical to Fort Stockton's existence. As the community grew in the 20th century, the springs also became the focus of a variety of social events. The landscape of the springs was repeatedly redesigned. On the back of this photograph, someone added the caption "along in the twenties, I guess."

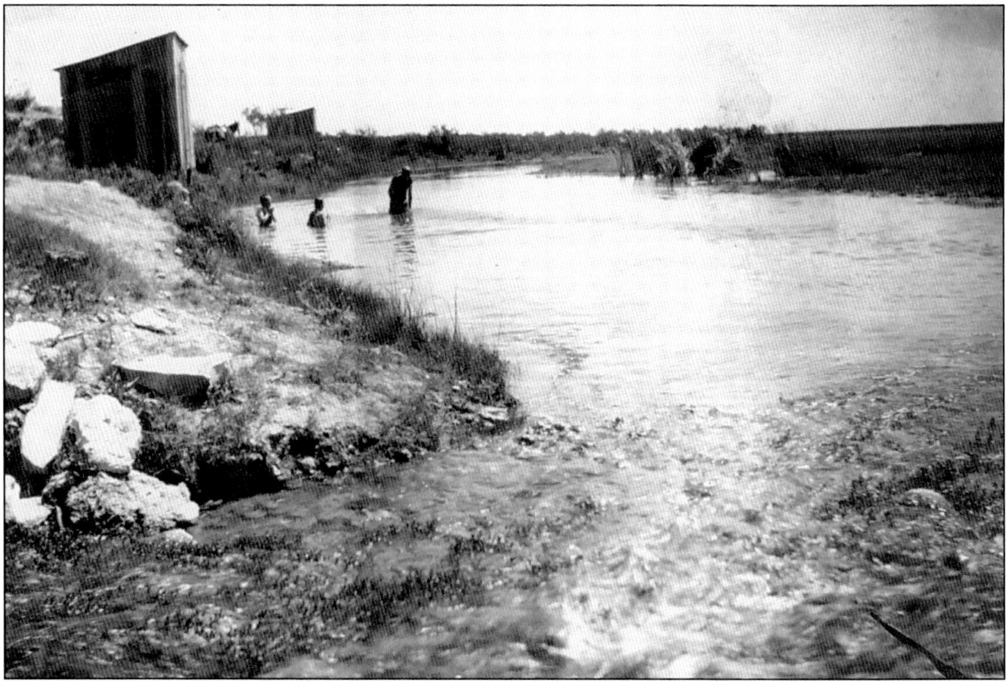

The springs provided water for drinking, cooking, and bathing. Early day bathhouses were simple wooden structures—one for women and one for men. Here, swimmers enjoy the water. A patient horse stands beside one of the bath houses. The water from Government Spring gushes out in the foreground. (See page 10 for a map of the springs.)

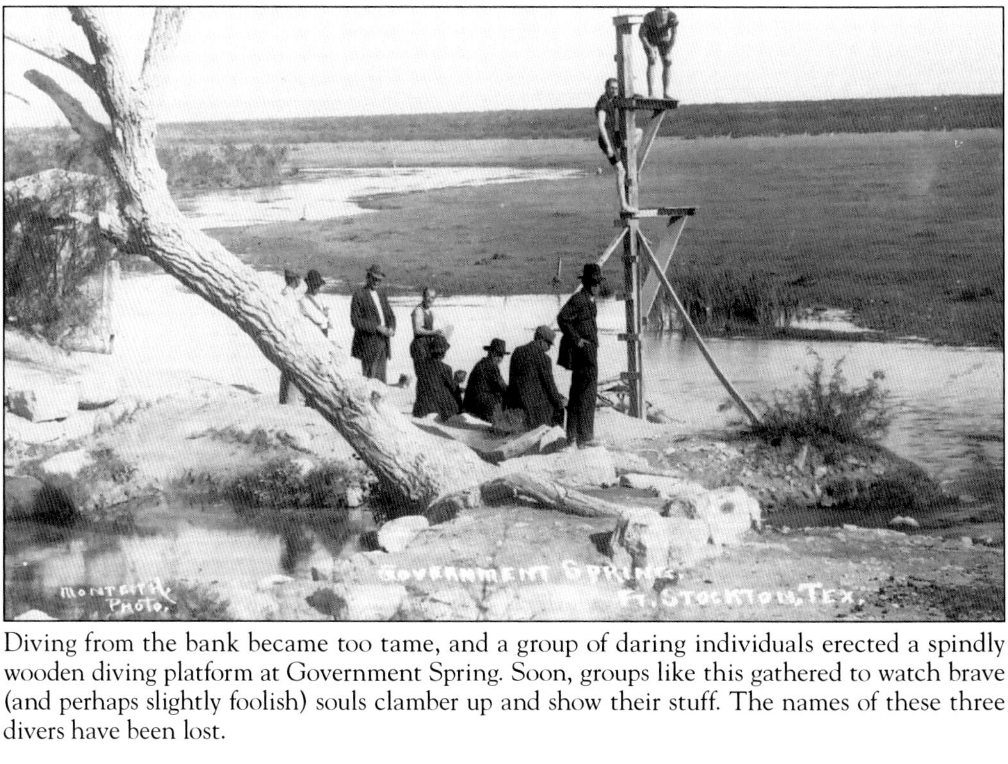

Diving from the bank became too tame, and a group of daring individuals erected a spindly wooden diving platform at Government Spring. Soon, groups like this gathered to watch brave (and perhaps slightly foolish) souls clamber up and show their stuff. The names of these three divers have been lost.

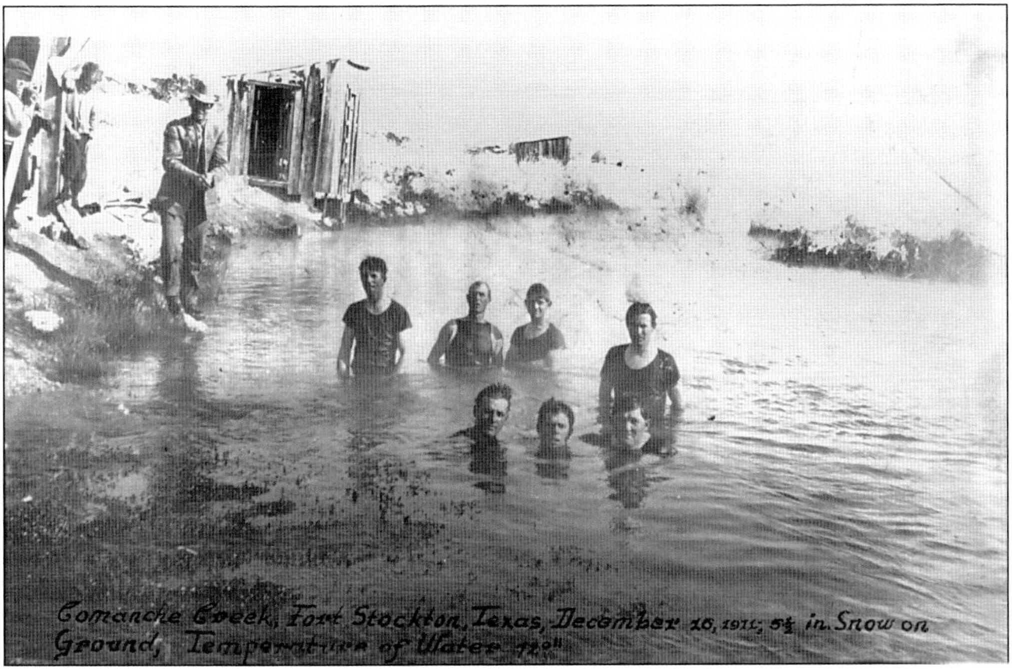

Young men continued to find new challenges. This caption states, "Comanche Creek, Fort Stockton, Texas, December 10, 1911, 5 and 1/2 inches of snow on ground, temperature of water 72 degrees." The group of swimmers included three sons of Judge O.W. Williams—Clayton Williams (far left, first row), Waldo Williams (second from left, second row), and J.C. Williams (right of Waldo).

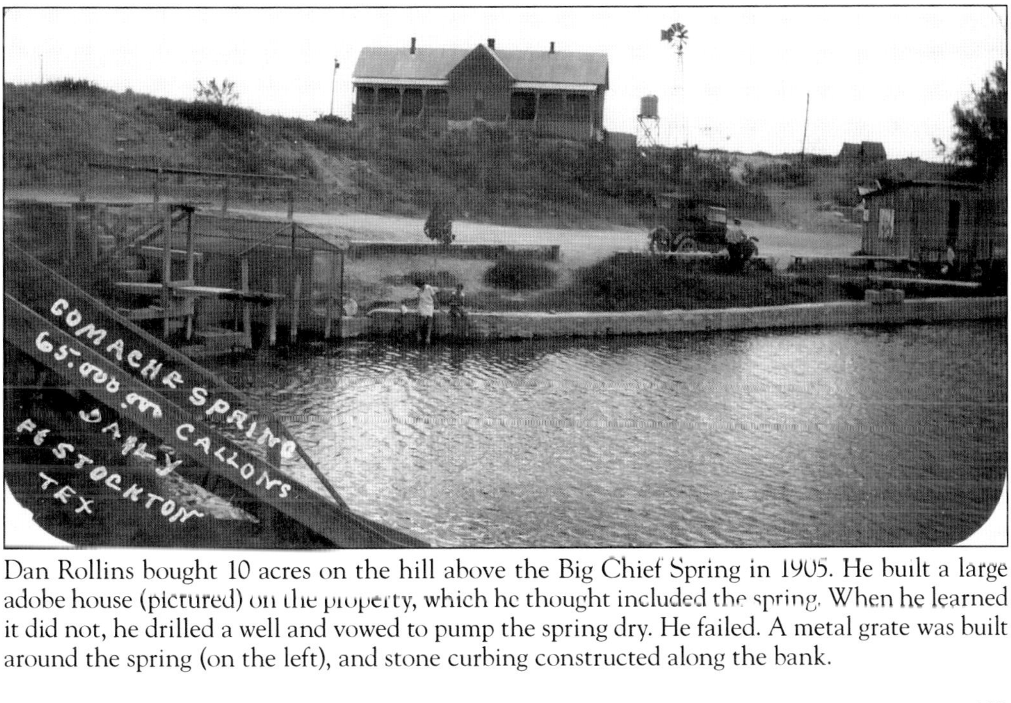

Dan Rollins bought 10 acres on the hill above the Big Chief Spring in 1905. He built a large adobe house (pictured) on the property, which he thought included the spring. When he learned it did not, he drilled a well and vowed to pump the spring dry. He failed. A metal grate was built around the spring (on the left), and stone curbing constructed along the bank.

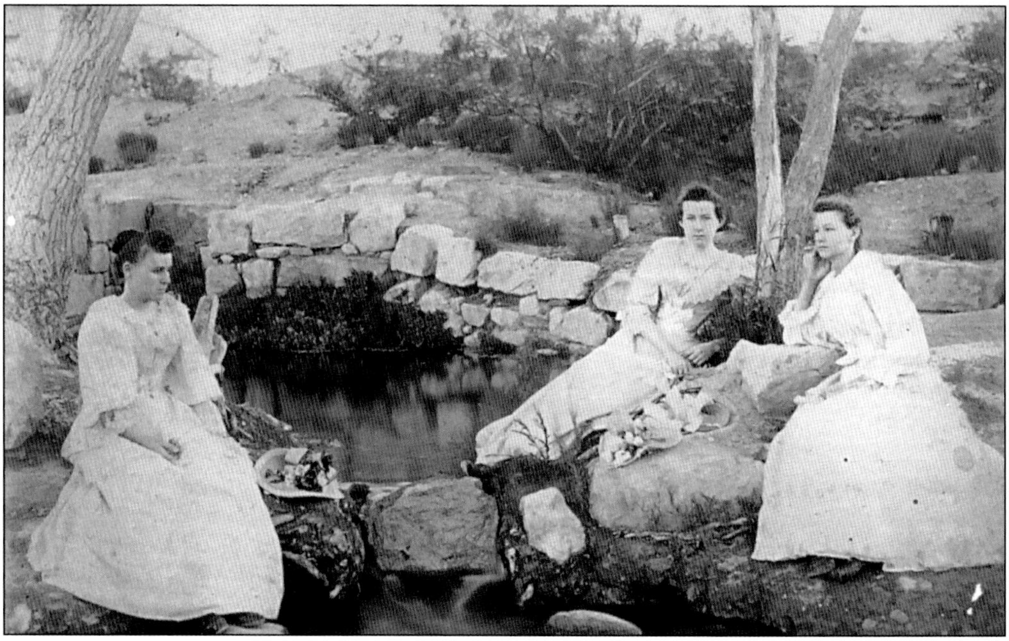

Young women found the springs suitable for more genteel outings. In 1894, Mary Rooney Richardson (left), Jannie Livingston (center), and Essie McDonald Rooney (right) had their portrait made at a summer banquet. In this early modification, the unidentified spring has been shaped into a pool lined with limestone blocks.

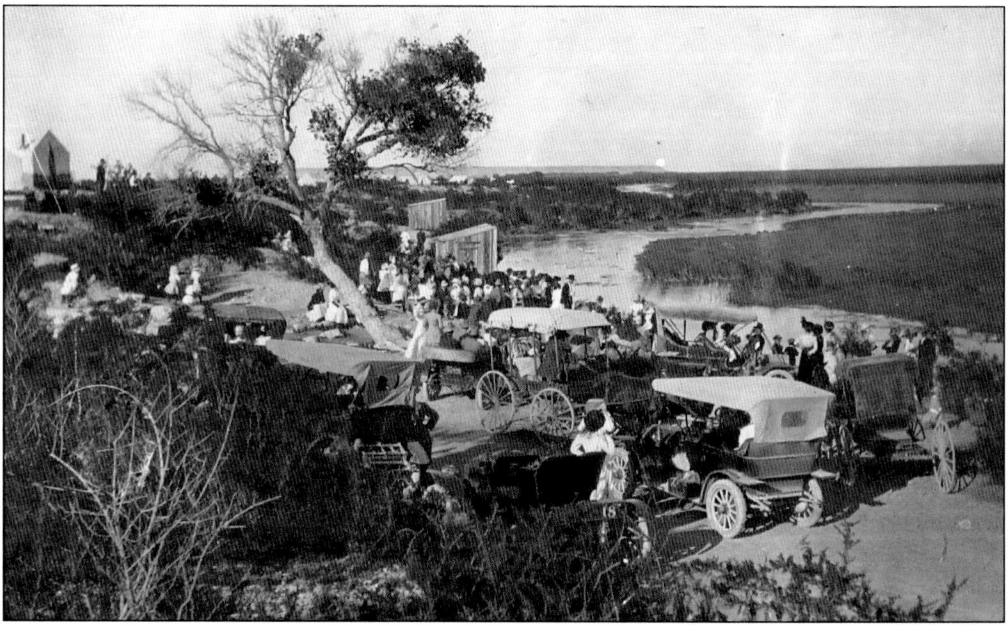

In addition to swimming and picnics, the springs served more solemn purposes. As the Protestant population grew after 1900, more churches were formed (page 86). This photograph records a Sunday afternoon baptizing that took place at the springs around 1913.

Shortly after arriving at his new parish (page 85), Fr. Gerardo Decorme was inspired to create a grotto, similar to that at Lourdes, at the spring behind St. Joseph. He and a few brave souls began construction, disturbing a huge snake in the process. By Thanksgiving 1916, the rocky grotto was taking shape. Rafaela Villalba contributed a statue of Our Lady of Lourdes. The grotto was blessed on January 9, 1917. (Courtesy of the Nita Stewart Haley Memorial Library.)

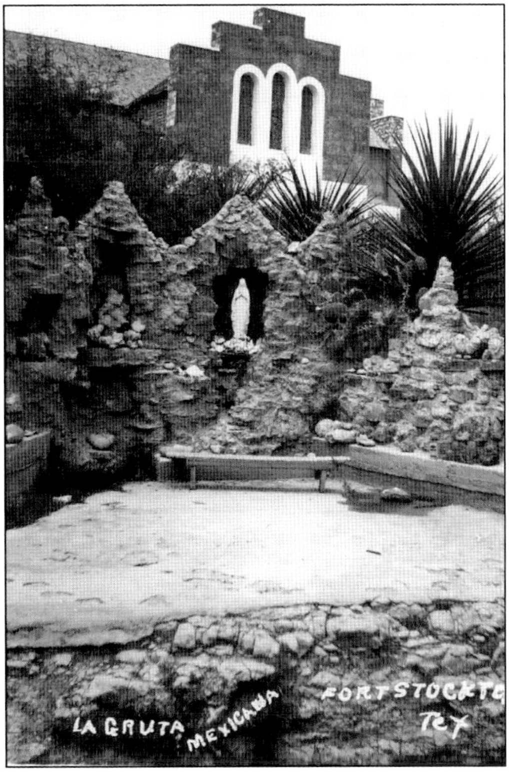

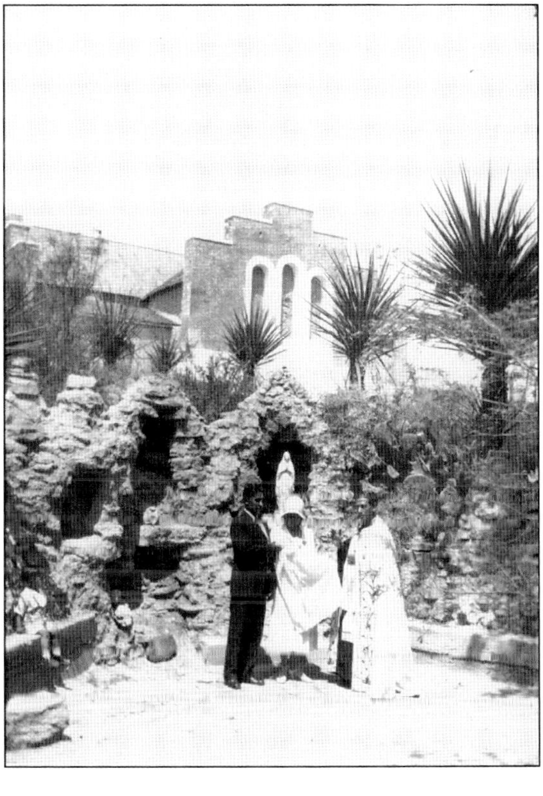

La Gruta became a popular site for many special events and celebrations, including baptisms. Alex Gonzalez, son of M.R. and Carmen Gonzalez (page 97), was baptized here in 1932 by Fr. Manuel Cuadrado. Godparents Lupe (left) and Esther Terrazas (right) hold Alex, while Alex's brother, also known as M.R., watches (left). After the church spring ceased flowing, the area was covered with church building expansions, and the spring's exact location was forgotten. (Courtesy of M.R. Gonzalez Jr.)

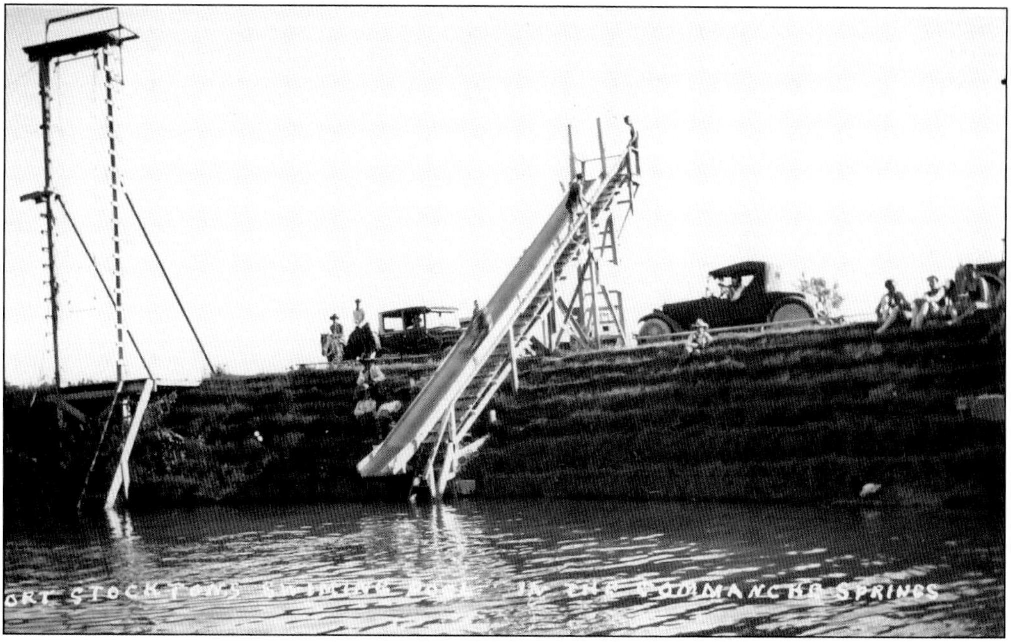

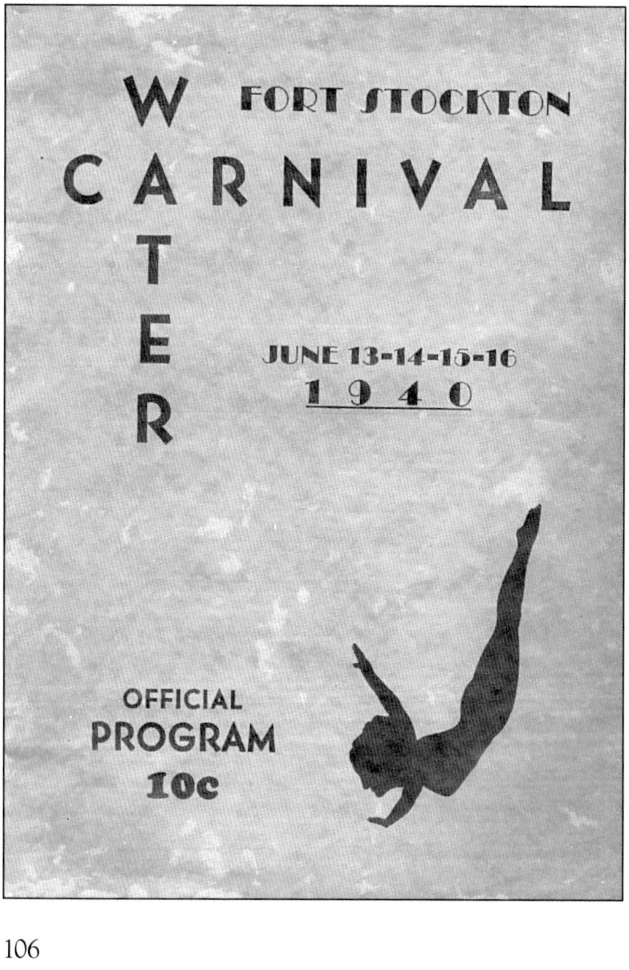

Improvements continued at the big spring. Slides, an area of grass-covered stadium seating, and better diving boards were added beside the spring, which still flowed 30,000,000 gallons per day (see page 101). To celebrate the Texas Centennial in 1936, H.M. Long, Lions Club president, helped launch a new event to focus attention on the recreational value of the Comanche Springs swimming pool.

The first Water Carnival consisted of a beauty pageant for older girls and a brief water show of swimming and diving. On June 12, 1936, a full 2,000 people paid the admission fee of 25¢ (children 15¢) to watch 60 young ladies promenade on a special boardwalk placed across a section of the pool. Sammie Lee Warnock became the first official Miss Fort Stockton. The Carnival grew each year. In 1940, the first official program was printed.

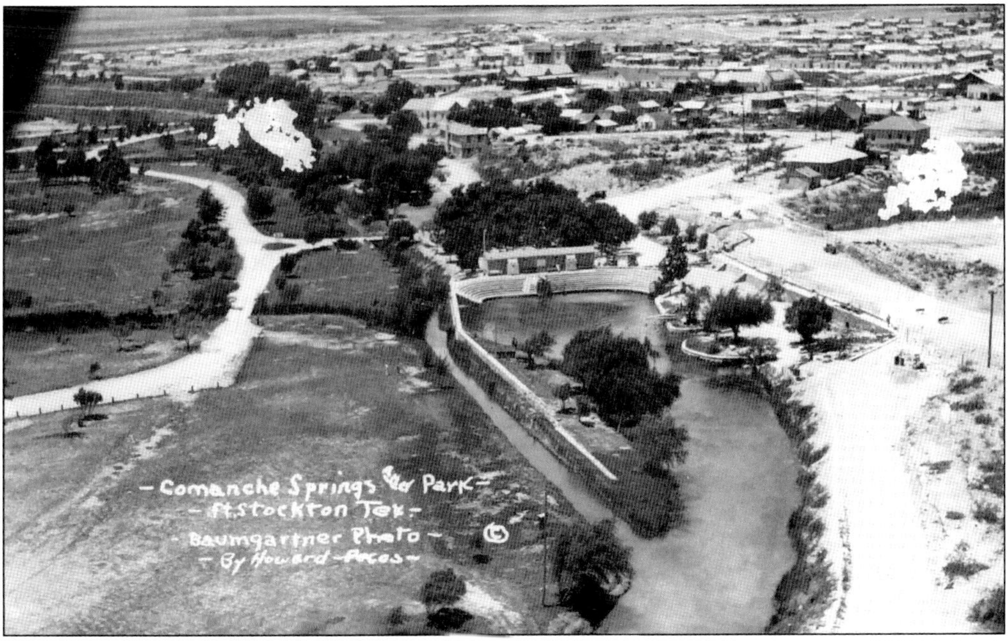

To improve the Water Carnival, the city obtained Works Progress Administration (WPA) funds for major revisions of the pool (pictured underway in this 1937 postcard). A new bathhouse and concrete steps were added. The foundations of the pavilion and a new road beside the springs take shape above the two spring outlets. Rooney Park, left of the pool, included a nine-hole golf course complete with sand greens oiled with local crude oil. A caddy earned 25¢ for each nine-hole round.

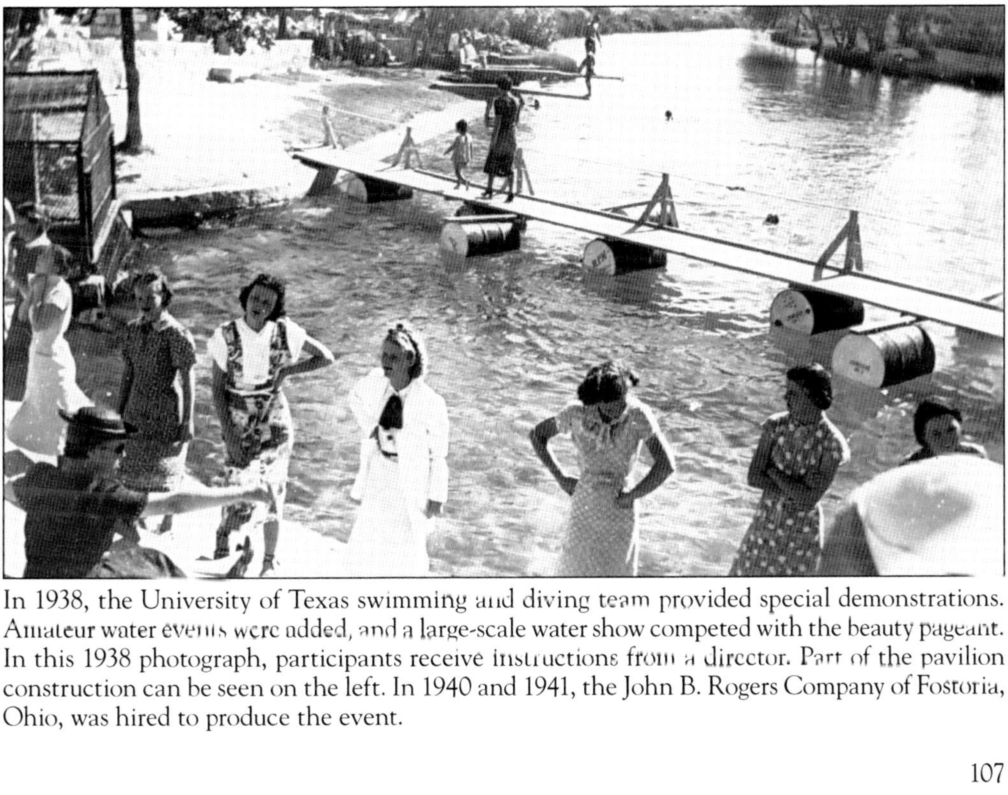

In 1938, the University of Texas swimming and diving team provided special demonstrations. Amateur water events were added, and a large-scale water show competed with the beauty pageant. In this 1938 photograph, participants receive instructions from a director. Part of the pavilion construction can be seen on the left. In 1940 and 1941, the John B. Rogers Company of Fostoria, Ohio, was hired to produce the event.

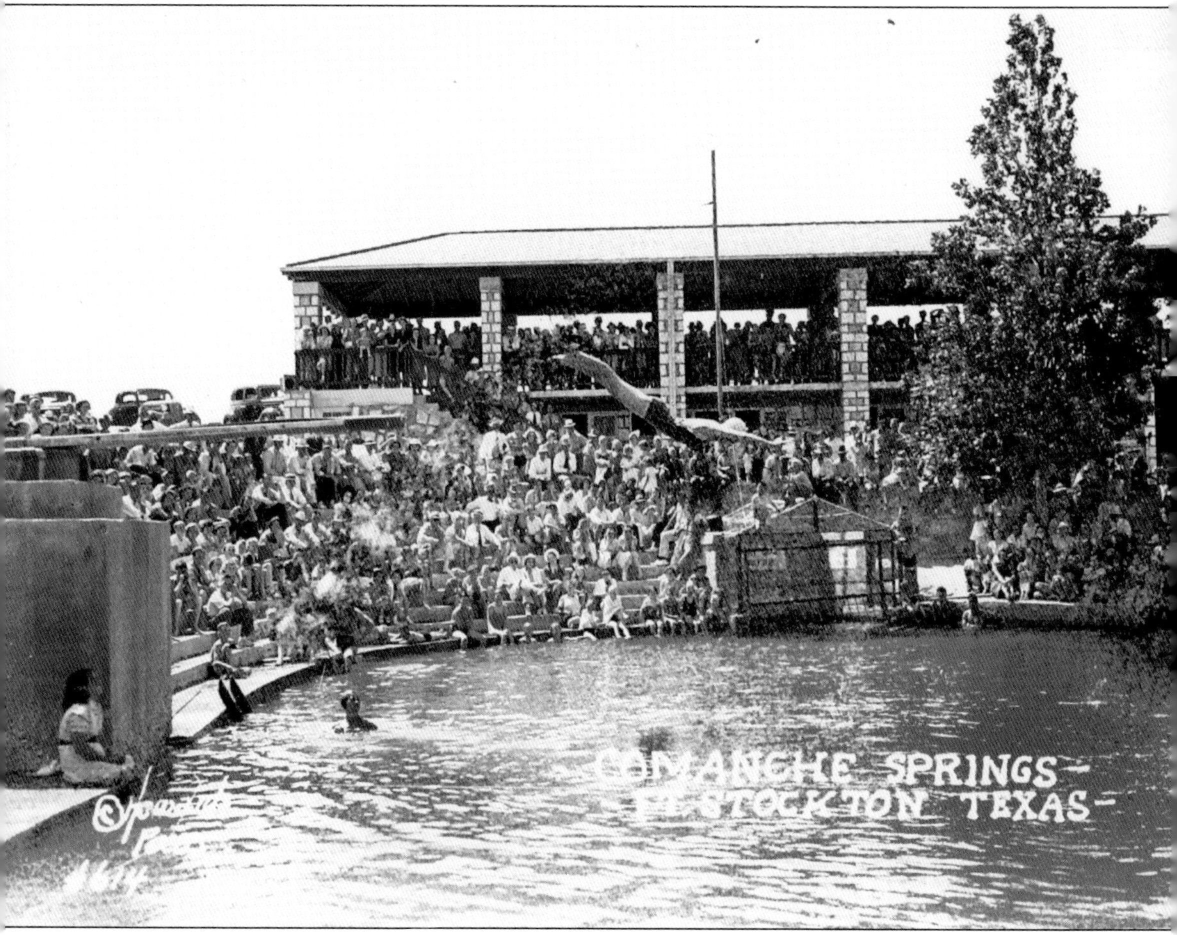

There were no Water Carnivals during the war years, but they resumed in 1947. In 1950, the declining flow of the springs temporarily halted the shows. In 1953, a new pool, specially constructed on concrete pillars, utilized the spring water for support, and the carnivals returned. When the spring flow fell too low to maintain the pool, it was redesigned and filled by a pump system. The Water Carnival has remained an important annual event in Fort Stockton, bringing pageantry, thrills, and entertainment to crowds such as this one from the 1940s. In 2005, at the 50th Water Carnival's "Queen of New Orleans" show, Alexis Ramirez was crowned Miss Fort Stockton.

Six

Growing a Diversified Economy

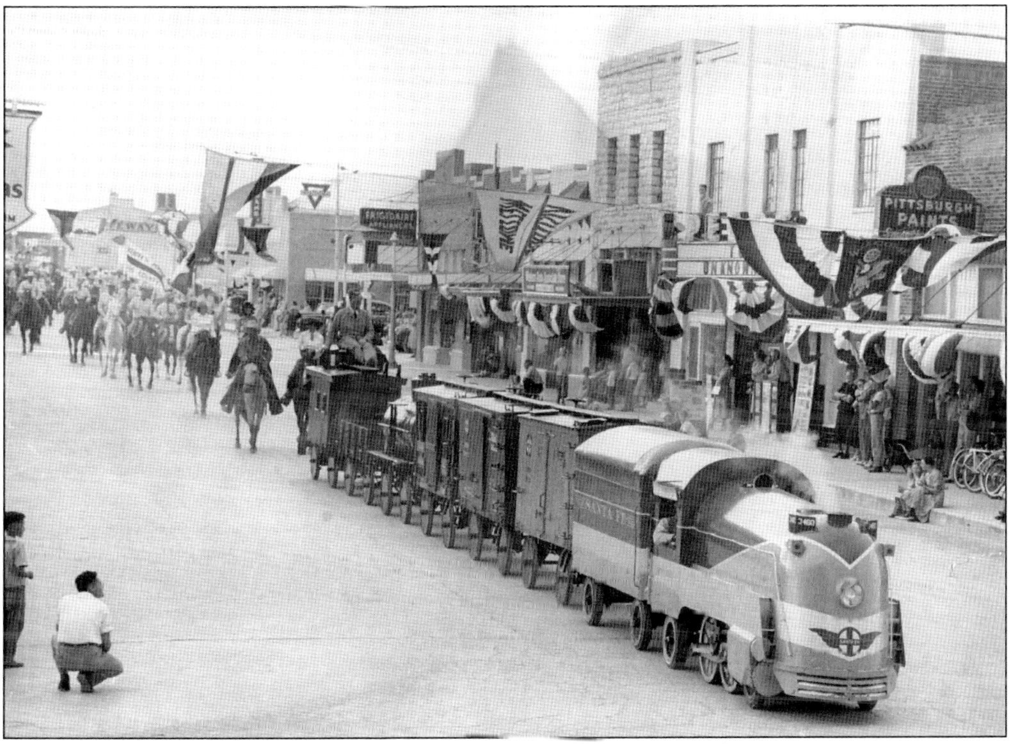

As Fort Stockton's economy diversified in the second half of the 20th century, the role of the railroad shrank (like the size of the train in this 1950s parade) as the automobile became the major means of travel and the truck the primary mover of goods. The role of oil and gas expanded tremendously, and the highway system redefined the community's shape.

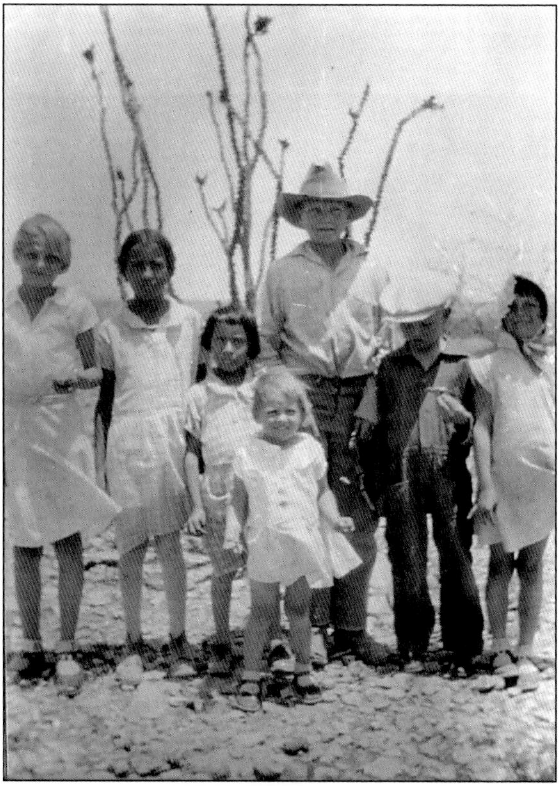

Fort Stockton and Pecos County, like most rural communities in the United States, struggled to survive in the years of the Great Depression. For many, like these Hovey students and their siblings pictured after an Easter egg hunt in 1931, there was little change in their hardscrabble lives. The Hovey school was always integrated. Railroad workers' children attended along with the children of ranchers. The school closed in 1938.

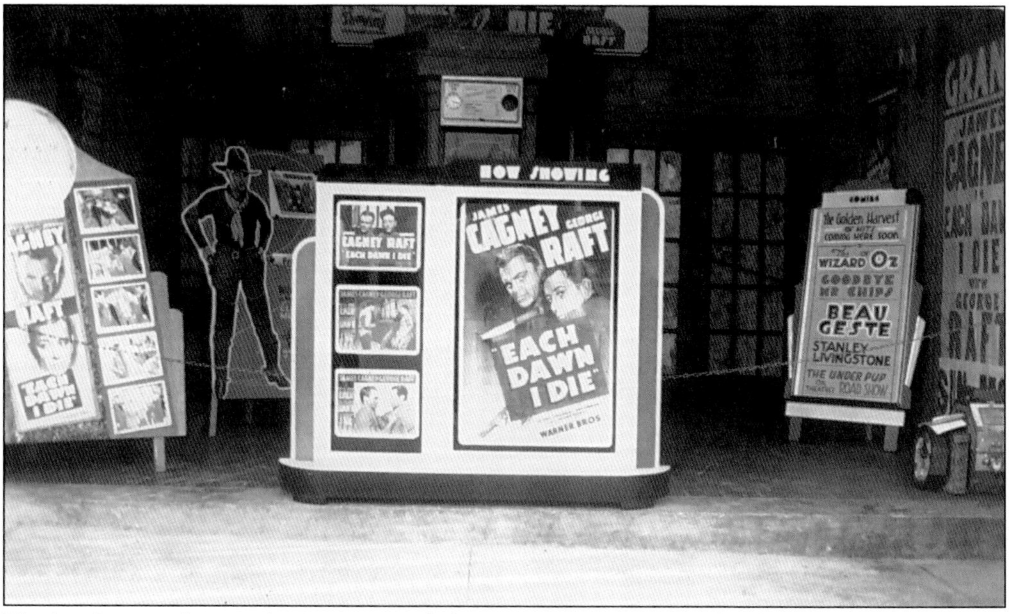

The local movie theater, the Pecos, provided momentary escape from hard times. In 1939, the year the Pecos ran these Hollywood classics, everyone could buy tickets, but Mexican Americans had to sit in the balcony, and African Americans had to sit in the top three rows of that section. The year before, a new school for Mexican American children was completed. Butz School opened in 1938 with approximately 250 students in grades 1 through 11.

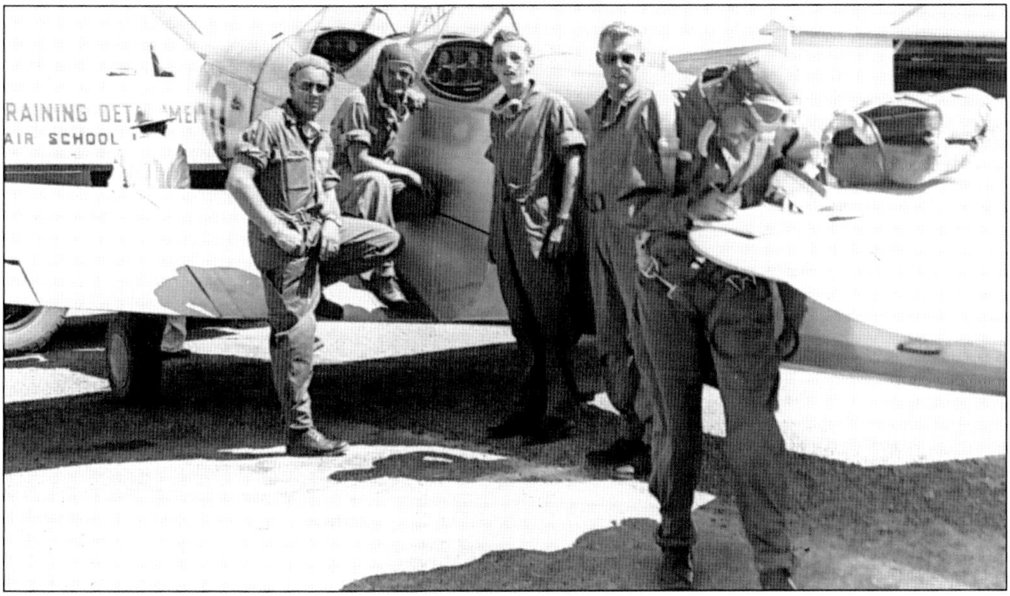

In 1942, the US Army announced its plan to build an airfield at Fort Stockton for the Pacific Air School to train pilots, taking advantage of open terrain and clear skies. Classes of 500 cadets would fly up to 120 Stearman and Childs aircraft at the facility, located northwest of town. In June, the first class arrived and consisted of young men such as these from a 1944 class.

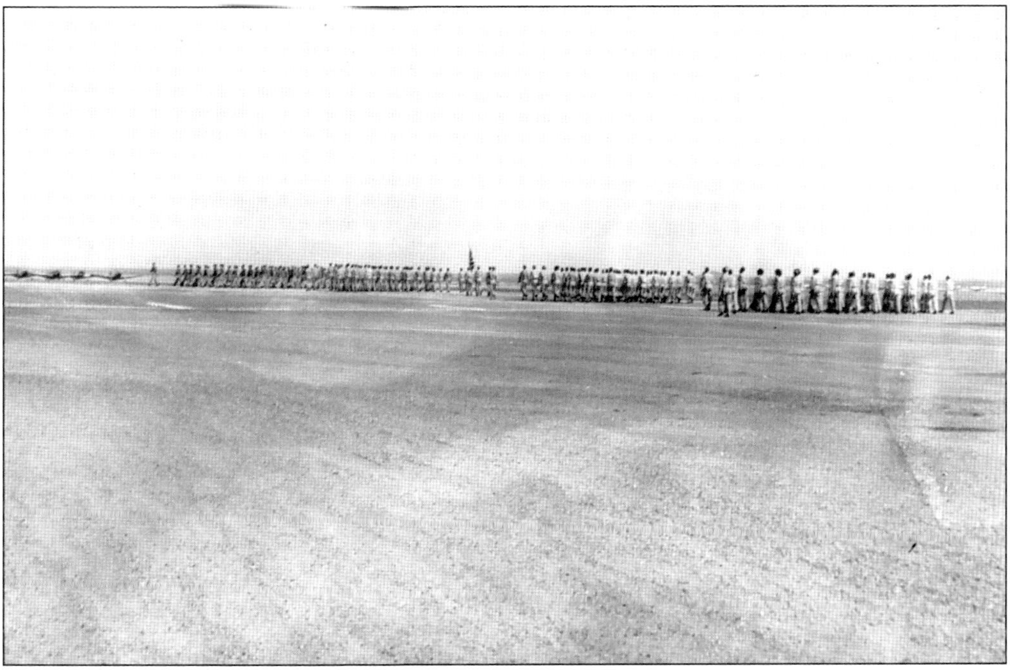

The first class, made up of 132 cadets, arrived by special train from San Angelo in June 1942. In October, the field was named Gibbs Field in honor of Maj. David R. Gibbs, who was killed in defense of the Philippines early in the war. Fort Stockton again became a military town. There were 18 classes of cadets, totaling over 4,000 students, trained at Gibbs Field. The 1944 class pictured was among the last. After the war, the airfield became a county airport.

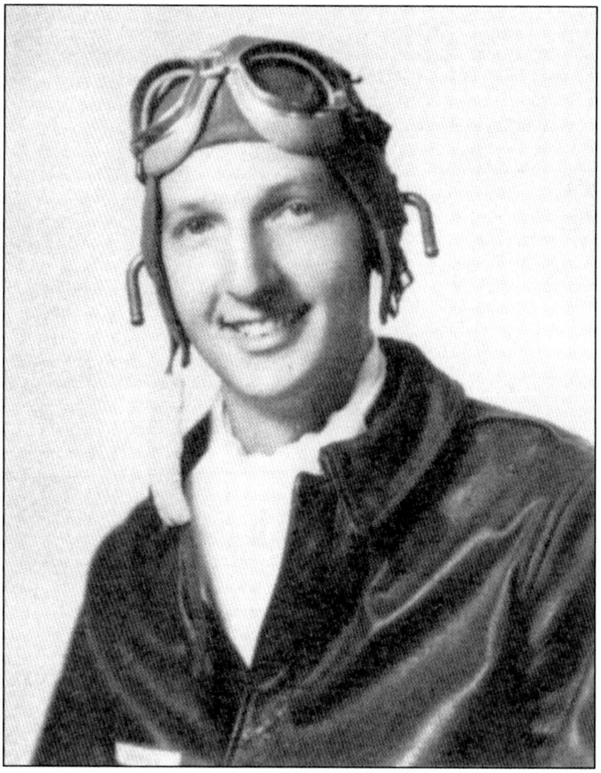

Like Captain Wedemeyer (page 15), Robert J. Fisher photographed his duty in Fort Stockton. Cadet classes were designated by the year and order of training. Each class produced a cadet book recording their service. Fisher (pictured in his cadet book) served on the staff of the 44A cadet book. As a retired Air Force lieutenant colonel, he sent the Annie Riggs Museum a collection of his photographs.

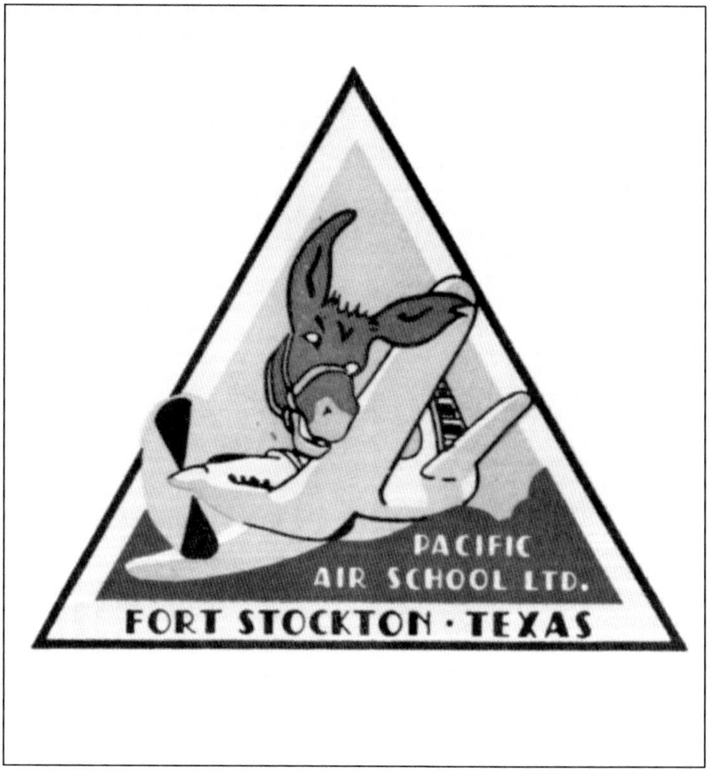

Classes arrived every four and a half weeks for the nine-week training, which included ground school and dual and solo flight instruction. The cadets adopted a local miniature mule as their mascot, Solo. When a cadet had a successful solo flight, he kissed Solo, and he could wear his goggles on his forehead. Local artist Cecil Casebier designed this popular field logo for the school. Casebier later became nationally recognized for his art in a variety of media, including 18 stained glass windows made for St. Luke's Episcopal Church in San Antonio, Texas.

The cadets provided a welcome stimulus to the local economy and proved a reminder of the Fort Stockton boys in uniform overseas. The caption on this photograph of unidentified cadets from Ben Games, a member of Class 43K, reads, "Cadets at pharmacy; the busiest place in Stockton; Mexican shoe-shine boys." While the young boys could ply their trade outside, Mexican Americans were not welcome at the soda fountain inside.

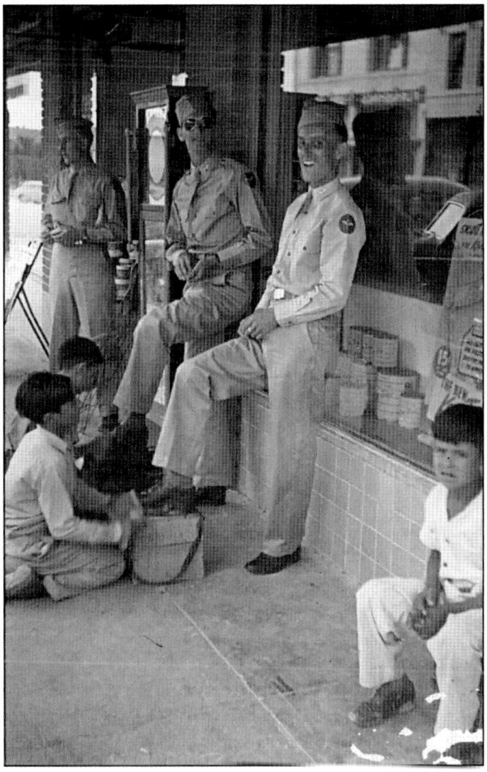

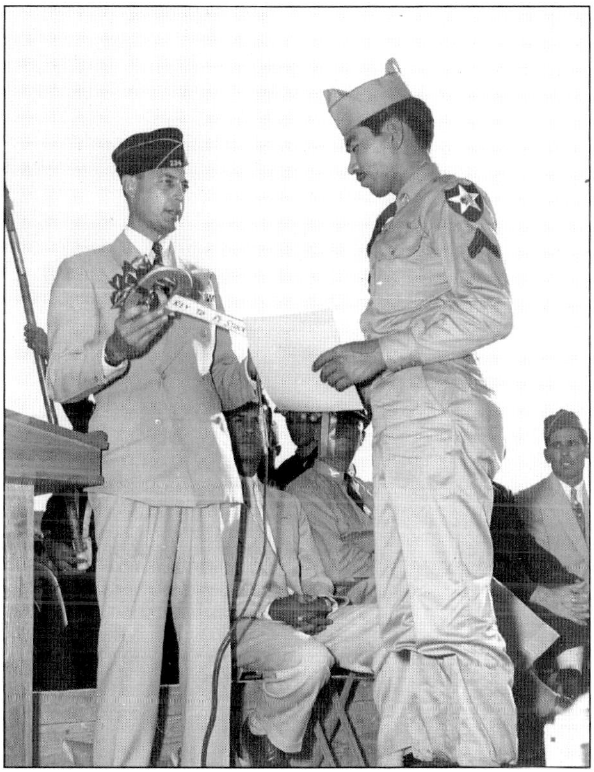

Many Fort Stockton men served in World War II. Jimmy Rooney was in the Pacific. Major D. Jacobi Sibley Jr., who had followed in his father's footsteps (page 96) by becoming a medical doctor in Fort Stockton, served with a mobile surgical unit in New Guinea and the Philippines. In this undated photograph, Walter Buengar, who won a Bronze Star under General Patton, presents the key to the city to former prisoner of war Abel Garcia.

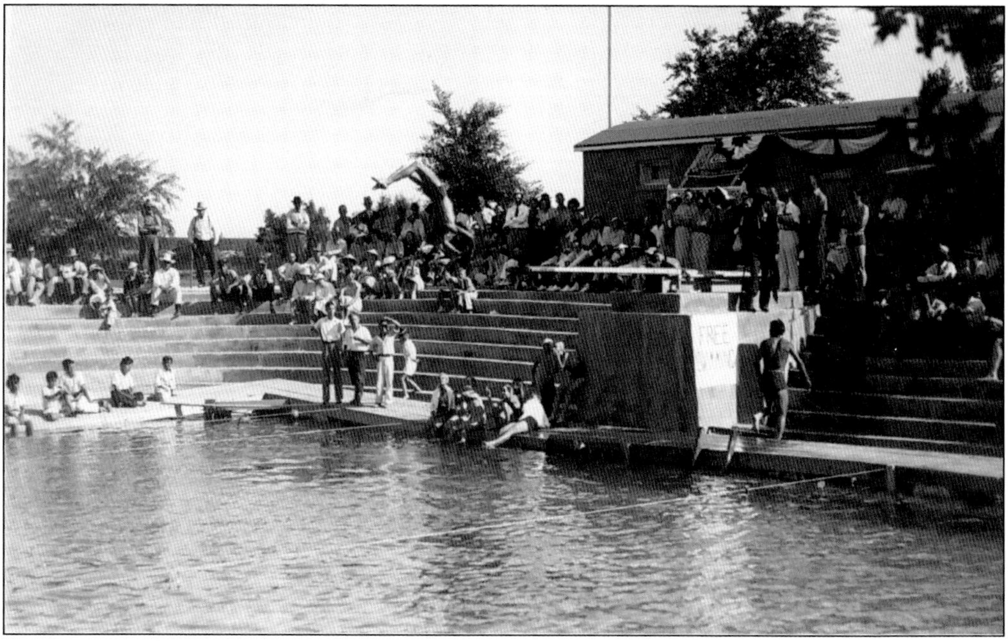

In a sense, World War II gave Mexican Americans the key to the city. Wartime service emboldened them to end local segregation. On July 6, 1943, Corp. Jesse Garcia wore his uniform to the swimming pool, but was turned away. After several near-violent incidents, the pool integrated in 1950 (as seen in this undated photograph). In March 1949, Adan Terrazas and his wife were turned away from the ground floor of the Pecos Theater, which prompted a fistfight. Theater manager Guy Moses fully integrated the theater by the end of April.

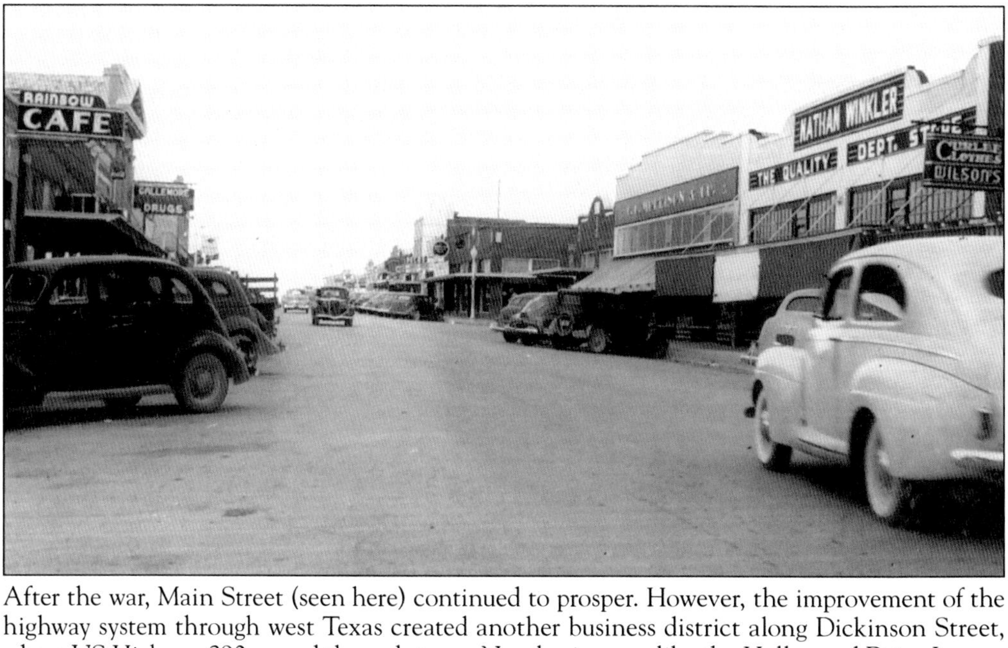

After the war, Main Street (seen here) continued to prosper. However, the improvement of the highway system through west Texas created another business district along Dickinson Street, where US Highway 290 passed through town. New businesses, like the Hollywood Drive-In, one block east of the railroad intersection, and the Gateway Lodge, a motor hotel, helped spread the city east and west of Main Street, which extended north to join Farm to Market 1053.

By the mid-1930s, Highway 67 ran from Dallas to Presidio on the Mexican border, but segments remained unpaved. In 1947, some 800 people turned out to watch Sixie Jo McGill (pictured), a local Hovey girl, shoot a paper ribbon, officially opening a completely paved road from Fort Stockton to Presidio. Arthur Stillwell's dream of a route to the Pacific became a reality with this La Entrada al Pacifico road, designed to increase efficient transportation of goods from Pacific coast ports like Topolobampo, Mexico, to Midland and Odessa, Texas, though heightened border restrictions after September 11, 2001, have limited its growth.

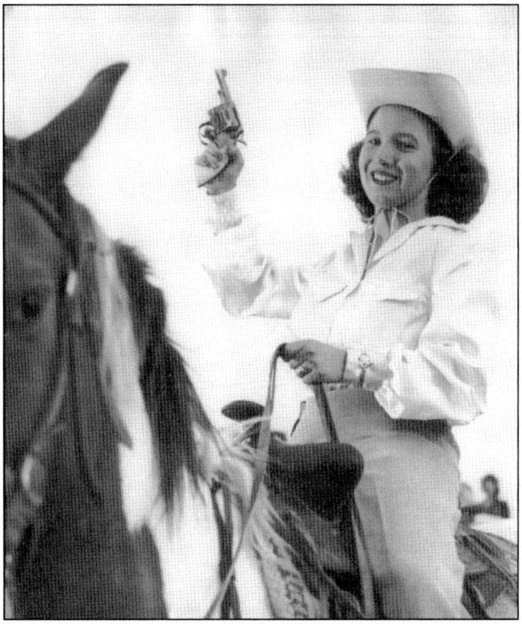

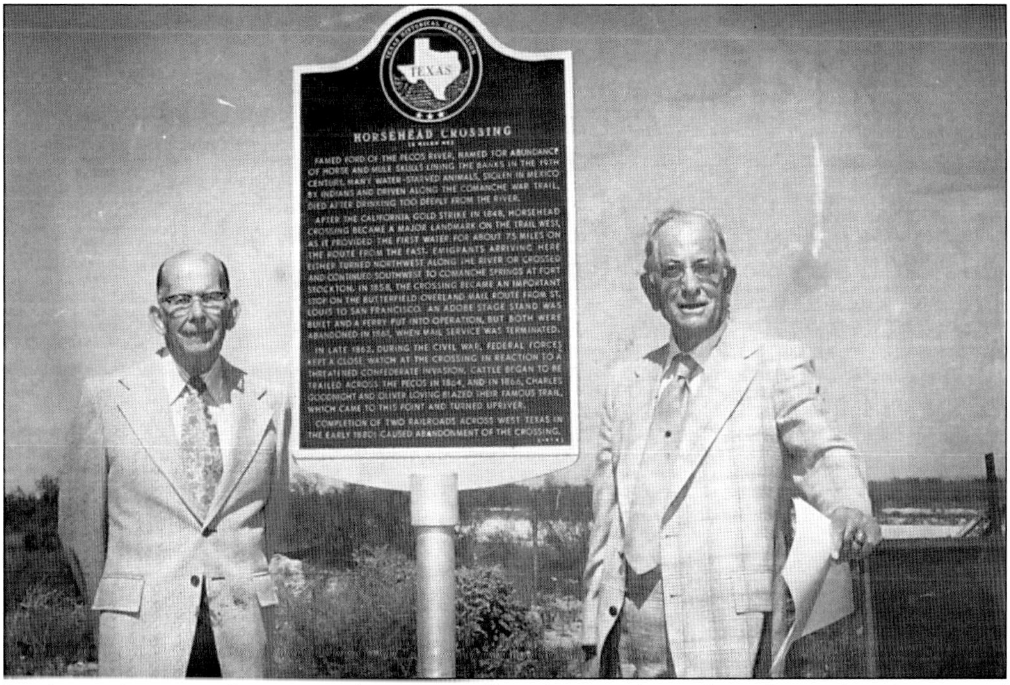

By the early 1950s, the Comanche Springs flow decreased significantly. Studies determined numerous irrigation wells were lowering the aquifer and drying the springs. A lawsuit to stop the irrigation, involving Clayton Williams Sr. (right), resulted in the 1954 Texas Court of Civil Appeals creation of the "rule of capture," which allowed Williams use of the underground water. The springs dried and soon only flowed infrequently. Williams, a noted local historian, joined Karl Butz, Pecos County Historical Commission chairman, in 1975 to dedicate a historical marker for Horsehead Crossing on the Pecos, a site used by Comanche raiding parties, stage and mail lines, and cattle drives.

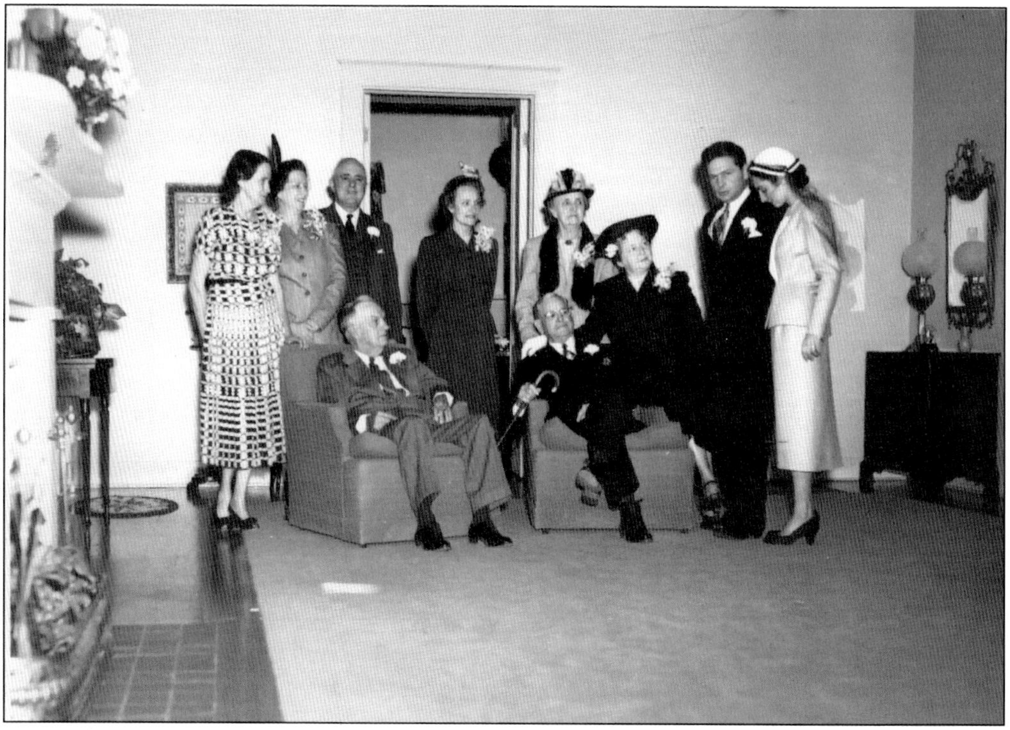

In March 1950, Dr. D.J. Sibley Jr. (standing on right) married Jane Dunn (right) in the Mendel home, former officers' quarters no. eight at Fort Stockton. The Sibley family acquired the Rollins home (page 103) and fort grounds several years earlier. Others attending included, from left to right, (standing) Myrtle Mendel, Mrs. Brewster, Dr. Thomas Brewster (Presbyterian minister), Minnie Dunn, and Lettisha Russell; (seated) Hood Mendel, Dr. D.J. Sibley, and Effie Sibley. Dr. Sibley Jr. served as physician for Fort Stockton for many years.

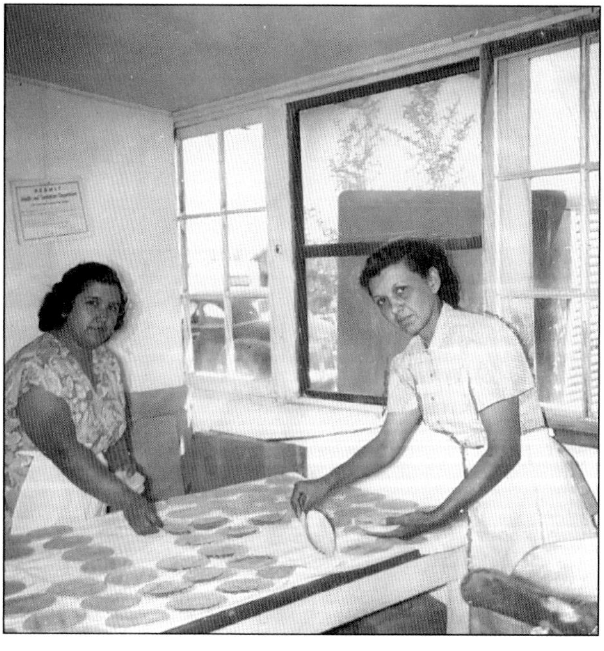

In 1948, Angel Terrazas and his wife, Elisa, began the Comanche Tortilla Factory in their home. In 1952, they moved to Nelson Street. The store employed several unusual adaptations of electric appliances, including a washing machine, to produce 50 dozen tortillas per day. Elisa Terrazas (right) and Mrs. Pacheco cool tortillas in the breeze from an evaporative cooler. In 2007, the factory celebrated 55 years of business.

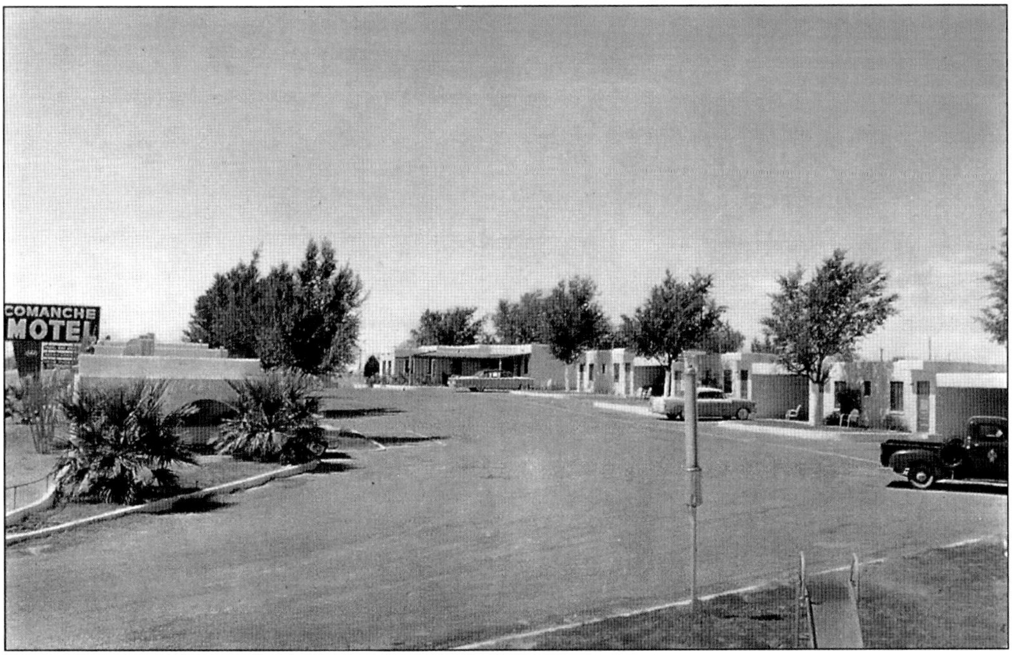

By the 1960s, local businesses increasingly faced competition from chain outlets and businesses focused on highway travel, such as the Comanche Motel (seen in this 1960s postcard). Some survived, and some did not. The Crockett Hotel closed after a devastating fire in 1955. Edward Winkler maintained his father's store (page 83) until he retired in 1995.

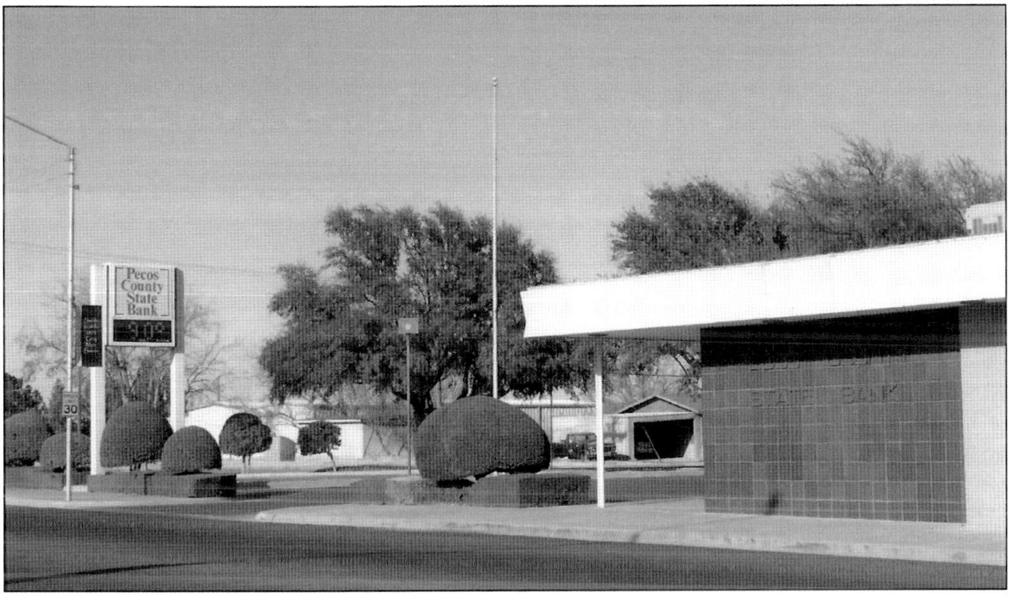

In 1923, First State and First National Banks consolidated as First National. In 1931, First National failed. The Pecos County State Bank opened in 1928 in the old First State Bank building at First and Main Streets and then moved into the remodeled First National building in 1935. In 1960, the bank relocated to 500 North Main Street (pictured) and continued operation from that location. A new First National Bank opened for business in 1958 and completed its fifth successful decade in 2008. (Photograph by James Collett.)

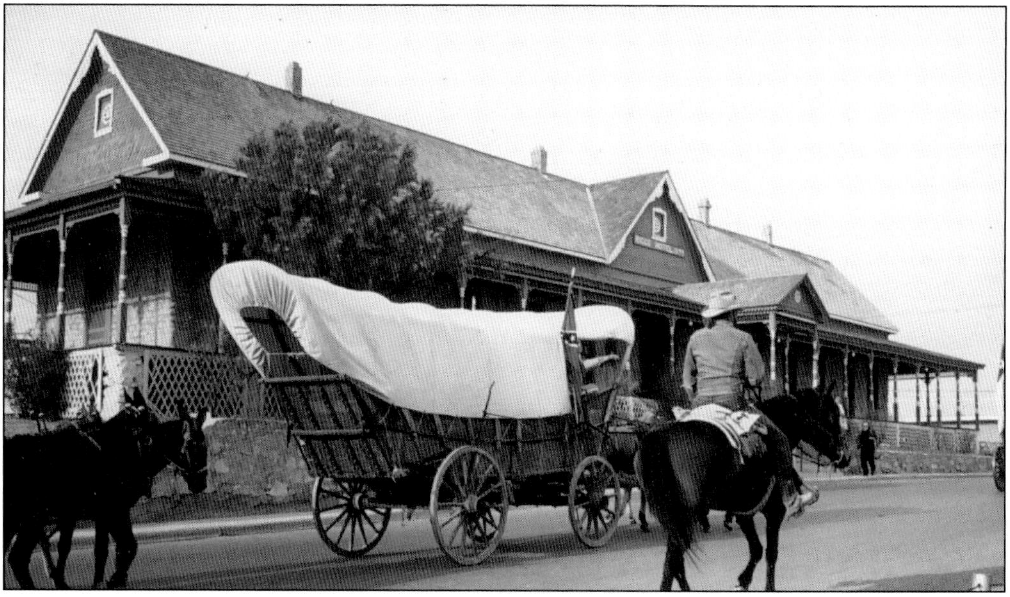

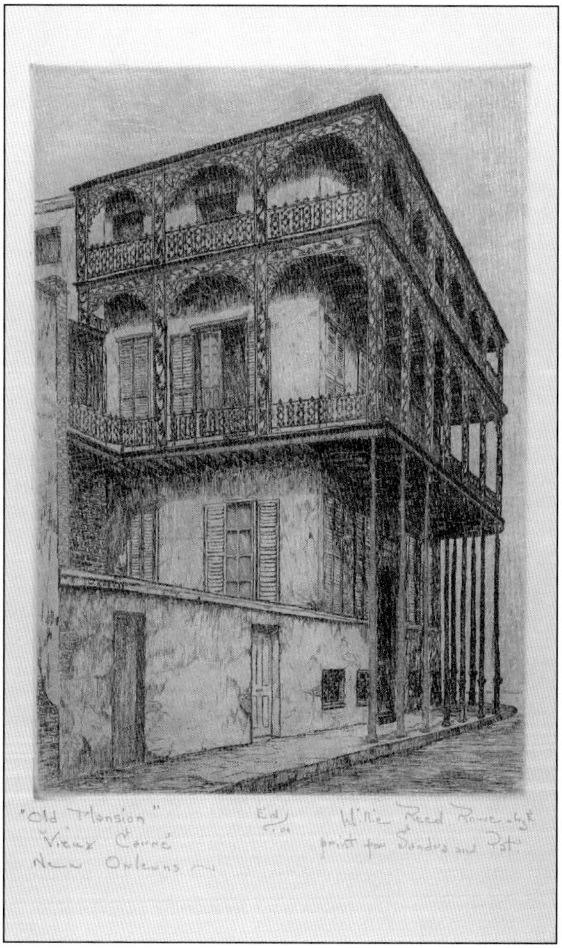

In the 1920s, the Riggs Hotel became a boardinghouse, which her family continued after Annie Riggs's death in 1931. In 1943, it became a private Riggs family residence. The Fort Stockton Historical Society organized in 1954 and acquired the hotel in 1955. Since that time, the Annie Riggs Memorial Museum has helped preserve local history in the old adobe building and is the site for many historic events, including the 1986 arrival of the Texas Sesquicentennial wagon train (pictured).

The Annie Riggs Memorial Museum also serves as a community resource for education and fine arts. Willie Reed Rowe began exhibiting etchings in New Orleans (an example is seen here) in 1938, winning several awards. In 1943, she exhibited at the National Academy of Design, and in 1947, she was honored with a solo exhibition at the Smithsonian Institution. Rowe served as the artist in residence for the museum for over 20 years, often painting and teaching on the museum porch. (Courtesy of Sheridan Porter.)

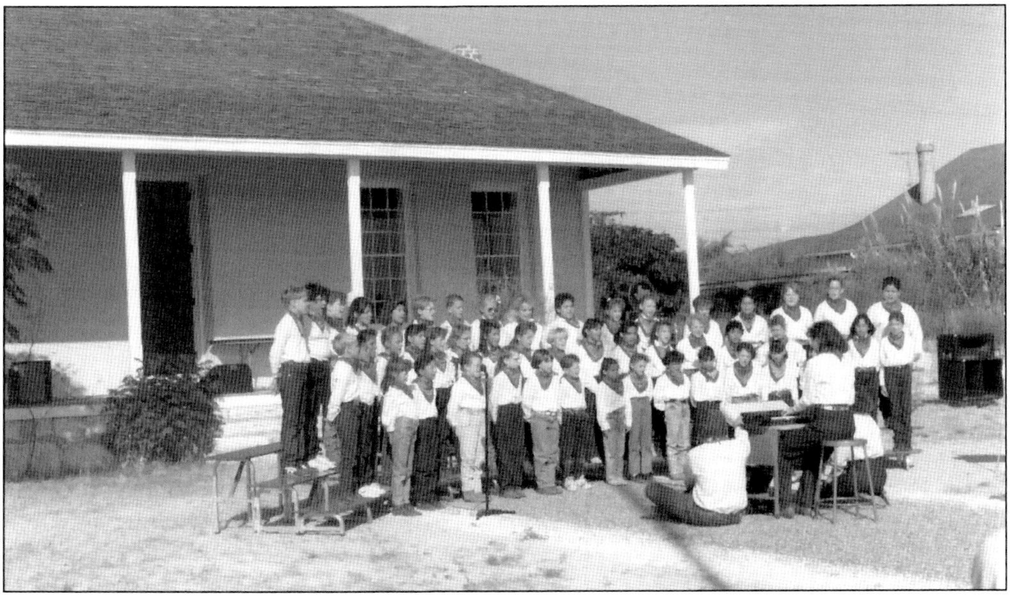

In July 1986, 100 years after the Fort Stockton post closed, Dr. D.J. Sibley donated a five-acre tract, including the parade ground, to the city. The property was developed as a historic site. Special events included education days for West Texas students. At the 1992 education day, the McCamey, Texas, Little Texas Singers, under the direction of Jo Ann Collett (seated), sang the national anthem for the flag raising. (Courtesy of Jo Ann Collett.)

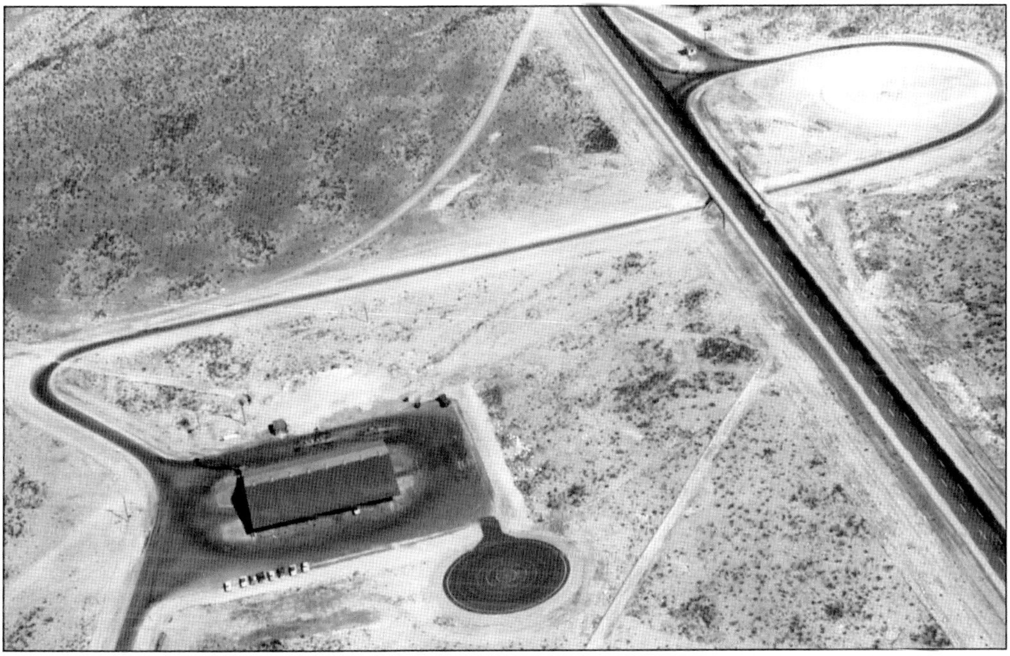

The 6,000-acre Firestone Test Center, with a 7.7 mile high-speed oval track larger than Daytona or Indy, opened in 1957 west of Fort Stockton. Pictured in this 1959 aerial photograph, it employed over 200 drivers at its peak. With access to interstate highways, excellent clear weather, and plenty of land to develop special roads and surfaces, this was an ideal location. In 2011, testing continued at this private facility closed to the public. (Courtesy of Bridgestone Americas.)

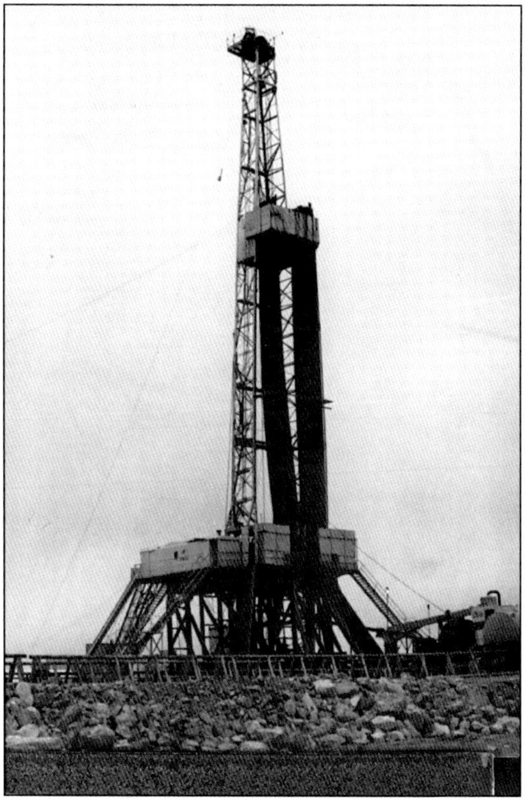

Oil and natural gas became the leading economic assets of Pecos County and fueled a housing boom in Fort Stockton that lasted into the 1970s. In 1952, the Puckett Gas Field opened. It was followed in 1963 by the prolific Gomez Field, which set world records. In 1981, the Emma Lou (pictured) set a depth record of over five and a half miles and produced over 20,000 cubic feet of gas. The Clayjon Gas Company, incorporated in Fort Stockton in 1961, became a major developer of the local gas fields.

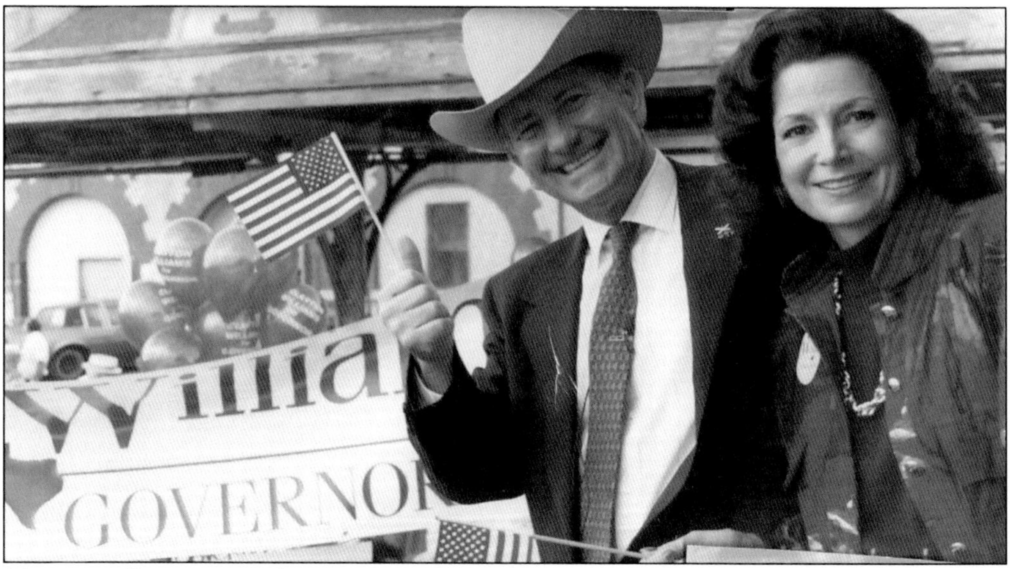

Clayton Williams Jr., grandson of O.W. Williams and a founder of Clayjon Gas, made a bid for the governorship of Texas in 1990. Williams, known as Claytie, gained the Republican nomination and ran against Democratic contender Ann Richards. Claytie (pictured campaigning with his wife, Modesta) lost to Richards by a narrow margin. Ann Richards was defeated as governor in 1994 by Republican George W. Bush, prompting Williams to later claim he helped make Bush president.

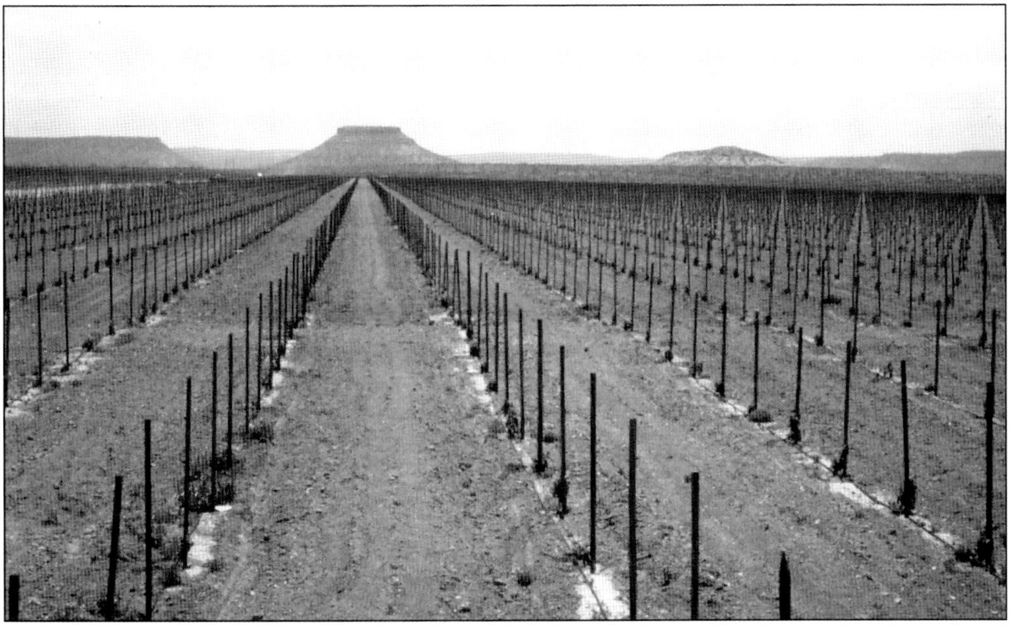

In 1984, Frank Carpenter, former alfalfa farmer, and his wife Carolyn, oversaw the expansion of the vineyards on University of Texas land east of Fort Stockton (pictured). Experiments begun in 1978 proved the environment was excellent, and the vineyards were expanded to over 1,000 acres. In 1985, a Texas-French consortium partnered with the University to produce Ste. Genevieve wines. The company constructed a 55,000-square-foot winery and named it for the patron saint of French vineyards. (Courtesy of Frank Carpenter.)

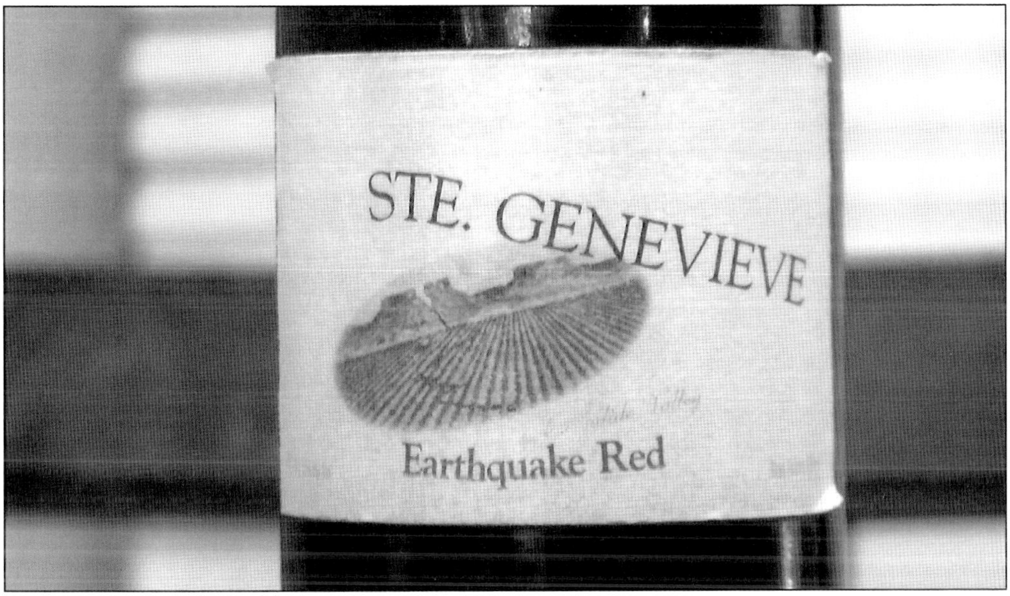

In 1995, a special Earthquake Red vintage was issued. The wine commemorated a rare Texas earthquake. Its epicenter was a few miles from the winery, and the quake blended together several hundred gallons of different red wines, which were sold as Earthquake Red with an off-center version of the Ste. Genevieve label. In 2007, the winery was sold to Mesa Vineyards, which became the largest wine producer in Texas. (Photograph by Diane Indorf.)

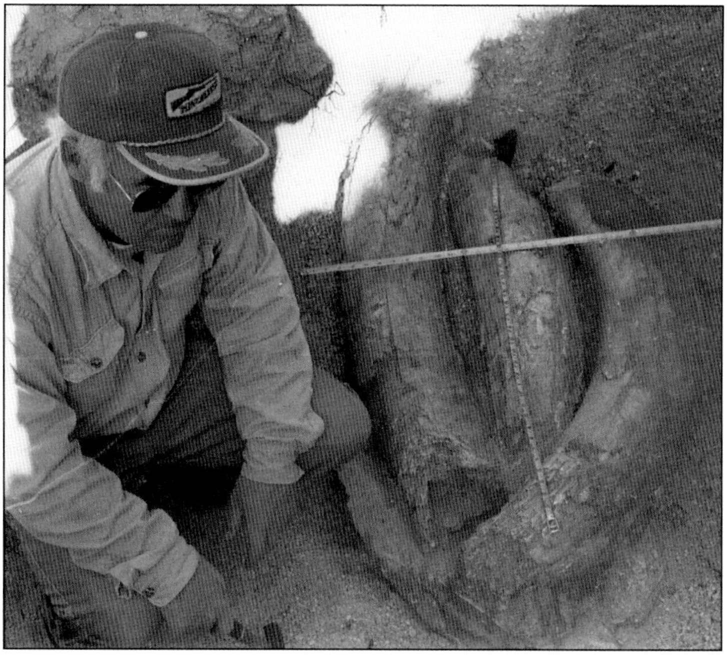

Biologist Frank Warnock (pictured), who grew up on the former Seven-d ranch, spent 35 years excavating a site at San Pedro Springs near Seven-Mile Mesa. There, Dr. Warnock discovered artifacts indicating human occupation 20,000 years ago. He also unearthed mammals, which the prehistoric people hunted, including Columbian mammoth tusks (pictured, and on display at the Annie Riggs Museum), bison, camel, horses, sloth, and hogs that were similar to the modern javelina.

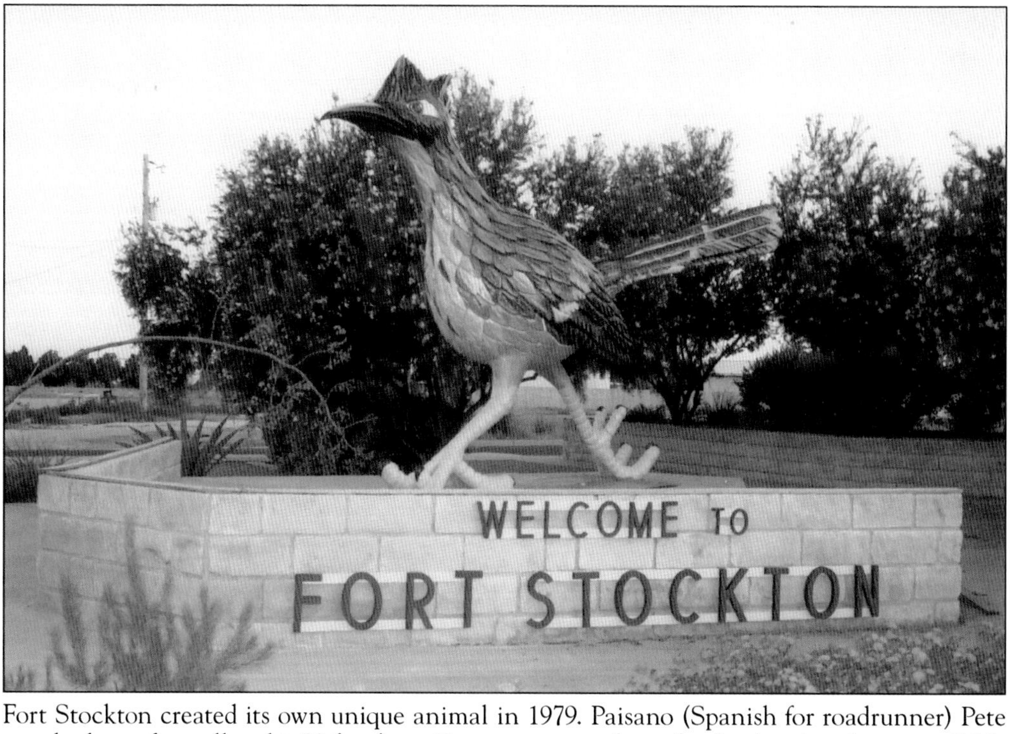

Fort Stockton created its own unique animal in 1979. Paisano (Spanish for roadrunner) Pete stands eleven feet tall and is 22 feet long. Pete serves as ambassador for the city, always available for photographs. He stands at the intersection of significant routes in the city's history—Main Street, the railroad tracks (though the trains no longer run), and Dickinson Street, the former Old Spanish Trail highway. (Photograph by Irma Dudley; courtesy of the Fort Stockton Convention and Visitors Bureau.)

Seven

Looking Forward, Looking Back

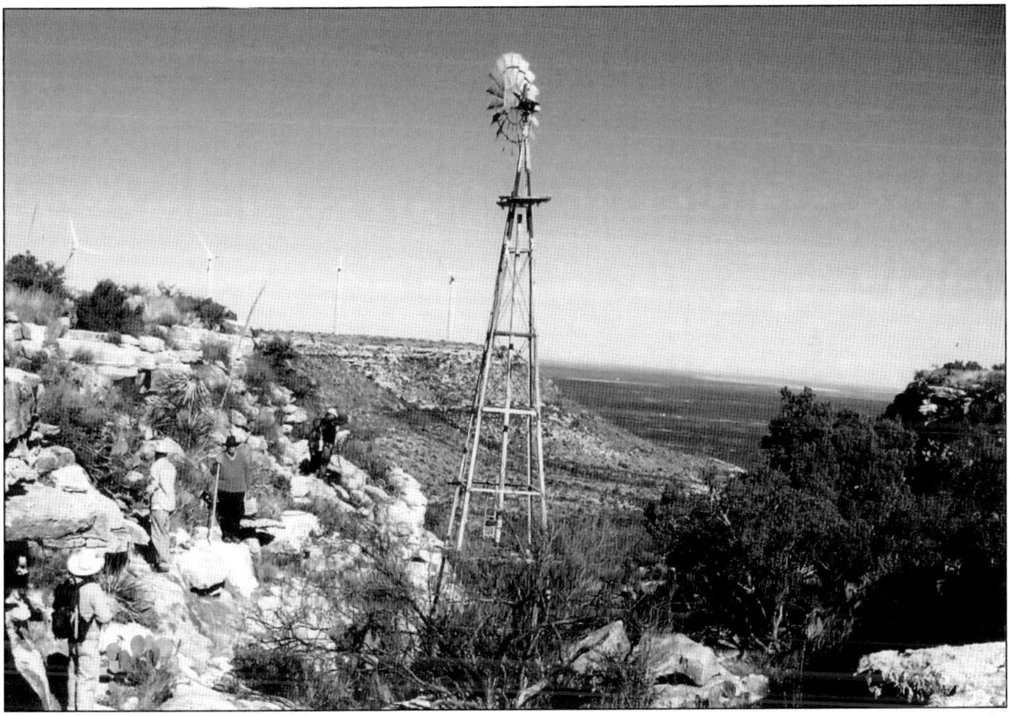

During a 2008 trip to a prehistoric art site in a rock shelter on a Pecos County mesa (pictured), the Iraan Archeological Society had a view reaching from prehistory to the high tech present. A ranch windmill pumps up water while a line of wind generators create electrical energy. The landscape behind them includes the Orient Railroad route and, farther north, the old trail to Horsehead Crossing. (Courtesy of Diane Indorf.)

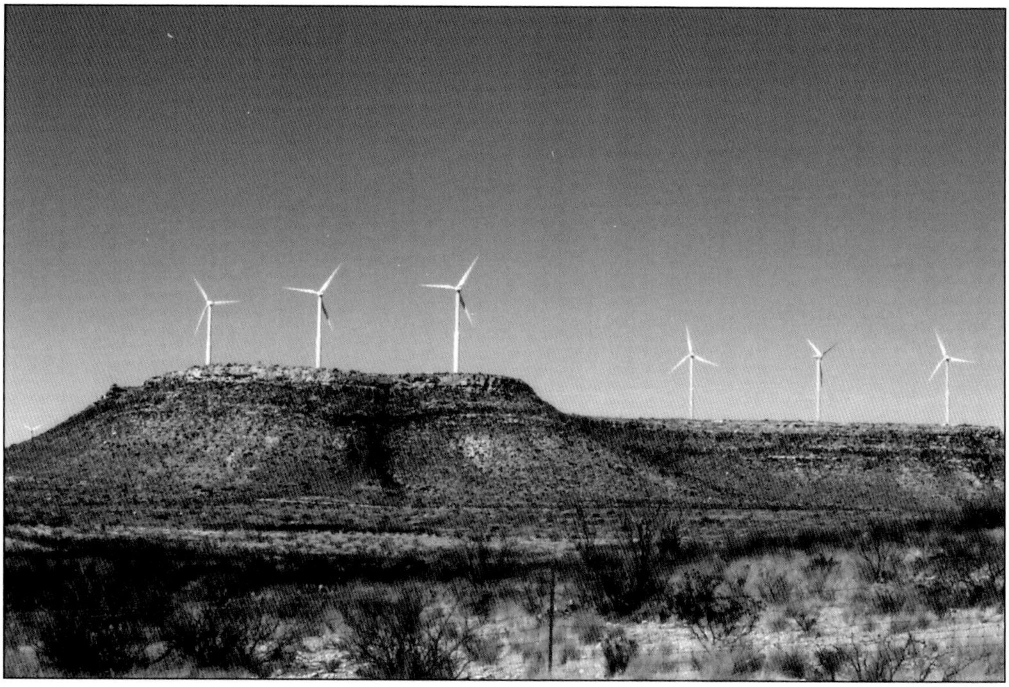

The first Pecos County wind farms were started in 2001. Texas governor Rick Perry provided the keynote address at the Desert Sky Wind Farm dedication in 2002. This wind farm produces energy for San Antonio. With several large utility grade enterprises, Pecos is the only Texas county to be a top 10 producer of renewable energy, oil, and natural gas. (Photograph by James Collett.)

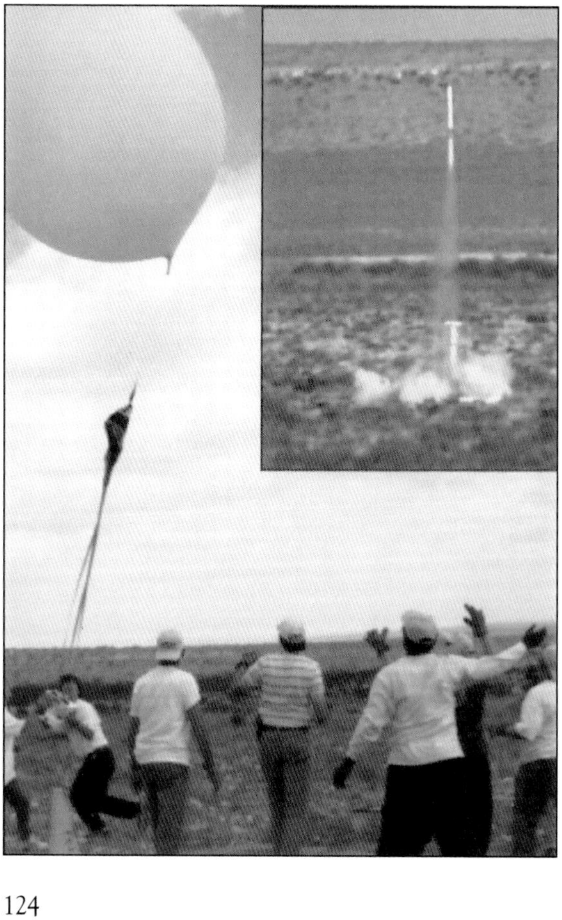

In 2002, JP Aerospace president John Powell launched a PongSat balloon (seen in this composite photograph) designed to carry electronic equipment to 100,000 feet, "the edge of space." A few hours later, a 12-foot-tall test rocket blasted 20,000 feet into the air to test a two-stage rocket process designed to place small satellites into orbit. Both were part of a plan creating a commercial spaceport on the La Escalera Ranch south of Fort Stockton. (Courtesy of the *Fort Stockton Pioneer*.)

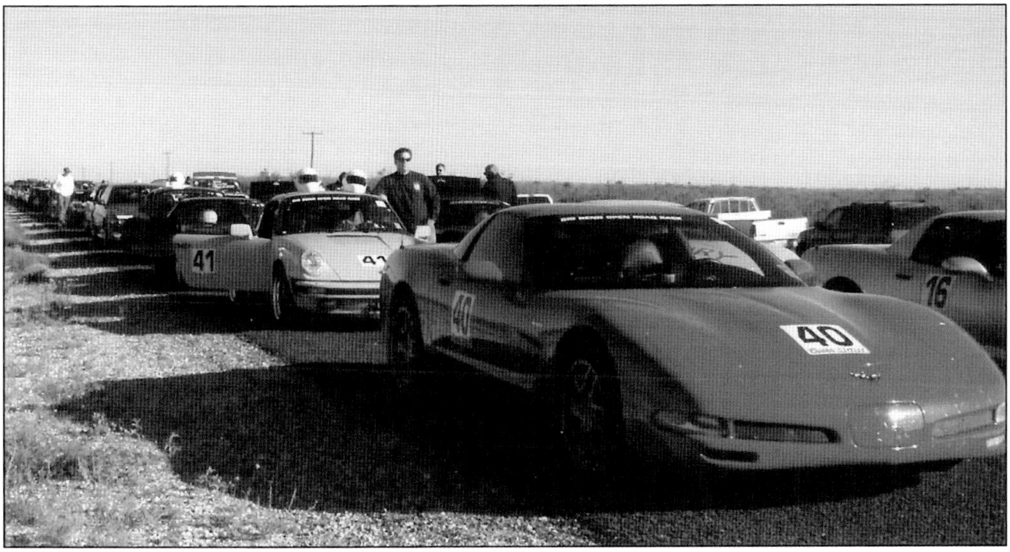

Since 2002, the Big Bend Open Road Race has pitted fast cars against a winding traditional roadway. Highway 285 from Fort Stockton to Sanderson, with over 59 curves, is closed for a day and drivers race 118 miles down and back with all speed limits removed. Drivers compete in average speed classes that range from 85 miles per hour to "unlimited." These cars await their turn in the 2009 competition. (Courtesy of the *Fort Stockton Pioneer.*)

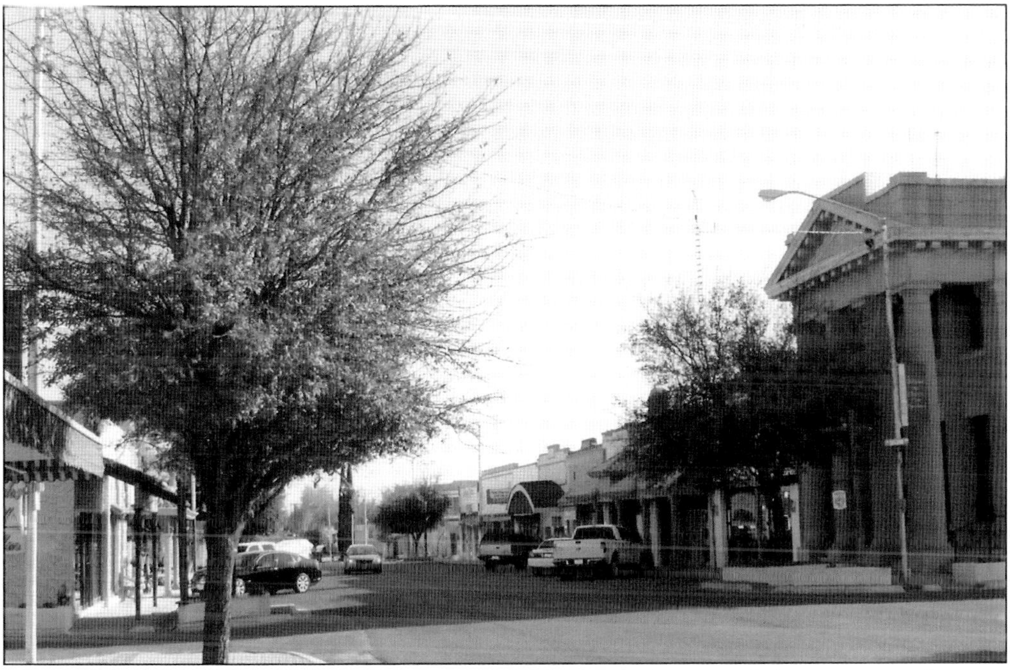

Main Street in 2011 may resemble Main Street in the 1940s (page 100), but it is part of a more cosmopolitan and high tech city. The old First National Bank serves as the police station, and Terrazas Furniture, over 50 years old, is its largest business. By the county courthouse, a new district court building is named for Alex Gonzalez (page 105), who presided over the 83rd Judicial District from 1984 to 1989. (Photograph by James Collett.)

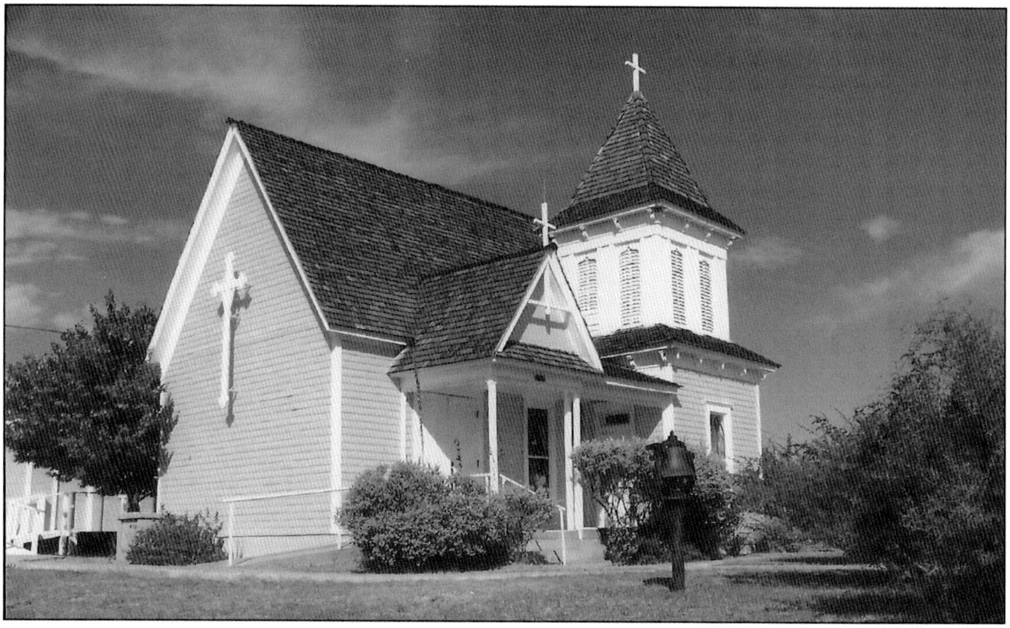

Fort Stockton leaders work to preserve and share the city's historic past. St. Stephen's Episcopal Church, built in 1896, is the oldest Protestant church building west of the Pecos River. It was moved from Pecos, Texas, in 1958 and placed on the fort property, which also contains the Sibley Home and the Hovey school building. All are part of a National Register Historic District created in 1972. (Photograph by Diane Indorf.)

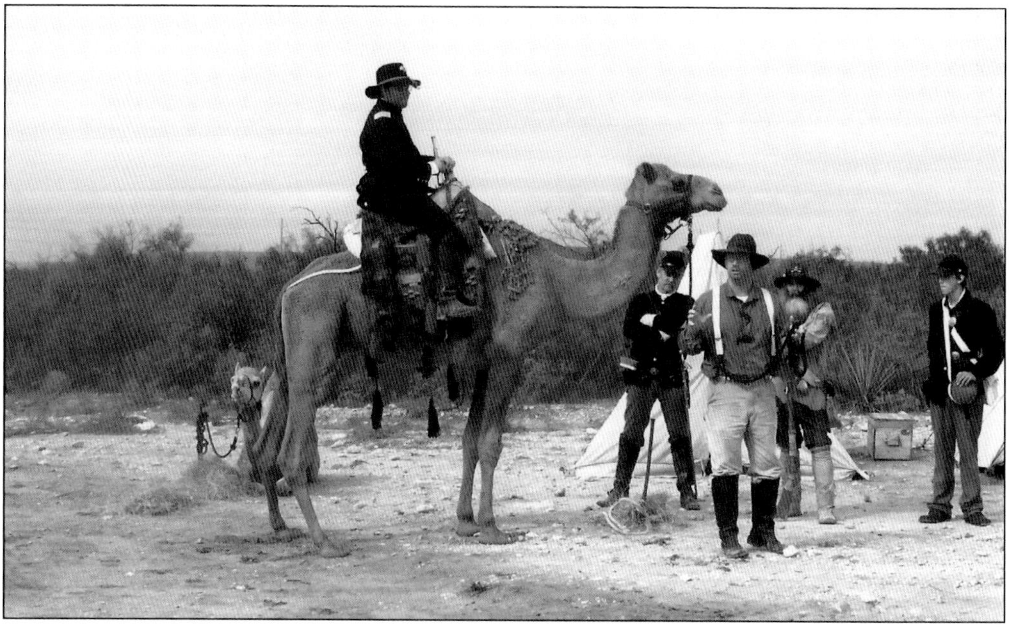

In 2009, Fort Stockton celebrated its 150th birthday. Special events included a reenactment by the Texas Camel Corps of the 1859 Hartz expedition (page 12). In a special live broadcast event from the trail, Doug Baum (at camel's nose) discusses the expedition story with students. Jeremy Lumpkins sits on the camel. Mike Baker (soldier) and Gil Hernandez stand behind Doug, while young recruit Clayton Dowell (right) observes. (Photograph by James Collett.)

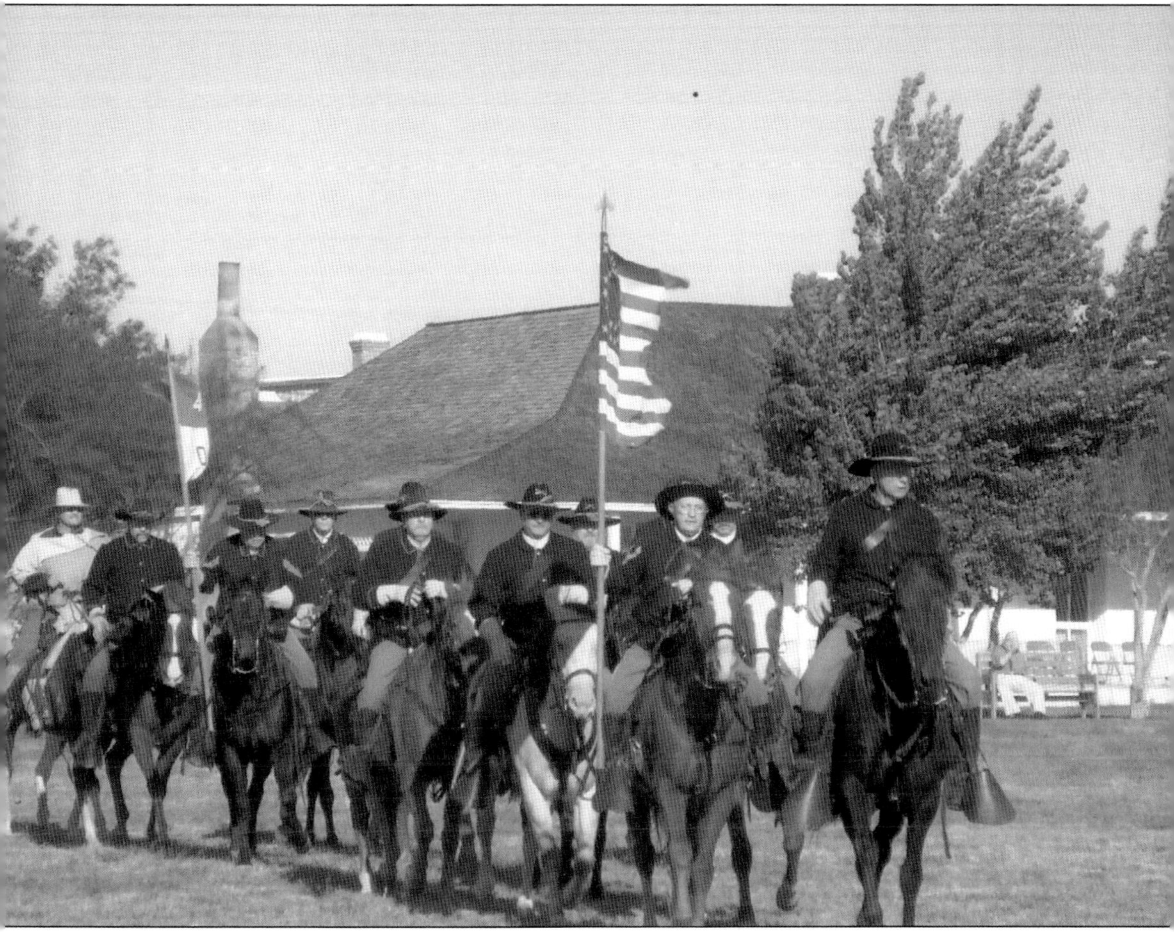

The 4th Regiment of US Cavalry Troop D rides out across the parade ground at the old Fort Stockton military post as participants in the 150th anniversary celebration in October 2009. Troopers include Roy Rob (leading), Rick Hooker (carrying flag), Larry McMurtry (second row, left), Bobby Blaylock (second row, right), and Bobby Bailey (third row, left), followed by members of the Fort Concho Cavalry. Except for a few modern items in the background, the scene could be from 1859, when the fort began, or the 1880s, when cavalry patrols were a regular sight (page 21). At 150 years old, Fort Stockton was a modern city with an economy combining agriculture, oil and gas, and high tech industry. The city shared its rich history with travelers and residents alike. As they had many other times over the years, Fort Stockton citizens gathered on the fort grounds to recall the past, celebrate the present, and share dreams of the future.